In The Fray

In the Fray

Contesting Christian Public Ethics, 1994–2013

DAVID P. GUSHEE

With Closing Reflections by
GLEN HAROLD STASSEN

CASCADE Books • Eugene, Oregon

IN THE FRAY
Contesting Christian Public Ethics, 1994–2013

Copyright © 2014 David P. Gushee. All rights reserved. Except for brief quotations in critical publications or reviews, no part of this book may be reproduced in any manner without prior written permission from the publisher. Write: Permissions. Wipf and Stock Publishers, 199 W. 8th Ave., Suite 3, Eugene, OR 97401.

Cascade Books
An Imprint of Wipf and Stock Publishers
199 W. 8th Ave., Suite 3
Eugene, OR 97401

www.wipfandstock.com

ISBN 13: 978-1-62564-044-4

Cataloguing-in-Publication Data

Gushee, David P.

In the fray : contesting Christian public ethics, 1994–2013 / David P. Gushee.

xiv + 238 p. ; 23 cm. Includes bibliographical references.

ISBN 13: 978-1-62564-044-4

1. Christian ethics. 2. Church and social problems. 3. Theology. I. Title.

BJ1251 G86 2014

Manufactured in the U.S.A.

New Revised Standard Version Bible, copyright © 1989 the Division of Christian Education of the National Council of the Churches of Christ in the United States of America. Used by permission. All rights reserved.

Holy Bible, New International Version®, NIV® Copyright © 1973, 1978, 1984, 2011 by Biblica, Inc.® Used by permission. All rights reserved worldwide. Scripture taken from the Holy Bible, Today's New International® Version TNIV®. Copyright 2001, 2005 by International Bible Society® Used by permission of International Bible Society®. All rights reserved worldwide. "TNIV" and "Today's New International Version" are trademarks registered in the United States Patent and Trademark Office by International Bible Society®.

For the sake of a faithful church

By David P. Gushee

Evangelical Peacemakers: Gospel Engagement in a War-Torn World. Cascade, 2013.

Glen Harold Stassen: Baptist Peacemaker, Global Christian Ethicist (Festschrift), with Reggie L. Williams.

The Sacredness of Life: Why an Ancient Biblical Vision is Key to the World's Future. Eerdmans, 2013.

Yours is the Day, Lord, Yours is the Night, with Jeanie Gushee. Thomas Nelson, 2012.

A New Evangelical Manifesto: A Kingdom Vision for the Common Good. Chalice, 2012.

Religious Faith, Torture, and Our National Soul. With Jillian Hickman Zimmer and Drew Zimmer. Mercer University Press, 2010.

The Scholarly Vocation and the Baptist Academy, with Roger Ward. Mercer University Press, 2008.

The Future of Faith in American Politics: The Public Witness of the Evangelical Center. Baylor University Press, 2008.

Only Human: Christian Reflections on the Journey toward Wholeness. Jossey-Bass, 2005.

Getting Marriage Right: Realistic Counsel for Saving and Strengthening Marriages. Baker, 2004.

Kingdom Ethics: Following Jesus in Contemporary Context, with Glen H. Stassen. Intervarsity, 2003.

Christians and Politics Beyond the Culture Wars: From Despair to Mission. Baker, 2000.

Toward a Just and Caring Society: Christian Responses to Poverty in America. Baker, 1999.

The Future of Christian Higher Education, with David S. Dockery. Broadman & Holman, 1999.

A Bolder Pulpit: Reclaiming the Moral Dimension of Preaching, with Robert H. Long. Judson, 1998.

Preparing for Christian Ministry: An Evangelical Approach, with Walter Jackson. Baker, 1996.

The Righteous Gentiles of the Holocaust: A Christian Interpretation. Augsburg Fortress, 1994. Second Edition: Paragon House, 2003.

Contents

Preface and Acknowledgments | ix

1 Learning from the Christian Rescuers: Lessons for the Churches | 1

2 Tears of a Generation:
Thinking about Divorce as if Children Matter | 20

3 Just War Divide: One Tradition, Two Views | 31

4 The Church, the Nazis, and the Holocaust: A Reconsideration | 38

5 Remembering Rwanda:
Lessons from the Church's Complicity in Genocide | 52

6 Can Christian Ethics Be Saved? | 58

7 Dietrich Bonhoeffer and the Evangelical Moment
in American Public Life | 75

8 Who Needs a Covenant? | 82

9 Evangelicals and Politics:
Convictions, Controversies, Challenges | 90

10 An Evangelical Declaration against Torture:
Protecting Human Rights in an Age of Terror | 103

11 Faith, Science, and Climate Change | 127

12 Church-Based Hate: A Review of Mitchell Gold's *Crisis* | 141

13 What the Torture Debate Reveals
about American Evangelical Christianity | 147

14 Scripture, Government, and the World's Poor | 164

15 Biblical Reflections on a World without Nuclear Weapons | 181

16 Religion, Science, and the Weakening Quest to Save Creation | 187

17 America's Unfinished Racial Reconciliation | 200

18 Christian Public Theology and Israel-Palestine | 212

19 Closing Reflections: David Gushee's Compassion and Realism, with Concreteness —*Glen H. Stassen* | 223

Works Cited | 231

Preface and Acknowledgments

I AM GRATEFUL TO Wipf & Stock Publishers for their interest in publishing this collection of essays produced over roughly two decades of work as a Christian ethicist.

The collection is called *In the Fray* because most of the essays were written in situations of ethical combat on the highly contested ground of Christian public ethics. Many have the scent of battle about them, because most were drafted amidst some kind of conflict over a controversial current issue—notably torture, climate, marriage and sexual ethics, war, nuclear weapons, race, global poverty, faith and politics, Israel/Palestine, and even whether Christian ethics is a real academic discipline.

Not every essay carries obvious polemical traces. The first essay reflects on lessons to be learned from that small minority of Christians who rescued Jews during the Holocaust. Another essay (chapter 4) reflects on the church struggle in Nazi Germany and how the churches fared in resisting Nazism and the Holocaust. A third essay (chapter 7) lingers over Dietrich Bonhoeffer. The Holocaust was the subject of my dissertation, and spending so many years of my life immersed in studying Christian behavior during that dark period has certainly shaped my moral vision. Its traces can clearly be felt in other essays as well. All reflect the desire for a church with resistance to racism, militarism, nationalism, and other social-ideological toxins, and with the discernment and courage to resist these *at the kairos moment, the time of testing, on behalf of the sacred worth and God-given rights of every person*—rather than merely lamenting the church's failures later.

The careful reader will notice considerable attention to the U.S. evangelical Christian community. The argument of several essays is directed against what I consider to be the sometimes aberrant or unconstructive public ethics of my co-religionists in this vast sector of the American religious community. I do not write as a disdainful outsider but instead as an insider who contests one primary version of evangelical public ethics—that represented by our most reactionary and narrow elements. I hope that my love for the church of Jesus Christ, and my desire for greater fidelity to Christ's lordship on the part of the church, is apparent in and through my criticisms.

The eighteen essays collected here were selected from dozens of speeches, articles, declarations, book chapters, and lectures presented over a busy two decades in Christian ethics and public life. They are presented in chronological order, oldest to most recent. I sought to include primarily single-author essays I wrote amidst some kind of public ethical conflict. I wanted a collection reflecting the broad range of issue areas I have engaged and a variety of literary genres and approaches. I also wanted to include materials that for the most part have not appeared in substantially similar form in any prior book.

Working with my extraordinarily talented and diligent graduate student partner Isaac Sharp, we have edited the essays to meet the style guide requirements of the publisher and have changed a few titles but otherwise have almost never altered texts as they originally appeared. I have included the date of presentation and/or publication and found some way of indicating the context in which it was written. Like several of my mentors in Christian ethics, I believe in an ethics that is situated and concrete, and I have long believed that no text can be read apart from awareness of its context.

A collection such as this reveals where a scholar-activist has been, not necessarily where she or he is going. I am painfully aware of issues I have not tackled or which urgently demand more of my attention in the next twenty years than they have received thus far. I am also aware of ways my mind has changed or is changing, but I have not sought to sanitize my writing to fit my current sensibility. One reason to undertake such a project as a sabbatical effort is precisely as a "halftime" exercise, if the sporting analogy may be excused. In that sense it has been extraordinarily illuminating, at least to me.

I am grateful to Mercer University for its generous sabbatical leave policy, which enabled me to undertake this work in relative peace and quiet.

I thank Wipf & Stock editor Rodney Clapp for his confidence in the significance of this project and his excellent editorial work on my second project under the Cascade imprint.

I am grateful to Isaac Sharp for his extraordinarily helpful editing, permissions work, and involvement in the decision-making process as to which essays made the cut for the book.

I am certainly grateful to my very busy teacher, colleague, and friend Glen Harold Stassen (1936–2014), of Fuller Seminary, for his willingness to add his thoughtful reflection on themes and implications he sees in the body of work collected here, as well as for helpful input on some pieces he felt sure must be included. Glen, my dear mentor, friend, and co-author, was suffering with cancer when he wrote this epilogue. It appears after his death on April 26, 2014—one of his very last published writings. No words can convey either my gratitude for his contributions to my life, or my grief at his passing.

I acknowledge with gratitude the following original contexts, partners, and/or publishers for the production of these essays:

Chapter 1: "Learning from the Christian Rescuers: Lessons for the Churches." Original research for Union Seminary (NY) doctoral dissertation (1993), which became *Righteous Gentiles of the Holocaust* (Fortress, 1994). This material was first presented in this form at the "Remembering for the Future II" conference in Berlin (1994). Published as "Learning from the Christian Rescuers: Lessons for the Churches," *The Annals of the American Academy of Political and Social Science* vol. 548 (November 1996) 138–55.

Chapter 2: "Tears of a Generation: Thinking about Divorce as if Children Matter." Original research for *Getting Marriage Right* (Baker, 2004), with considerable overlap of material between this essay and that book's chapter 2. Appeared in this particular form first as "Tears of a Generation: Divorce as if Children Mattered." *Prism* 5, no. 7 (November–December 1998) 9–14, 23–26. Used by permission of *Prism* (Evangelicals for Social Action).

Chapter 3: "Just War Divide: One Tradition, Two Views." An early version was presented as "Soft and Hard Just War Theory: A Proposal and Analysis," at 2002 Christianity in the Academy Conference. Later published in William R. Marty and Bruce W. Speck, eds., *Christ and Culture and "Who Is My Neighbor?" Christian Conduct in a Dangerous World: Proceedings of the 2001 and 2002 Christianity in the Academy Conferences*, Southern Pines, NC: Carolinas Press, 2004, 1–8. The version printed here resembles most closely "Just War Divide," *Christian Century* 119, no. 17 (August 14–27, 2002) 26–29. Used by permission of the *Christian Century*.

Chapter 4: "The Church, the Nazis, and the Holocaust: A Reconsideration." A review-essay originally published under the title "'Rescue Those Being Led Away to Death': The Church, the Nazis, and the Holocaust," *Books & Culture* (March–April 2002) 22–23, 40–42.

Chapter 5: "Remembering Rwanda: Lessons from the Church's Complicity in Genocide." Originally published as "Church Failure: Remembering Rwanda," *Christian Century* 121, no. 8 (April 20, 2004) 28–31. Later republished as "Why the Churches Were Complicit: Confessions of a Brokenhearted Christian," in *Genocide in Rwanda: Complicity of the Churches,* edited by Carol Rittner, John Roth, and Wendy Whitworth. Minneapolis; Paragon House, 2004. Used by permission of the *Christian Century*.

Chapter 6: "Can Christian Ethics Be Saved?" An early version was presented as a lecture at Union University in 2002. Published as "Can Christian Ethics Be Saved?" *Christian Ethics Today* 10, no. 4 (Fall 2004) 4–10.

Chapter 7: "Dietrich Bonhoeffer and the Evangelical Moment in American Public Life." Originally presented as "Bonhoeffer as a Model for Religious Activism," Boston College/Hebrew Union/Andover Newton Seminary conference (2006). Later published as "Dietrich Bonhoeffer and the Evangelical Moment in American Public Life," *Studies in Christian-Jewish Relations*, vol. 2, Issue 1 (2007) CP8–12.

Chapter 8: "Who Needs a Covenant?" Originally published under the same title in *Christian Reflection* (Spring 2006) 11–18. Used by permission of *Christian Reflection* (Baylor University).

Chapter 9: "Evangelicals and Politics: Convictions, Controversies, Challenges." Originally presented as a lecture in 2006 at Hamline University. Published as "Evangelicals and Politics: A Rethinking," *Journal of Law and Religion* 23, no. 1 (Fall 2007) 101–14. Small parts of this essay were used later in my own *The Future of Faith in American Politics* (Baylor, 2008).

Chapter 10: "An Evangelical Declaration against Torture: Protecting Human Rights in an Age of Terror." As chair of the new organization Evangelicals for Human Rights, and working with the skilled assistance of staff person Mary Head, I was the principal drafter of this declaration (the only collective declaration included in *In the Fray*). The declaration first went public when it was approved by the board of the National Association of Evangelicals in February 2007. Since then it has been reprinted in multiple venues. I am grateful to the drafting team, whose names are listed with the document in chapter 10.

Chapter 11: "Faith, Science, and Climate Change." Presented as a lecture to the Christian Life Commission, Baptist General Convention of Texas, March 2008. This is its first time in print.

Chapter 12: "Church-Based Hate." A review-essay published under that name in *Christian Century* (June 2, 2009) 28–30. Used by permission of *Christian Century*.

Chapter 13: "What the Torture Debate Reveals about American Evangelical Christianity." An early version was presented at our Mercer University conference on torture (2008), and then at the Society of Christian Ethics, 2009. Published under the title "What the Torture Debate Reveals about

American Christianity," *Journal of the Society of Christian Ethics* 30, no. 1 (Spring/Summer 2010) 79–98. Another version was included in my *Religious Faith, Torture, and Our National Soul* (Mercer Press, 2010).

Chapter 14: "Scripture, Government, and the World's Poor." A co-authored piece with Andi Thomas Sullivan, presented at Wheaton College/Bread for the World conference, May 2010. This is its first time in print. I thank Andi Thomas Sullivan for permission to include it in this volume.

Chapter 15: "Biblical Reflections on a World without Nuclear Weapons." Paper prepared for a 2011 conference at the University of Notre Dame that was canceled due to weather; first appearance of any type for this brief essay.

Chapter 16: "Religion, Science, and the Weakening Quest to Save Creation." Published under this title at website of Center for Health and the Global Environment, Harvard University, May 4, 2012. http://chge.med.harvard.edu/resource/religion-science-and-weakening-quest-save-creation. Used by permission of Center for Health and the Global Environment.

Chapter 17: "America's Unfinished Racial Reconciliation." Paper presented at Carl v. Ossietzky Universität, Oldenburg, Germany, 2012. It appears in print here for the first time. I am grateful to Kyle Stokes and Isaac Sharp for the significant research they contributed to this essay.

Chapter 18: "Christian Public Theology and Israel-Palestine." Presentation at Fuller Theological Seminary, April 2013. It appears in print here for the first time.

1

Learning from the Christian Rescuers
Lessons for the Churches

1996

WHILE NAZI GERMANY WAS undertaking the destruction of the Jews of Europe during World War II, only a very small proportion of Europe's non-Jews took action to help their Jewish neighbors survive. At the same time, the Nazis found a significant number of Europeans willing to collaborate with them—on grounds of self-interest or conviction or both. Meanwhile, until 1945, no power on Earth was both able and willing to take the kinds of political and military actions that would end or even seriously hinder Nazi Germany's mass killing of Jews. And so, preyed upon by the most powerful nation in Europe, murdered by some of their neighbors, abandoned by almost all of the rest of them, and largely unaided by the world, the Jews of Europe were slaughtered.

The spirit of an examination of the Holocaust, it seems to me, ought to be something like the spirit of an investigation of a fatal airplane crash (though, of course, even this metaphor is not nearly grave enough). As tears sting the eyes and the stench of death overwhelms the senses, the investigators nonetheless pick through the rubble, in search of the answer to two critical questions: Why did this catastrophe happen? How can another disaster like this be prevented in the future?

This article concerns that tiny minority of non-Jews who attempted to help Jews survive the Holocaust. As such, it attends to what must be seen as the only glimmer of light in the Holocaust's overwhelming darkness.[1] The danger of examining this light-in-darkness is that a focus on the light should make the darkness seem, somehow, less dark than it was. This is an especially acute concern when the examination is made by a Christian researcher, whose community loyalties might incline him toward too much celebration of European Christian moral goodness and too little grief over European Christian moral evil. Maybe rescuers should not be studied, or perhaps they should be studied only by Jews, who are unlikely indeed to mistake a glimmer of light in the Holocaust for a bright and sunny sky.

It seems probable, however, that the shattering moral failure of a community of people—and the scattered moral successes of some within that community—might best be understood by other members of that community. As well, it seems likely that members of the community in question are the ones best positioned to interpret the historic failures and successes of the group in a way that can effectively improve the behavior of that community today, which must be a fundamental goal of such explorations. Perhaps these are among the reasons why at least two Jewish scholars who have researched the rescuers have asked Christians to join them in this work.[2] As a Christian scholar working in the U.S. setting and primarily with Southern Baptists and other evangelicals, I am among those who have taken up that invitation. My task, as I see it, is to help to interpret for my faith community—and others who listen in—the contemporary significance for us both of the Holocaust and of those Christians who tried to save Jews from it. Why? In order that my community will be a morally healthier place than it would have been otherwise, especially with regard to antisemitism; in order that it might do better today in facing its moral challenges than most Christians did in Europe during World War II; in order, frankly, that it might be more faithful to the one it claims as Lord. Mine is an exercise in "remembering for the future."

THE RELIGIOUSLY MOTIVATED CHRISTIAN RESCUERS

Mordecai Paldiel, director of the Department for the Righteous Among the Nations at Yad Vashem, Israel's Holocaust museum and research center, has said that one hundred thousand is a conservative estimate of the number of European non-Jews who aided Jews during the Holocaust.[3] At this writing,

---

1. Tec, *When Light Pierced the Darkness*; Huneke, "Glimpses of Light in a Vast Darkness."
2. Fleischner, "Can the Few Become the Many?," 233.
3. Paldiel, interview by author.

more than eleven thousand Gentiles have been verified as rescuers by Yad Vashem, and more names continue to be submitted even now. Celebration of these one hundred thousand or so rescuers is appropriately muted, however, by knowledge that three hundred million European non-Jews lived in Nazi-controlled areas during the Holocaust.[4] Even if we generously assume that only one-third of these non-Jews had any kind of realistic opportunity at all to help their Jewish neighbors, the numbers still mean that no more than one-tenth of 1 percent of Europe's Gentiles did anything to help Jews survive the Holocaust.

Thus the study of rescuers is the study of a tiny minority. This tiny minority has been the subject of a number of social-scientific and other types of research projects, especially within the past ten years or so.[5] Most of these projects have involved interviews with persons verified as rescuers by Yad Vashem. These interviews have probed not only the rescuers' wartime deeds but also their motivations, personalities, family backgrounds, and any other shred of evidence that can help illuminate why the rescuers risked their lives to help Jews when their neighbors did not.[6]

Consistently, these studies have found that a certain percentage of rescuers—on average, in the vicinity of 20 percent—cite religious motivations as one of the reasons why they rescued Jews.[7] Likewise, these inquiries and primary and secondary documents—memoirs, profiles, postwar testimonies, biographies, films, interviews, and so forth—give evidence of the religious practices, convictions, and way of life of some religiously motivated rescuers and rescuer networks. These religious motivations and practices were, of course, overwhelmingly Christian in origin, as one would expect in the heart of (post-) Christian Europe. But, given the history of virulently anti-Jewish Christian thought and practice in this same Europe, the existence of understandings of the Christian faith—and of ways of being Christian—that led to compassion and care for Jews is a matter of considerable interest.

In work published elsewhere, I have attempted to isolate and explore some of the most important religious motivations and practices of those rescuers who claim their Christian convictions as significant for their wartime activities or give other kinds of evidence of the behavioral significance

---

4. Friedman, *Their Brothers' Keepers*, 13.

5. Tec, *When Light Pierced the Darkness*; Fogelman, "The Rescuers"; Oliner and Oliner, *Altruistic Personality*; Gushee, *Righteous Gentiles of the Holocaust*.

6. Gushee, "Many Paths to Righteousness," 372–401.

7. Ibid., 388.

of their Christian faith.[8] It has seemed to me that these particularly and explicitly Christian reasons for rescue offer especially useful clues to those of us working with and in Christian faith communities today. Here I want to return to the theme not by repeating findings presented elsewhere but by reflecting briefly on eight lessons that religiously motivated Christian rescuers might offer to the churches as the latter seek to improve the quality of their moral practice today. Though these reflections will be rooted in evidence that has emerged from the rescuer literature, and though I will offer stories and other data from this literature, I do not claim that this material *proves* anything about what the churches should be and do today. I simply believe that these narratives and research findings speak quite powerfully to the churches in my own North American, Southern Baptist, and evangelical context, and I hope that they might speak effectively to other contexts as well.

LESSON 1: FREEING CHRISTIAN FAITH FROM ANTISEMITISM

The horrors of the Holocaust have caused a number of Christians to take seriously at last the long-standing and accurate accusation that aspects of traditional Christian theology and church life have been fundamentally important in generating and inflaming hatred of Jews. For fifty years, much of Jewish-Christian dialogue has focused on this history of Christian anti-Judaism and antisemitism and the moral obligation incumbent upon Christian leaders to articulate and practice a non-antisemitic faith. At the same time, a considerable body of Christian theological and biblical scholarship has emerged that clearly reflects the impact of the Holocaust and postwar Jewish-Christian dialogue. This trailblazing scholarship and the changes it has sometimes generated in church life are to be commended.

Yet the impact of the Holocaust and of this dialogue has not been distributed evenly across the Christian world. In terms of American church life, with which I am most familiar, it appears that post-Holocaust theological and ecclesial reformation has not significantly penetrated the self-identified evangelical world, including Southern Baptists. The Christian side of the Jewish-Christian post-Holocaust dialogue has been led, on the whole, by Catholic and mainline Protestant intellectuals and church officials. Protestant evangelicals have not played a prominent role. Two unfortunate results have followed. First, evangelical theology and evangelical churches have not confronted, or been confronted by, the Holocaust. Second, a considerable

---

8. Gushee, *Righteous Gentiles of the Holocaust*.

amount of Christian post-Holocaust reflection is built on presuppositions that are rejected by evangelical Christians, or results in theological claims that would likewise be rejected if evangelicals paid any attention to them. For example, evangelical Christians will not accept any theological claim that abandons classic Christian beliefs about the person of Jesus: his messiahship, incarnation, bodily resurrection, or divinity. Likewise, most will reject any claim that the New Testament itself, erroneously and tragically, is antisemitic. The net result of these two problems is that the fastest-growing portion of the American church today, and the sector with the fastest-growing political and cultural strength, is coming to its ascendancy without serious reflection on the meaning of the Holocaust for its theology and church life. This is both lamentable and potentially disastrous.

What might the Christian rescuers have to offer those of us who want to articulate a Christian faith free of antisemitism? The following excerpts from interviews with Christian rescuers offer some guidance:

> We were brought up in a tradition in which we had learned that the Jewish people were the people of the Lord.
>
> The main reason [for rescue] is [that] we know that they are the Chosen People of God. We had to save them.
>
> My background is Christian Reformed; Israel has a special meaning for me. We have warm feelings for Israel.[9]

Research on the religiously motivated Christian rescuers has revealed that a significant percentage of such people refer to a special sense of religious kinship with Jews as a key motivation for their rescue work.[10] The most prominent single group of Christians thus motivated appear to have been those of the Dutch Reformed tradition. But the same pronounced religious philosemitism-of-a-sort can be found among representatives of other theologically orthodox or even fundamentalist groups involved in rescue. Examples of philosemitic French (Reformed) Protestants, French Darbyites, Ukrainian Baptists, Hungarian Methodists, and German Plymouth Brethren are available in the literature.[11] It should also be noted that individual rescuers who did not come from these kinds of Christian groups also sometimes held understandings of the Christian faith in which Jews were singled out not for particular contempt but for particular appreciation. This understanding of Jews and Judaism more than occasionally proved fruitful in motivating rescue.

9. Oliner and Oliner, *Altruistic Personality*, 154–55, 157.

10. Oliner and Oliner, *Altruistic Personality*, 154–55, 157; Baron, "The Holocaust and Human Decency," 244–45; Fleischner, "Can the Few Become the Many?," 239.

11. Gushee, *Righteous Gentiles of the Holocaust*, 119–25.

What clues might this Christian sense of special religious kinship with Jews, and the rescue that sometimes followed from it, offer the churches today?

The "special kinship rescuers," as I have called them elsewhere, show that there are resources available within well-established and theologically orthodox Christian traditions, such as the Calvinist tradition, that can generate respect and even admiration rather than contempt for Jews. That these traditions are theologically conservative and rooted in the Bible means that they can be of great usefulness in contemporary Christian faith communities that are themselves theologically conservative and Bible centered. These are communities that will not be open to extra- or contra-biblical theological claims emerging in response to the Holocaust, however well intended. It should be noted that most Protestant evangelicals draw a sharp line between the authority of Scripture and that of Christian tradition; the latter can be and is criticized relentlessly where criticism is due. This provides an opening for uprooting anti-Judaism in Christian tradition so long as that uprooting can be justified in biblical terms. Christian scholars and church leaders working in such communities, who want to articulate a Christian faith free of antisemitism, must fight the battle in the only place it can be won: within rather than beyond the established theological boundaries of those communities.

What can be offered within such boundaries is a non-antisemitic way of reading the biblical witness concerning the Jewish people, the Jewish covenant with God, and its status vis-à-vis the church's relationship with God, first-century Judaism, the life, teachings, and death of Jesus, the self-definitional struggles of the early church, the nature and meaning of the Torah and its significance after the coming of Jesus, and so on. This understanding can, at the least, defuse the very intense Christian antisemitism that can be found in the Scriptures if viewed through the lens of an (unconscious or conscious) anti-Jewish hermeneutical tradition. Indeed, those Christians who rescued Jews because of a religiously rooted love for the Jewish people show us the possibility of something far better than a Christianity merely purged of antisemitism. They show us a Christianity with positively philosemitic elements that helped motivate Christians to risk everything to save the lives of Jewish strangers. Surely, the witness of these rescuers must be taken very seriously.

LESSON 2: REDISCOVERING CHARACTER, REDEFINING CHRISTIAN VIRTUE

"A German woman knocked at my door. It was in the evening, and she said she was a German Jew, coming from northern France, that she was in danger... Could she come into my house? I said, 'Naturally, come in, and come in.'"[12]

The speaker is Magda Trocmé, who, with her husband, André, was at the heart of the well-known rescue efforts of the French village of Le Chambon-sur-Lignon. My interest here is in one striking word: "naturally." In offering shelter to a German Jewish woman, Magda Trocmé did what came naturally.[13] She offers no hint that she paused, considered, hesitated, or weighed pros and cons. One might suppose that such spontaneous, risk-taking moral action on behalf of a stranger would be extremely rare. But a number of rescuer researchers have discovered the same phenomenon: rescuers reporting that their involvement in rescue began as a spontaneous action or reaction, that little or no conscious reflection was required, and that their behavior was completely "natural" or obvious, what "anyone would have done."[14] Of course, such conduct was not what everyone actually did, as the historical record reveals so starkly.

How are we to account for the spontaneity and naturalness of rescue for so many rescuers? What might it mean for the churches? Though a number of other explanatory models might be offered from the point of view of different disciplines, as a Christian ethicist I am drawn to the category of character. Character can be defined as those distinctive personal attributes and predispositions developed during childhood and (normally) relatively stable through adulthood that are fundamental in shaping a person's moral consciousness and behavior. Character has to do with the moral being from which actions, moral doing, most often flow. Those who want to nurture moral goodness must attend to the formation of sound character, those deeply rooted perceptions, intentions, motives, dispositions, attitudes, habits, values, and so on that characterize a person over time and deeply shape his or her behavior. At least, this is the assertion of a number of Christian ethicists, who in recent years have argued for a rediscovery of the centrality of character in the genesis of human behavior, and for a consequent emphasis on character formation.

---

12. Hallie, *Lest Innocent Blood Be Shed*, 120.
13. Sauvage, *Weapons of the Spirit*.
14. Sauvage, interview by Bill Moyers.

An ethics of character poses a fundamental challenge to an ethics of decision making, which for many decades was offered by both Christian and other ethicists as the fundamental paradigm of the moral life. In this view, the moral life consists primarily of an individual's series of decisions about weighty moral dilemmas. The task of ethics is thus to propose a sophisticated model for decision making that enables people to weigh the relevant variables and come to a morally defensible choice. Certainly, the moral life of most people includes instances in which such decision making occurs and should occur. Models for decision making can be of great usefulness in such cases. But much human behavior simply does not occur in this way, even on matters of the greatest moral significance. Actions simply come naturally—they are predetermined or at least driven by the fundaments of a person's character. To talk with people about their decision-making method under such circumstances will strike them as nonsensical. They know what they have to do. Magda Trocmé and other spontaneous and natural rescuers illustrate the truth of this claim.

If this is true, then the churches' efforts in the arena of ethics should focus on character formation rather than—or more than—approaches to decision making. The goal of Christian ministers and teachers would then be to nurture Christian people, from birth, toward an authentic and morally constructive kind of Christian personhood or character, that is, toward the kind of character that would lead a Christian person to say to a stranger in need, "Naturally, come in, and come in." If Magda Trocmé is any indication, the presence of such character makes the development of elaborate decision-making theories unnecessary or at least secondary.

This discussion leads to a final point. The rediscovery of character alone is not enough. The churches must also attend to the normative content of character; that is, what kind of settled habits, dispositions, attitudes, and so on they want to see Christian people develop. For example, it is possible to develop an ethics of Christian character that is heavily privatized and focused on personal moral abstemiousness and the avoidance of the classic personal vices. This has been a pattern among many American evangelicals and Southern Baptists. In a culture in which such virtues seem in increasingly short supply, and their lack leads to considerable human misery, I do not disparage them. But the rescuers point us toward such social or public virtues as tenderheartedness and mercifulness, justice and fairness, courage and fortitude with a boundary-crossing love for the stranger and the persecuted. No account of Christian virtue or normative Christian character can do without these kinds of virtues.

LESSON 3: CREATING MORALLY FRUITFUL CHRISTIAN COMMUNITY

Character is learned and shaped in communities, beginning with the communities we call families. Communities themselves, moreover, accurately can be said to have a kind of character. Those who are concerned about the quality of human character must attend to the character of the groups that shape human lives and human conduct.

In the first section of this article, I pointed to the significance for some rescuers of membership in religious communities characterized by at least partially philosemitic theological beliefs. It would be a mistake to consider the behavior of these philosemitic rescuers in abstraction from the religious communities that nurtured such morally fruitful convictions. In the last section, we considered the character of Magda Trocmé. Pierre Sauvage, Philip Hallie, and others who have studied rescue in Le Chambon have pointed out the fundamentally communitarian nature of rescue in and around that village. Rescue was the work not simply of Chambonnais individuals but of the community of Le Chambon. This was true not only to the extent that the community worked together to organize rescue activities but more broadly in the sense that rescue emerged from the collective and historical consciousness and commitments—that is, the corporate character—of that community of people in southern France. The same can be said of rescue in the predominantly Protestant Cévennes region nearby, which has been the subject of more recent scholarly attention.[15]

In fact, it seems increasingly clear that rescue was far more often the activity of communities, broadly defined, than of lone individuals. This was true not only of rescue in Le Chambon, the Cévennes, the Dutch village of Nieuwlande, the entire nation of Denmark, Bulgaria's rescue of its Jews, and the handful of other instances of corporate rescue that have been uncovered. Over a decade ago, Douglas Huneke proposed that "communal rescues" were one of the three major types of rescue activity that can be identified. He defined communal rescues as those undertaken by groups of people living in close proximity with each other, sharing long-established values, functioning as a cohesive group prior to the war, associating with one another voluntarily, and establishing an intentional rescue plan and network.[16] Likewise, Samuel and Pearl Oliner have claimed that nearly every rescuer they interviewed was involved in some kind of supportive network. Just under half of these were formal resistance or rescue groups like the Polish group

---

15. Oline, "Rescuing the Hidden Story," 4–7, 11.
16. Huneke, "Glimpses of Light in a Vast Darkness," 488.

Zegota; the rest were informal, ad hoc, clandestine networks of families and friends, neighbors and nameless strangers, Jews and Gentiles, all working together to rescue Jews.[17] A close reading of most rescuer memoirs also reveals the existence of such fluid, free-form rescue networks.

Rescuer communities and networks performed two distinct kinds of tasks for those involved in rescue, both of fundamental importance. On the one hand, they provided the physical resources—safehouses, transport, clothing, money, connections, information, and so on—that made rescue possible, and on a much larger scale than that which a lone individual could do. On the other hand, rescuer networks also provided intangible but critical communal moral support and reinforcement for frightening and very difficult activities, activities that, again, were much easier to undertake if done with a group rather than on one's own. Rescuer networks were in this sense moral communities, often quite diverse in their membership, which both reflected and nurtured the kind of character necessary to rescue Jews during the Holocaust.

One of the deepest griefs I have felt in wresting with the Holocaust has been in thinking about the churches' lost opportunities to function as precisely such rescuer communities, or as parts of such rescuer communities. Churches, religious orders, seminaries, orphanages, church-run hospitals, and the like could be found throughout Nazi-occupied Europe, even in the most remote areas. Each such religious institution was linked or could easily be linked with others in its community and region, and most were part of a national and even international network of like institutions. After the Nazis crushed all rival political parties, first in Germany and then throughout most of the lands they occupied, no other set of institutions survived that had comparable organizational potential to thwart their plans—and the Nazis knew and feared this. Even a casual reading of Holocaust and rescuer literature reveal that what might be called the Christian infrastructure of Europe was indeed involved in the rescue of Jews. But if this infrastructure had been mobilized to its full potential, it could have done so much more.

The lesson I would draw for Christian leaders and ministers from the foregoing is simply that we must seek to nurture morally fruitful Christian communities. Such communities would be the kind of communities that would produce rescuers working alongside friends and strangers, Jews and other Christians, in skillful and supportive networks. These would be Christian communities that understood both their faith and their times well enough to know that rescue was required of them in this situation. They would learn together how to organize that rescue and to carry it out as

---

17. Oliner and Oliner, *Altruistic Personality*, 93.

effectively as possible. They would cling together and encourage each other amid the suffering of rescue, reminding one another that such suffering is part of what it means to be a people of God. The development of this kind of community with these kinds of skills and commitments ought always to be the churches' goal, regardless of the particular immediate crisis or lack thereof. This commitment is simply the character of an authentic Christian community—a community ready at all times to act on behalf of the victimized, the powerless, the hungry, the homeless, and the stranger.

LESSON 4: NURTURING A PIETY THAT DOES JUSTICE

The devout of every religious tradition have available to them what might be called a repertoire of piety and spirituality. This repertoire consists of those religious practices, experiences, and feelings that infuse religious faith with the spiritual vitality that makes it come alive in practice; it empowers believers, enabling them not only to know but to do what they are religiously obligated to do. This repertoire is mediated to each believer through the faith community; though believers in each generation deepen and enrich the repertoire itself—and both faith community and individual believer normally see the spiritual vitality resulting from this piety as a gift from God.

Research on the religiously motivated Christian rescuers has shown that this repertoire of piety was critical both in leading these Christians into rescue and in sustaining them in their very demanding and frightening efforts. In a previous work, I have identified the following elements of such rescuer piety:

> staying alert to communication from God, initiating communication with God through prayer, reading the Bible for guidance and strength to endure, searching for God's will and being utterly devoted to its performance, desiring to please God and avoid God's displeasure, experiencing a sense of God's living and providential presence in one's life, and involving oneself in a group of Christians doing rescue and together seeking sustenance in the faith.[18]

For those of us steeped in the study of the Holocaust, it is easy to want to dismiss everything Christian, including the Christian repertoire of piety. We know the moral collapse of Christian Europe during the Holocaust far too well. Where we see any sign of Christian devotion or piety in that darkness,

---

18. Gushee, *Righteous Gentiles of the Holocaust*, 169–70.

it is all too often the horrifying Christian piety of the devout antisemite, the one who collaborates with the Nazis in the name of Christ and then returns to his prayers at church on Sunday morning as if nothing has happened. This is an ancient form of Christian antisemitic piety, one that long preceded the Nazis and one that continues today. Alternatively, we can look to the tortured lands of the former Yugoslavia, in which some Christians recently were motivated in their misdeeds by the unholy amalgam of religion, ethnicity, and nationalism. It is hard to be enthusiastic about a Christian piety expressed in the form of men carrying religious icons with them while they rape Muslim women and burn mosques to the ground. There is indeed a kind of Christian piety that works hatred and even death.

Among evangelicals in North America today, Christian piety rarely takes such a virulent form. More often, its flaw is its self-centered privatism. The purpose of prayer, Bible study, worship, and corporate Christian experiences of all types is to meet the individual's needs, to help the individual find meaning, to help him or her cope with the frustrations and challenges of everyday life. Many observers have noted a resurgent interest in spirituality in the United States today. It looks as if our cultural experiment with secularism is collapsing all around us, and people are groping for alternatives. But much of the newly available literature simply reinforces the pattern; it is aimed at the individual seeking meaning, hope, and healing.

The piety of religiously motivated Christian rescuers was neither hate-reinforcing nor self-centered. It was a piety that began with a faith characterized by compassion and an orientation to others' needs. All aspects of piety reinforced this basic orientation. The search for God's will and the commitment to obeying it deepened the compassion and empowered Christians to act on it, as did the desire to please God and the fear of God's displeasure. Religious practices such as prayer, Bible study, and worship provided living moral power for the hard work of rescue. Those of us who live and work among Christian people know that there are among us certain people consistently involved in acts of love, compassion, and justice on behalf of others. One finds that not only do such people believe an authentically compassionate version of Christianity but they also practice a piety that empowers them to do what they believe. It is not enough to have compassionate convictions but no spiritual vitality; nor is it sufficient to have spiritual vitality but coldhearted convictions. What is needed is a compassionate version of the Christian faith and the spiritual power to act on it. The Christian rescuers help to show us the way.

LESSON 5: RECOVERING THE CONSTRUCTIVE MORAL POWER OF THE BIBLE

"We were all taught the second great commandment, 'You shall love your neighbor as yourself.' So I knew what I must do . . . It was no big thing." These were the words of Tadeusz Soroka, a Pole who rescued several Jews during the Holocaust.[19] His words can serve as one example among many of the times in which the Bible served as a critical resource for Christian rescue. Other biblical passages often cited by rescuers included the parable of the Good Samaritan, the Golden Rule, the Great Judgment, and the story of Cain and Abel ("Am I my brother's keeper?"). An array of other biblical texts appear on occasion in rescuer testimony and research.[20]

In considering the constructive moral power of the Bible, we must do so again in the shadow of the Holocaust, for we cannot and must not forget the many ways in which the Bible has been used to serve morally destructive purposes. The most germane misuse of the Bible, for my purposes here, has been in advancing Christian antisemitism, as discussed previously. But looking more broadly, we cannot fail to note the use of the Bible to defend slavery; to oppress women, to justify religious wars, and to buttress the hatred of homosexuals. The latter is a particularly pressing issue in the North American setting today.

Some have viewed the horrendous misuse of the Bible as reason enough to reject it and the Christian faith that so cherishes it. But the situation is more complex than this; all of the evidence must be considered. One piece of that evidence is that there were Christians in Nazi-occupied Europe who risked their lives to rescue Jews because they believed that the Bible demanded such action. Close attention to the texts that proved most important for rescue indicate that these indeed demand love and compassion on behalf of others, even (especially) the needy stranger. When read by a Christian who believes that the Bible authoritatively reveals the will of God (and who believes that Christians are obligated to do the will of God once it is revealed to them, as discussed in the last section), these biblical texts provide especially powerful incentive for rescue. Those who preach and teach the Bible in Christian faith communities should hear in the foregoing a word both of warning and of encouragement. The word of warning is that the Bible has been and is easily misused and that oppression and destruction have been the result. This warning is especially needed in evangelical circles, where a high view of the authority of the Bible makes it harder to

---

19. Paldiel, "Hesed and the Holocaust," 104.

20. Huneke, "Glimpses of Light in a Vast Darkness," 490; Gushee, *Righteous Gentiles of the Holocaust*.

acknowledge its history of, and potential for, destructive misuse and where the potential for future misuse is thus all the greater. It is the responsibility of Christian leaders to prevent this from happening, through vigilant watchfulness over the use of the Bible in the churches, as well as through the appropriate stewardship of the Bible in their own work with Christian people. A key aspect of this stewardship is to make sure that central biblical teachings enjoining compassion and love for all people, including the stranger—the teachings that most frequently inspired rescue—return to the forefront of Christian preaching and teaching.

The word of encouragement is that even today the Bible, read rightly, can be a source of constructive moral power for Christian people who understand it as the authoritative revelation of the will of God. One of the central tasks of the Christian leader is to see to it that the community of faith understands the Bible in a morally constructive rather than morally destructive way. It seems to me that this is the "battle for the Bible" that is the one most worth fighting.

LESSON 6: ACHIEVING THEOLOGICAL CONVICTION WITHOUT INTOLERANCE

One of the great challenges that faces the churches in every age is the task of nurturing serious Christian theological conviction without simultaneously encouraging intolerance, especially religious intolerance. Surely, the same challenge is faced by those of many other faiths.

The link between serious theological conviction and religious intolerance is very easy to identify. Historical Christian antisemitism, for example, has been fed by deeply felt belief in Jesus as Messiah and as the only way to salvation; grief over his death (marked weekly in many churches in somber Eucharistic ceremonies) has been transmuted easily into hatred for those inaccurately deemed responsible for it, the Jewish people. Likewise, it is no accident that those in American society most vehemently opposed to the acceptance of homosexuality as a legitimate form of sexual expression are those who most ardently believe that the Bible carries divine authority and that it condemns homosexuality.

Is the solution, then, to discourage serious religious conviction? Perhaps if believers were encouraged toward less ardent religious conviction, they would be more tolerant. If they held their beliefs with less assurance and were more willing to "listen to reason," intolerance would decline. Some would argue, and have argued, that this is the path to take.

The religiously motivated Christian rescuers offer one reason for a reconsideration of that kind of solution to religious intolerance. One finds in the testimony of these rescuers a set of rock-solid theological convictions, some of which were outlined earlier in this article—convictions about the special place of the Jewish people in God's plan, about the responsibility to act with love and compassion toward the needy, about the duty to do God's will, about the providential care of God, about the reality of God's final judgment of one's life. Here I would add one more, which elsewhere I have identified as one of the major religious motivations for resistance and rescue—theological conviction about the incompatibility between Nazism and Christian faith.[21] These were Christians who listened to Hitler's hate-filled rantings, watched the SS round up Jews in the streets and commit random murder, and simply knew that here they were witnessing the antithesis of their most deeply felt religious and moral convictions. These revolting experiences then moved them to act on behalf of Jewish people in need and to oppose the Nazis in any other feasible way.

So perhaps the problem is not serious religious conviction, but the precise nature of those convictions; likewise, perhaps the issue is not whether intolerance is produced by those convictions, but what it is exactly that is not tolerated. Christian rescuers were convinced that their faith demanded compassion and love on behalf of the oppressed, and this is a conviction we rightly celebrate. It was a conviction that moved them to risk life and family for Jewish people. Likewise, they were intolerant of Nazism and its evil fruits, and this intolerance we rightly celebrate.

Some human beings do not partake of serious religious conviction and are not moved by what such conviction tolerates and does not. The challenge for them is to find another ground of serious conviction and another way of determining what kind of behavior to celebrate and what to abhor. It is by no means self-evident that a religious path toward conviction and tolerance (or intolerance) is inferior to a nonreligious one. It is clear that religious conviction is a powerful source both for appropriate and inappropriate conviction and for appropriate and inappropriate intolerance. The Christian rescuers show us praiseworthy religious conviction and appropriate intolerance of evil. The challenge for the churches is to see to it that other Christians follow the same path.

---

21. Gushee, *Righteous Gentiles of the Holocaust*, 129–32.

LESSON 7: SHAPING AN APPROPRIATE CHRISTIAN PATRIOTISM

Patriotism is one of humanity's abiding passions. As such, it is a source both of good and of evil. Christian thinking about patriotism, at least in the American setting, has tended toward polarization. Some have argued that there is no place for any significant kind of love for country in the Christian life, since we are pledged to Jesus Christ and him alone as Lord. The tendency here is to move toward some version of pacifist internationalism. At the other pole are those who embrace a militant or at least enthusiastic patriotism and who link it in one way or another with Christian faith, as in the concept that the United States is God's chosen nation. This is the path more frequently taken by American evangelicals.

The Holocaust and the rescuers starkly illustrate both the peril and the promise of patriotism, and especially the relation between patriotism and Christian faithfulness. The peril of patriotism is exemplified by every Hans, Friedrich, and Wilhelm who left his Christian home and church in Germany and went east, unquestioningly murdering Jews (and Poles and Russians and others) in the name of the Reich and on its orders. But the promise of patriotism is exemplified by those who resisted Nazism as an act of fidelity to their nations. Every major study of rescuers has found that a certain percentage of them acted to save Jews on the basis of loyalty to national values.[22] This occurred both counterculturally, as when Dietrich Bonhoeffer resisted Nazism in the name of what he considered authentically German national values, and with the culture, as when Danes helped Jews escape to Sweden as a collective expression of loyalty to Danish identity and national convictions.

These expressions of patriotism—one with and one against the prevailing cultural climate—had one thing in common: both reflected a kind of patriotism that included the equality of diverse groups within the nation as a central value. On the basis of their research, Samuel and Pearl Oliner have reported that rescuers did not differ from nonrescuers in the level of their patriotism. They did differ in the nature of their patriotism; rescuers were more likely to embrace this kind of democratic and pluralistic patriotism than were nonrescuers.[23] This was the kind of patriotism that led to rescue.

Here is where patriotism and the Christian rescuers meet and where a lesson for the churches can be drawn. There is a kind of exclusivistic and

---

22. Oliner and Oliner, *Altruistic Personality*, 157; Tec, *When Light Pierced the Darkness*; Fogelman, "The Rescuers," 162–71; Gushee, "Many Paths to Righteousness," 387–88.

23. Oliner and Oliner, *Altruistic Personality*, 159.

chauvinistic patriotism with which most nations are at least occasionally tempted, especially powerful ones. On the basis of their theological convictions, Christians can only reject this kind of patriotism. All too often we do not do so, as was the case with so much of the German church during the Nazi era. Yet there is a kind of patriotism that complements rather than contradicts authentic Christian beliefs. This is a patriotism that is inclusive, democratic, compassionate, and just in its orientation. For religiously motivated Christian rescuers, patriotism was not normally the most fundamental motivating force for action on behalf of Jews, but it could be a complementary factor, flowing together with religious conviction to reinforce the compulsion to rescue Jews from Nazi hands. Where patriotism is seen in the testimony of the religiously motivated Christian rescuers, this is the version of it that almost always appears.

LESSON 8: IDENTIFYING COMPETENT CHRISTIAN MORAL LEADERSHIP

Holocaust researchers often and rightly argue that Christian officials in Europe during the Holocaust—at international, national, regional, and local levels—in general did not acquit themselves well. It is not too much to claim that there was a collapse of Christian leadership during that catastrophe. It is a collapse that the churches have had to reflect upon and respond to for some fifty years. This does not mean that no Christian leaders acted on behalf of Jews and guided their flocks in that direction; it does mean that those who did were the exception and not the rule.

Those of us involved in seminary education deal daily with the development of Christian leaders. We are the ones who train the men and women who will lead churches and religious institutions for many years to come. When we send them off to the churches, we certify that they have completed a rigorous course of study that has prepared them for the Christian ministry. The question that must haunt every one of us after the Holocaust is this: have we identified and trained ministers who will offer competent moral leadership?

In American evangelical circles, the phrase "moral leadership" will most readily bring to mind leadership in the area of personal morality. Thus a minister offers competent moral leadership if he or she models and teaches a rigorous personal moral code and if his or her flock responds well to this instruction. Alternatively, "moral leadership" might also bring to mind contemporary social issues such as abortion, racism, and the environment.

More politically minded congregations might seek a minister who can mobilize the church to become engaged with these kinds of issues.

Yet the churches' response to the Holocaust (mainly failed, occasionally faithful) is the paradigm that shapes my sense of competent Christian moral leadership. Christian moral leadership in this case would have included the ability and the courage to articulate a faith filled with love and compassion, even for the stranger; even for the Jew. It would have articulated the limits of legitimate political authority and the duty to resist rulers who write laws that violate the moral laws of God. It would have outlined the theological incompatibility of Nazism and Christian faith. It would have instructed Christians in the high price to be paid sometimes for fidelity to authentic Christian faith. It would have reinforced in the congregants' minds the constant requirement to do God's will, whatever the situation. It would, of course, have sought opportunities to aid Jews and to enlist parishioners in such activities. It would have called on the faith community to cling tightly and faithfully to one another in the midst of such actions, drawing strength from Christian community. It would have taken advantage of whatever possibility it might have had to offer public moral leadership in the community, region, or nation on the question of the persecution of the Jews. It would have established a moral atmosphere in which actual involvement in support of such persecutions was completely beyond the pale. This was the kind of Christian moral leadership offered by André Trocmé and his associates in Le Chambon and by a handful of other Christian ministers across the continent of Europe.

It might be argued that surely this is a path to death. But, just as surely, the possibility of death as a consequence of following Jesus is constitutive of Christian faith: "Anyone who does not carry his cross and follow me cannot be my disciple" (Luke 14:27, NIV). The possibility of death should come as no surprise at all. To train competent Christian moral leadership requires us to train men and women who are prepared to suffer and die in the service of Christian moral fidelity

CONCLUSION

After the Holocaust, the Christian faith and Christian churches stand indicted. We must show how we can be a morally constructive part of the human future after Auschwitz. We must show how our wartime failures will serve as the source of reformation.

I have argued that the religiously motivated Christian rescuers help us to see a way forward. These were people whose version(s) of the Christian faith and whose practice of the Christian life led them to the rescue of Jews. They show us morally constructive and empowering resources at the heart of traditional, orthodox Christian faith—and morally inspiring people who embodied those resources. They give us hope that other Christians can "go and do likewise."

They do not offer any guarantees of Christian moral goodness, however. As we surveyed the different aspects of their Christian faith and practice, we saw that at every point there is the possibility of a slide into moral ineffectualness or even disaster. Commitment to the Bible can be turned to antisemitism; Christian character can be weak or priggish; Christian community can be nonexistent or vapid; Christian piety can nurture hate or self-centeredness rather than compassion; theological conviction can be turned to exclusivist intolerance; Christian patriotism can be jingoistic and chauvinist; Christian leaders can be swept away by cultural currents and in other ways fail to offer genuine leadership.

What is required of the churches after the Holocaust is neither the mass production of just any kind of Christian and Christianity nor the stripping down and abandonment of Christian faith altogether. Instead, it is the production and reproduction of a quality of Christian person and Christian faith that is both true to the Founder and morally constructive in a world such as this. Imitation of those Christians whose faith inspired them to risk everything to rescue Jews during the Holocaust seems a good place to start.

2

Tears of a Generation
Thinking about Divorce as if Children Matter
1998

A VIGNETTE

I OPEN WITH A letter from a father to the daughter he hasn't seen in ten years, since he divorced her mother:

> Dear Sally,
>
> Thank you for the Father's Day card. I do not wish to appear cynical, but this is the first Father's Day card you sent; so I suspect you want something (Furthermore I feel your mother's hand in this.)
> To be honest Sally, if you want something, why don't you ask for it straight out. I know this is not the way you were brought up . . . but you now have the opportunity and hopefully the maturity to be straightforward.
> In your last letter (again motivated by your mother), you stated you were attending college. I wish you the best most sincerely.
> In the same letter, you stated you didn't hate me . . . but you hated what I did. Specifically, what did I do that you hated [?] I doubt your mother would want you to say; most assuredly she would not want me to answer.
> Hopefully we will continue corresponding, with the criteria we be honest. I abhor hypocrisy (1 had ten years of it)
> Love,
> Jim Patterson

And here is an excerpt from Sally's response:

> Hey! Where do I begin? I suppose that "You're Welcome" is appropriate. Actually, you don't have to thank me for the Father's Day card, I should have been sending them all along . . .
>
> I want nothing but a relationship with you. I have finally come to my senses. I've realized that I've missed out on a big part of my life . . . My only intention in writing includes patching up our differences and trying to make my wrong right. I'm sorry if I caught you off guard . . .
>
> As for hating you, I could never do that, you are my father. As for hating what you did, well, did you forget me? Or did you just give up? Did you care what I was doing or . . . the person that I developed into? My last letter was sent only to inform you of what is going on in my life. I thought that maybe you wondered . . .
>
> I hope that you believe my sincerity in that I truly want to know about you. Again, mom has no hand in this. I promise to be as honest as I can. . .
>
> Sally[1]

INTRODUCTION

What would a Christian ethical treatment of divorce look like if the experiences of children of divorce were taken seriously? Can we construct an ethic of divorce as if children matter?

This question lies at the heart of an ongoing book project on which I am working. I have believed for some time that Christian moral reflection (not to mention moral practice) on divorce is grossly inadequate. Old categories have been displaced by the tidal wave of cultural change, and no new paradigms have emerged to take their place. Thus Christian ethics and the church have remained uncomfortably silent on one of the most significant moral issues of our time.

Christian silence on a significant moral issue is itself deeply problematic. It means that we who are called to provide moral leadership in and to the church are not doing our job. Aware of this, I have dabbled in moral reflection on divorce for a number of years.

However, the focus on the children of divorce is relatively new. It emerged—appropriately enough, given this setting—through the pastoral ministry in which I informally engage as a Christian studies professor at a Baptist university. Last spring—the first year of my teaching at Union

---

1. Provided by interviewee.

University—I found myself in a series of unplanned pastoral visits with students, like Sally, who were struggling with the impact of divorce on their lives. These visits were extraordinarily intense. For a brief period it seemed as if every day brought a new child with a broken heart.

At that time it became clear to me that the impact of divorce on children should function as a key point of entry, if not the very core, of Christian moral reflection on divorce. It did not take much biblical study or moral reflection to recall that the heart of the biblical moral witness is concern for the voiceless, wounded, powerless, and oppressed. Scripture teaches that God is One who hears the cries of the victimized and intervenes to deliver them from their bondage into wholeness and community—and that the community of faith is to participate with God in siding with the oppressed and acting on their behalf in whatever way is needed.

One could hardly think of a contemporary group of sufferers who betters fits the biblical definition of the oppressed than the children of divorce. They are the quintessential powerless group of our time. Like Sally (a pseudonymous college student, whose all-too-typical exchange of letters has been excerpted with permission), their suffering is entirely the result of someone else's decisions. There is nothing they can do about what happens to them. They are the weakest party in the ongoing drama of divorce and its aftermath. All clinical evidence is clear that divorce has a negative psychological impact on every child who experiences it, though the form and extent of this impact varies considerably, and conflict within marriages also causes stress. To stand up for the children of divorce is akin to speaking up for the orphans of biblical times. To provide a platform from which they can voice their pain is—or must be—a significant dimension of contemporary moral response to divorce. This is so even if it makes us grownups entirely uncomfortable.

On the basis of these convictions I have undertaken a series of interviews with children of divorce, ages eighteen to twenty-five. My conversation partners are almost entirely Union University students, though I have had a handful of interviews with others. The homogeneity of the group could be seen as a problem except for two things: first, the fact that these students overwhelmingly come from so-called Christian homes affords a significant glimpse into what exactly is going on behind the scenes in the lives of those who are members and even leaders in our churches. Second, in a sense, that homogeneity is more apparent than real. Every person's experience is different and compelling in its own way.

Thus far I have completed thirty interviews. I would like to report some early gleanings from these interviews and reflect very briefly on their significance for Christian ethics and the church. These findings are undergirded by and filtered through research in the most significant current works on the experience of divorce.

MAIN FINDINGS: INSIDE THE DIVORCE CULTURE

The stories of children of divorce do not fit into a single coherent narrative pattern. Much depends on when divorce comes upon children, how divorce is handled both at the time and in the years that follow, and what shape family life takes after divorce. However, thus far I am finding that divorce is the single most significant event in the lives of children who must suffer it. As one of my children of divorce has written:

> Every day I think of my parents' divorce at least once. I consider the ramifications of their decisions and actions. I wish that I could remember the good memories from my childhood. I wonder what my life would be like today if my past were different... I think about what a childhood without adult responsibility would have been like... Every day I relive the pain in some way. *Every day*.[2]

Life before Divorce

Children of divorce have had various experiences of either joy or misery prior to divorce. For some, divorce comes as a total shock, disrupting a childhood they experienced as quite positive and relatively free of marital troubles. In the shadow cast by divorce, these childhood memories are particularly bittersweet:

> I remember my younger sister and I would sit on the roof and my Dad would hit plastic golf balls up to the roof, and he would say 'Scoot back. Don't get too close to the edge.' And we would catch those. My favorite meal was ribs, rice, and green beans, and we had this little grill... and my dad would cook the best ribs on that...[3]

A surprising number of my interview subjects in fact report many positive impressions and memories from childhood. Life was once good, but then there was a turn in the road, a change of atmosphere. Dad changed, Mom changed, or their marriage took a turn for the worse.

2. Interview by author.
3. Interview by author.

Reasons for Divorce

Divorce researchers are particularly interested in the causes of divorce. My interviews reveal a distressing litany of marriage destroyers. They include a surprising number of cases of adultery; financial disagreements; communication breakdowns; work-related stresses and absences from home; midlife crises, personality changes, and other character-related causes. Some divorces happen for no reason that either the abandoned spouse or the children can articulate. Thus far it appears that the "amicable mutual divorce" is very rare indeed. Regardless of the legal fiction of no-fault divorce, most divorces do indeed involve some action or series of actions that break the marriage covenant. Children of divorce certainly never experience it as an amiable, faultless parting of the ways.

The Experience of Divorce

Sometimes divorce comes upon the household with great suddenness. Other times the tension level has reached such a crescendo that everyone knows separation or divorce is imminent. In either case, children of divorce never forget the moment in which they get the news. It is seared in their memories:

> When [my mom, sister, and I] pulled into the driveway Dad had all of his things packed into his car. As we opened the door to go in he was on his way out. He was very surprised that we were there. It was a strange confrontation. He was just slipping out . . . I don't know how he was planning to tell us . . . Dad sat us down and said that he was leaving and that he had an apartment . . . It was fake because he was saying how much he was going to miss us and that he loved us. I was on an emotional rollercoaster and not able to sort out everything . . .[4]

Divorce and the Law

Children of divorce are struck by how easy it is for one or both of their parents to obtain the divorce that shatters the kids' world; yet they also suffer through legal struggles over custody, alimony, and child support:

---

4. Interview by author.

> As hard as it was I think it was too easy. They both went to lawyers and they said okay fill out these papers ... It was almost like buying a car. You have decided to do something and the lawyer says yeah give me this much money and I'll milk the other for all he or she has. There is no justice there ...[5]

Life After Divorce

The most common pattern of post-divorce life for my interview subjects, as for children of divorce nationally, is to live with their mothers while struggling to establish some workable relationship with their fathers. As Judith Wallerstein (*Second Chances*) in particular has argued, post-divorce life creates particular strains and stresses, and children frequently lose emotional if not physical access to not just one but both parents.[6]

Very few of my children of divorce enjoy a satisfying relationship with their fathers. Interstate moves, as in the case of Sally, make such relationships nearly impossible; yet the entire concept of the visiting father, even if local, is a difficult one—as David Blankenhorn has so cogently argued in *Fatherless America*.[7] Thus the spectacle of Sally, quoted above, who has not seen her father in ten years yet apologizes to him for her supposed failure to maintain the relationship—and her father, whose sense of himself as Sally's father has become so attenuated that he signs his letter, "Jim Patterson."

Meanwhile, my children of divorce tend to admire their mothers for their heroic efforts to maintain the family. My findings confirm those of Lenore Weitzman and others that the standard of living for single mothers and their children tends to drop, sometimes precipitously, and that the father who pays all ordered child support is a rare thing.[8] As Bill testifies,

> There was an economic impact on our lives ... He did not pay child support and alimony ... My mother suffered tremendously so my sister and I would not feel the impact. I remember her sitting down with us and showing us her paycheck and saying this is all we have. These are the things we need and let's all make out a budget and see how we are going to make this work.[9]

---

5. Interview by author.
6. Wallerstein and Blakeslee, *Second Chances*.
7. Blankenhorn, *Fatherless America*.
8. Weitzman, *The Divorce Revolution*.
9. Interview by author.

And yet the effort of working two or more jobs, raising a family alone, and dealing with the grief of divorce takes its toll on single mothers. Children end up in many cases raising themselves, and even, at times, caring for their mothers in a strange role reversal. Divorce all too frequently costs children both of their parents.

Post-Divorce Family Forms

Life after divorce is profoundly affected by whether or not a child's parents date, cohabit, and remarry. I have been surprised at the extent to which serial cohabitation and monogamy have penetrated the heartland, including the supposedly Christian homes from which many of these children of divorce come. Listen in on the following interview exchange:

Q: How many times has your father been married?

A: Let's see—There was Jill number one, then my mom, then Jill number two, then he married again in there, then Belinda. So I think we are on number five.

Q: How many times has your mother been married?

A: I think this is number ten. I kind of lost count, and one of them she married twice so I don't know how you count that. But ten's a good guess.[10]

While this is the most extreme case in my interviews (so far) it is by no means unique. For all too many children of divorce, childhood consists of a dizzying array of unstable and ever reconfiguring families, with the various moves, homes, and fluctuating step- and half-siblings and other in-and-out relatives that this means. I was not prepared to discover the depth and breadth of the relational chaos that has come to constitute family life in America today. The consequences for children are severe. Several of my students remind me of trauma survivors. While I'm no specialist, I think some could qualify as post-traumatic stress syndrome candidates.

Violence

Divorce is sometimes preceded by family violence—and in my interviews I find that violence *follows* divorce even more frequently. Perhaps the most shocking moment in my interviews thus far was the following comment from one of my older interview subjects, who along with her brother was asked by her mother and her mother's new lover to kill their father. She describes her recovery of this memory in the following way:

---

10. Interview by author.

Years later when I had kind of pushed things aside . . . I kept thinking to myself, "I must have dreamed this." I started having flashbacks. I had had my first child, and I didn't even tell my husband because I couldn't believe that this really happened. I was talking to my brother one day [on the phone]. I said, "Do you remember, I hope I really imagined this, but do you remember that they talked about killing [Dad]?" And he said, "Don't you remember? He [the step-father] had said that we should do it, and that was the only way to solve the problems." I just broke down because I can't imagine someone telling a child that . . . "Oh," he [the step-father] said, "You might get sent to a reform school, but we'll come visit you." He's an evil man.[11]

Impotence of Christian Faith and the Church

While most of my children of divorce come from Christian homes, they almost universally report that the supposed Christian faith of their parents played no role in inhibiting the move toward divorce and the behaviors that led to it. These were ministers, deacons, "every-time-the-[church]-doors-were-open" Christians who committed adultery, got in trouble with the law, beat their spouses, and otherwise destroyed their families. There is little evidence that these men and women thought coherently about how their behaviors fit with their supposed faith.

Likewise, the churches in which these crises occurred offered few if any programmatic, counseling, or relational resources that could make a difference. While there were some constructive exceptions, the churches generally stood impotently by as their members' families disintegrated. Usually, though not always, the divorced were pressured to remove themselves from church leadership positions. Frequently, they stopped attending church altogether. So if there can be said to be a common church response in these interviews, it was the response of informal exclusion of the divorcing adults from leadership positions.

The children of divorce sometimes sought out Christian friends for personal support, and thankfully this support was sometimes available. But other times children of divorce experienced rejection as their friends' parents—due to a strange kind of logic of tainting—sought to sever their children's ties with children of divorce. The overall picture of the role of the church in either preventing divorce or helping to pick up the pieces is distressing in the extreme.

11. Interview by author.

Emotional Impact on Children

The children of divorce respond to their experiences with different emotional mechanisms. Some, especially the young men, have clearly flattened out their grief into a kind of hard, cynical anger. For others, especially women, the grief is at or very near the surface. I remember Jenny, who began to cry even before we started talking, and ended her interview with the same tears and these wrenching words: "I think I would have been a daddy's girl."[12]

There are no children of divorce for whom divorce is an insignificant event. A minority experience it as a kind of relief after the stresses of marital conflict, but not the majority. Many report a continuing sadness and grief, and this shows on their faces. Many have struggled with depression. Frequently they experience difficult or nonexistent relationships today with one or both of their parents. They tend to have fewer financial resources for college (due to the fact that fathers are not obligated to pay college tuition, which is a great injustice) and so they struggle to make it through school. Their emotional base of support from "the folks back home" is also far less stable than the average student enjoys.

They desire trusting and intimate relationships but report difficulty in establishing them, some more than others. They have no model for how to make an opposite-sex relationship succeed, and so they grasp in various directions for help on that score. Some fear the prospect of marriage, while others are eager to get married and to do better than their own parents—a nearly universal refrain among them. Many have a clear sense of what is required to make that happen. There is reason for hope as one talks with them. Many are quite inspiring.

I would be remiss not to report on the role of Christian faith for these children of divorce. While many are not all that articulate about it, they usually indicate that it was their faith that helped them to survive their childhood trials.

Beth told me of the time that her father was moving out—he and her mother were sitting at the kitchen table exhaustedly sorting out details of his departure after one last frantic fight. Beth, who was not close to her father, found one of his shirts, put it on, and climbed up onto her roof. It was raining. As the rain mixed with her tears, she seriously considered jumping in an attempt to put an end to her pain. Yet as she considered this she felt a strong sense of God's presence. She reported to me that she sensed the love of God and a message that God had a purpose for her life. She did not jump.

---

12. Interview by author.

Now she wants to be a minister to youth, especially children of divorce. Her story is similar to that of many others in my research thus far.

PRELIMINARY GLEANINGS FOR CHRISTIAN ETHICS

The Christian moral tradition began with a very strong presumption against divorce. Rooted in the teachings of Jesus and Paul, divorce was understood to be a violation of the intentions of God. The Catholic Church took the position, and holds it to this day, that divorce is not only immoral but metaphysically impossible: (validly contracted) marriages are literally indissoluble. While Protestant churches have always been less absolutist than this, the Reformers and those who followed after them believed that divorce should be a rare exception. Western law has historically reflected Christian moral tradition in its restrictions on access to divorce.

As the reality of deeply troubled marriages became more visible in recent centuries, and as the pressure for divorce grew in the latter stages of our century, Christian moral thinkers (outside of the very most conservative voices in Catholic and Protestant circles) have generally tended to weaken their absolute or near-absolute opposition to divorce. Indeed, the issue has tended to drop from the ethical radarscope, while churches have focused attention on divorce recovery and other pastoral post-divorce initiatives. Progressive-minded church leaders have wanted perhaps above all to avoid the taint of previous "legalisms" and the piling on of guilt onto the heads of the divorced.

But as we make the turn into the twenty-first century, fully thirty years or so into the age of mass divorce, the times call for a new approach. The need of the hour is not to help the divorced feel good about themselves but instead to push back with energy and creativity against the divorce culture (Barbara Dafoe Whitehead's phrase)[13] in which we all are now engulfed.

There are many reasons for this revision in approach but perhaps the testimony of the children of divorce is the most compelling. More than one million children each year in this nation experience the kind of trauma I have outlined above. Their lives are indisputably marred by the actions that others visit upon them. We now see that divorce is a justice issue—not only for its children but frequently for single mothers and sometimes for men. If we approach the ethics of divorce as if its victims matter, we will find ourselves engaged in a total rethinking of our current stance.

A revisiting of the Christian ethics of divorce will begin with a fresh examination of the theological/moral meaning and purpose of marriage.

---

13. Whitehead, *The Divorce Culture*.

It will take seriously the requisite qualities of character and relationship for effective marriages. It will craft creative and effective church programs for marriage preparation and divorce prevention as well as care for those experiencing divorce, including children. It will seek to create disciplined communities of faith in which joyful marital unity for a lifetime is not a pipedream but common practice. It will explore ways in which divorce can be restigmatized and delegitimized as a normal, everyday "lifestyle choice," at least for Christians. It will learn to speak the language of justice, equity, and oppression when it comes to divorce and its victims. It will rethink the morality of divorce in a way which recognizes marriage's divinely intended permanence and yet makes appropriate provision for the rare, occasional, necessary evil of divorce. It will think about incremental public policy measures that can encourage strong marriages and discourage divorce. Perhaps above all, and in every matter just discussed, it will treat divorce as if children matter.

3

Just War Divide
One Tradition, Two Views

2002

SPEAKING AT THE US Military Academy in June [2002], President Bush offered an expansive statement articulating a doctrine of preemptive action against rogue states and terrorist groups. Iraq was not mentioned, but subsequent statements suggest the West Point speech laid the foundation for war against that nation. If the president moves ahead with these plans, Christians will once again face a decision about whether to support military action.

If that day comes, Christian thinkers undoubtedly will break out the just war theory. Every time US leaders sound the alarm for war, this ancient tradition is put to work. The counterterrorist war in Afghanistan was the latest occasion. In the 1990s just war theory was applied to actions in Iraq, Bosnia, Somalia, Kosovo, Haiti, and elsewhere.

But a chorus of dissatisfaction with just war theory is gaining strength in the US, and not just from pacifists and others who dissent from the tradition on principle. The tradition itself has been split apart. Politically conservative Christians tend to find in the just war theory grounds for support of nearly all US military actions. Politically liberal Christians tend to find in the theory grounds for opposition to nearly all US military actions.

The most pessimistic reading of this divide is that the just war theory has decayed into an ornament used by partisans to shroud their political loyalties under an illusion of "objective" confirmation. The deeper reality is that there are two different kinds of just war theories, rooted in what appear to be theoretical differences and especially in different assessments of American behavior: there is "soft" just war theory and "hard" just war theory.

While I use the term "soft" for the more dovish stance and "hard" for the more hawkish perspective, I do not mean to prejudice the discussion by these terms. The labels could be reversed: the antiwar position could be called "hard" because it tends to apply just war criteria stringently and thus rule out support for most wars. Yet it makes more intuitive sense to me to label them as I have.

The soft just war stance is assumed in "The Challenge of Peace" (1983), a key Cold War era document by the US Catholic bishops. The hard just war position is taken by a writer such as Keith Pavlischek, who serves at the Center for Public Justice in Washington.[1]

Soft just war theory is characterized by seven key components: a strongly articulated horror of war; a strong presumption against war; a skepticism about government claims; the use of just war theory as a tool for citizen discernment and prophetic critique; a pattern of trusting the efficacy of international treaties, multilateral strategies and the perspectives of global peace and human rights groups and the international press; a quite stringent application of just war criteria; and a claim of common ground with Christian pacifists.

"The Challenge of Peace," for example, presents a stark condemnation of the savagery and horror of war, especially modern warfare and an envisioned nuclear war. While governments have the right to defend their people, the bishops emphasize that conflict resolution and nonviolent means of national defense are most in keeping with the call of Jesus.[2]

Only if "extraordinarily strong reasons" exist "for overriding the presumption in favor of peace and against war" may war be considered.[3] Even then, just war theory's primary function is to "restrict and reduce" war's horrors.[4] "The presumption that binds all Christians" is that "the possibility of taking even one human life is something we should consider in fear and trembling."[5]

---

1. National Conference of Catholic Bishops, "The Challenge of Peace"; Pavlischek, "Just War Theory and Terrorism."
2. National Conference of Catholic Bishops, "The Challenge of Peace."
3. Ibid., 38.
4. Ibid.
5. Ibid., 26–27.

The classic "entry into war" criteria are then reviewed—just cause, competent authority, right intention, and so on. Christian citizens must apply these criteria carefully in analyzing any government's call to war. The discussion of competent authority notes bitter divisions in American life over whether many US military actions have met this test. The bishops' reflection on comparative justice emphasizes limiting both the ferocity of war and any kind of moral absolutism on our part. It also notes the role of propaganda and the danger of national self-righteousness.[6]

The treatment of war as a last resort laments the difficulty of applying this requirement given the lack of "sufficient internationally recognized authority" to mediate disputes.[7] The bishops call for support for the United Nations, the "last hope for peace" on earth.[8] Discussion of proportionality emphasizes the grave costs of war, recalling that this same body of bishops publicly rejected the Vietnam War in 1971 due to its failure to meet this test.[9]

The section on just war theory closes with a warm affirmation of the value of a pacifist witness within the Catholic Church, claiming that it shares with just war theory "a common presumption against the use of force as a means of settling disputes."[10]

Hard just war theory reverses these emphases, replacing them with the following: a presumption against injustice and disorder rather than against war; an assumption that war is tragic but inevitable in a fallen world, and that war is a necessary task of government; a tendency to trust the US government and its claims of the need for military action; an emphasis on just war theory as a tool to aid policymakers and military personnel in their decisions; an inclination to distrust the efficacy of international treaties and to downplay the value of international actors and perspectives; a less stringent or differently oriented application of some just war criteria; and no sense of common ground with Christian pacifists.

In an October 2001 lecture titled "Just War Theory and Terrorism," later published by the Family Research Council, Keith Pavlischek lamented what he called the "blame America first" perspective of many religious leaders after September 11. In response, he called for rigorous retrieval of "classic" just war theory.[11]

6. Ibid., 26–34.
7. Ibid., 30.
8. Ibid.
9. Ibid., 31.
10. Ibid., 37.
11. Pavlischek, "Just War Theory and Terrorism."

For Pavlischek, the foundational presumption of just war theory is the government's mandate to pursue justice, order, and peace. Government is ordained by God to prevent the victimization of the innocent, the violation of public order, and the disruption of peace. It is granted a monopoly on coercive, even lethal, force in order to accomplish this mandate. In a fallen world, such force will be required both in domestic and international relations. This use of force is to be restrained and law-governed, but it is a necessary, good and proper exercise of "God's governance in a fallen world."[12]

This argument is not intended as a "realist" embrace of a stance implying that no moral considerations apply to governmental conduct. Governments must be held to stringent moral criteria. Nonetheless, in a tendency apparent in hard just war theory, at no point in Pavlischek's essay does he indicate a concern about the overall trustworthiness of the US government in its use of force.[13]

Pavlischek's hard just war theory reflects no yearning for the establishment of an international governing authority. The normative "political community" for Pavlischek is the relatively just individual nation-state.[14] "The Challenge of Peace" emphasizes the limited ability of states to resolve conflicts peaceably; indeed, Vatican II documents called for the formation of some kind of world government.[15] Pavlischek will have none of this.

Pavlischek offers some strikingly different interpretations of just war criteria. Under just cause, for example, he includes retributive justice; that is, punishment for evil.[16] The bishops reject this as a just cause for modern war. Pavlischek disagrees. This debate was played out many times in the days after September 11.

Whereas "The Challenge of Peace" offers an extensive discussion of conscientious citizen objection to unjust uses of government power, Pavlischek instead emphasizes the role of just war theory in statecraft and military planning.[17]

Finally, Pavlischek has no use for pacifism and what he considers a "crypto-pacifist" corruption of just war theory. Pavlischek argues that pacifists and "crypto-pacifists" are profoundly unbiblical when they claim that governments should not use force or threaten to use it, or when they argue

---

12. Ibid.
13. Ibid.
14. Ibid.
15. National Conference of Catholic Bishops, "The Challenge of Peace."
16. Pavlischek, "Just War Theory and Terrorism."
17. National Conference of Catholic Bishops, "The Challenge of Peace"; Pavlischek, "Just War Theory and Terrorism."

that the use of force is evil. He claims that their stance threatens to weaken our national resolve to fight terrorism as it needs to be fought currently.[18]

Complex issues in Christian ethics, international relations and political theory lie at the heart of this dispute. I will focus on four essential interpretive questions.

First, is there a way to probe beneath this divide in just war theory to discern deeper reasons for it? Glen Stassen and I suggest in *Kingdom Ethics* that people's loyalties affect how they perceive their contexts, and that their loyalties and perceptions together affect their ethical outcomes more powerfully than their style of reasoning.[19] I suggest that it is no coincidence that the more hawkish version of just war theory is most often deployed by those most loyal to the (US) military, or to the nation-state and its authorities, or to a particular regime, leader, or party in power at the time of moral analysis. Their reasoning follows their loyalties and perceptions. Likewise the more dovish versions of just war theory tend to be employed by those who do not share such loyalties, at least not to the same degree.

Second, which approach to just war theory is more in keeping with its historic proponents? Pavlischek and others view their version of just war theory as the classic tradition and treat a soft just war position as an unfortunate corruption. Yet the soft just war theory of the Catholic bishops and others lays claim to the same intellectual inheritance.

After rereading the classic Christian voices it is clear to me that hard just war theorists have the tradition right, in large part because most historic Christian exponents of just war theory had the same loyalties to the state and its authorities that their contemporary followers have today. The twentieth-century development of just war theory is clearly an evolution of the historic tradition in response to the carnage of the era. Events from 1914 to 1989 scalded the international Christian consciousness. Many Christian leaders became convinced that the world was rushing to incineration and that historically Christian nations were largely responsible. They lost confidence that states and their leaders could be so easily trusted to make wise decisions about the use of military force. Pacifism nearly converged with a deeply chastened just war approach to yield soft just war theory.

Those revising the tradition have not always been fully transparent about what they were doing. Honest exposition of its sources would enable us to understand the classic theory for what it is, and to see the limits imposed by its pre-modern composition. Just war theory was crafted in nondemocratic, quasi-theocratic contexts, with far less destructive military

18. Pavlischek, "Just War Theory and Terrorism."
19. Stassen and Gushee, *Kingdom Ethics*.

technology. If the theory needs to be democratized and updated to account for modern technology, so be it. Genealogy does not settle the argument, though it is important to get the history right.

Third, which approach to just war theory is more likely to bear the good fruit of justice, peace, and order today? How we construe just war theory must bear good fruit or that construal must be altered or the theory abandoned.

Hard just war theory can make American Christians too likely to support marginal or unjust wars and in general to be unreflective about our nation's activities in the world. Yet soft just war theory can weaken our moral clarity on those occasions when we must have sufficient resolve to fight truly just wars. Which is the greater problem today? A struggle against groups that fly jetliners into buildings requires the steely resolve that hard just war theory contributes. But if this occurs at the expense of peacemaking efforts mandated by Jesus that can get at the roots of global terrorism, or costs us the ability to think critically, we will go badly astray.

Fourth, which approach to just war theory is more likely to help American Christians discern our particular responsibilities? The gravest flaw of recent discussions of just war theory has been their ahistorical and acontextual quality. When we Americans talk about war and its justice, we're not Swedes or Malaysians, we're Americans; we're the most powerful nation on earth, with the largest military, the single nation in the world today most likely to threaten and use military force. Which version of just war theory best helps us to remember both the opportunities and the dangers of our extraordinary international power?

It is no coincidence that the origins of American soft just war theory can be traced to the nuclear arms race and the turn against the Vietnam War. The American Christian debate about just war theory is in a sense nothing other than a debate about America's role in the world, a debate little changed since, say, 1968. In the end, competing perceptions of our national moral virtue lie at the heart of the division between soft and hard just war theory.

What is America, after all? Are we the leading international force for "human dignity, the rule of law, limits on the power of the state . . . private property, free speech, equal justice, and religious tolerance,"[20] as the president said at West Point? Or are we instead the global hegemon—the Rome of the modern world—throwing our military weight around, pursuing economic excess while parsimonious in our generosity, demonstrating

---

20 Bush, "Commencement Address."

indifference to how our actions negatively affect other nations, and consuming far more of the world's resources than we should?

The US is, in fact, both. And the split in just war theory partly reflects the tension between our cherished ideals and our power-distorted selfishness, both of which reflect who we are as a nation.

4

The Church, the Nazis, and the Holocaust

A Reconsideration

2002

OF HUMAN PASSIONS AND the actions that follow from them, Aristotle wrote the following famous words:

> Fear and confidence and appetite and anger and pity and in general pleasure and pain may be felt both too much and too little, and in both cases not well; but to feel them at the right times, with reference to the right objects, towards the right people, with the right motive, and in the right way ... this is characteristic of virtue.[1]

The five books under consideration in this review essay tell the story of a time not so long ago when the churches of Jesus Christ failed this Aristotelian test of virtue. When Adolf Hitler rose to power in Germany, initiated his anti-Jewish policies, launched World War II, decided on extermination as the Final Solution of the Jewish Question in Europe, and pursued this policy without mercy for four long years at the cost of six million Jewish lives, the churches failed the moral test this escalating calamity imposed. In general and with notable exceptions, the churches felt too little anger and too little pity; directed that anger and pity too weakly and too late, with

---

1. Aristotle, *Nicomachean Ethics*, 352.

mixed motives, and without adequate courage and vigor. The failure of the church (and the churches) continues today in its inadequately strenuous reckoning with what happened from 1933 to 1945. These five books attempt to offer that historical reckoning, and generally do so well.

One of the besetting difficulties of writing or teaching about the Nazi era is that the Holocaust tends to be the filter through which all data are interpreted. Every moment of the period, from the days of Hitler's rise to power until his death in 1945, is viewed with an awareness of Auschwitz, gas chambers, mass murder. This is perhaps inevitable. It certainly reflects an appropriate moral revulsion.

Those of us on the other side of the Holocaust find it extraordinarily difficult to imagine a world in which Auschwitz did not yet exist. We follow the historical trajectory knowing that it ends in the gas chambers. But the people and institutions whose actions we are studying did not, of course, know at the time that the story would culminate in factories of mass murder.

If we would seek to understand and evaluate the actions of Christians and church leaders in Germany and around the world in 1929 or 1933 or even 1941, we must attempt to reenter their pre-Holocaust world. We must try to imagine Hitler, and perceptions of Hitler, before he became the paradigm of human evil. We also must undertake the arduous task of understanding German and European political, cultural, and religious conditions.

Wolfgang Gerlach offers an excellent account of these conditions as they existed in Germany in his important book *And the Witnesses Were Silent*, focusing on the response of the German Evangelical Church to Nazism. Some of the same ground is covered in essays collected by Robert Ericksen and Susannah Heschel in their work, *Betrayal*. It is also the background for *The Popes Against the Jews*, David Kertzer's book on the Vatican's stance toward the Jews from 1814 until World War II.

The story begins at the end of the eighteenth century, with the tentative flowering of an Enlightenment-inspired tolerance toward Jews in Germany and elsewhere in Europe. After centuries of religiously inspired anti-Judaism, and the expression of that anti-Judaism through the political and social subordination and isolation of the Jews, many European nations slowly made provision for the emancipation of Jews and their participation in civil society.

Freed from both social and metaphorical ghettoization, some of the emancipated Jews of Germany and other nations joined vigorously in the creation of what became the modern world. In philosophy and the arts, business and government, Jews contributed energetically and quite visibly to the secularized liberal culture of the modernizing Western nations, including Germany.

A social change of this magnitude perhaps inevitably creates a backlash. Indeed, that very backlash, in the form of antimodernism, antiliberalism, and antisecularism, is with us to this day. It characterizes much Christian public rhetoric. The nineteenth and early twentieth centuries saw this backlash begin and later intensify. It took a variety of forms, both traditional and strangely modern. Traditional antimodernism yearned for the return of an earlier day of cultural and religious homogeneity, and was spearheaded especially by Christian leaders alarmed by growing secularization. But at the same time, a modern antimodernism rooted in pseudoscientific racism began to flourish, offering Social Darwinian theories asserting the superiority of "Aryans" over other races. The focus of these theories, the primary racial enemy, was the newly emancipated Jews.

During the first third of the twentieth century, Gerlach shows, German Protestant leaders were susceptible to both religious anti-Judaism and modern antisemitism, though the former rather than the latter held greater sway. Christian anti-Judaism had a very long history.[2] The essay by Shelley Baranowski in *Betrayal* shows that antimodernist anti-Judaism, which blamed Jews for their contribution to deleterious social changes in the secularizing Germany of the era, was an important theme in mainstream Protestant thought during the Weimar era.[3] It dovetailed nicely with this older religious anti-Judaism and proved deeply appealing in German church life. Gerlach documents the expression of anti-Judaism in the German Protestant press during this period, demonstrating that egregious expression of anti-Jewish sentiment was quite common in the widely read Sunday papers as well as sermons and other popular outlets. A section of a sermon by Basel theology professor Dr. Adolf Koberle captures the mood quite well:

> The secular, areligious Jew . . . has followed the path of outrage against God to its final consequence. In his heart, he has bid farewell to the last bits of faith and reverence before God. His ideal is the spirit of the French revolution, the spirit of liberalism and materialism, Marxism and Bolshevism, but also, when possible, the spirit of unprincipled Mammonism and the unbridled greed of a Caesar-like world domination. He is everywhere where there is something to subvert . . . whether it be marriage and family, love for the Fatherland or the church, discipline and order, chastity and decency, wherever there is something to gain.[4]

---

2. Gushee, "All Things Jewish."
3. Baranowski, "The Confessing Church and Antisemitism," 90–109.
4. Gerlach, *And the Witnesses Were Silent*, 7.

Discussing the Koberle sermon, Gerlach incisively concludes: "As the struggle of the German Evangelical Church with the Nazi regime began, such attitudes were widespread in the churches. These prejudices would make any genuine Christian activism on behalf of the Jews virtually impossible."[5]

It was not only Hitler's antisemitism that struck a chord in the churches. The Nazi Party positioned itself in the 1920s and early 1930s as the only force standing between Germany and utter social collapse. The chaos of the tottering Weimar Republic is well known, as is the economic crisis that helped Hitler's rise to power. Hitler and the Nazis promised to reestablish a strong central authority and bring order, restore Germany's honor after the double humiliation of defeat and a punitively imposed peace, rebuild the German military, prevent Soviet-style communism from prevailing in Germany, and feed a hungry people. The Nazis also—and this is often overlooked—promised a return to traditional values, proclaimed a strengthening of Germany's fragmented sense of national community, and demanded the suppression of enemies who undermined these bulwarks of traditional German identity. Nationalism, militarism, community, prosperity, law and order, tradition, authority, anti-communism: not only in Germany have culturally conservative Christians found these themes attractive.

But it would be grossly unfair, as well as historically false, to suggest that Christians in Germany simply welcomed Nazism with open arms. Some did, to be sure, but many did not. The failure of the German church cannot be attributed solely to its own weakness. On the contrary: from their beginnings, the Nazis regarded the church—Protestant and Catholic—as a formidable obstacle to achieving their goals. Gerlach and other scholars tend to downplay or ignore this part of the story, which is illumined by documents from the Nazi era recently posted on the website of the *Rutgers Journal of Law and Religion* under the auspices of the Nuremberg Project. Compiled and edited by Rutgers law student Julie Seltzer Mandel, whose grandmother survived Auschwitz, the documents reveal that "the destruction of Christianity was explicitly recognized as a purpose of the National Socialist Movement."[6] Only the need to consolidate power on the way to totalitarian rule kept the Nazis from openly attacking the church at the outset.

To acknowledge this is not in any way to excuse the ultimate failure of the church in Germany (with some notable exceptions). At a time of great testing, it buckled. But as we look back on the contest between those Christians and a brutal, implacable foe, we have no cause to feel complacent.

---

5. Ibid., 7.
6. Sharkey, "The Case Against the Nazis."

The testing of the German Church began with the rise the Nazis in the 1920s, but it began in earnest in 1933. On January 30 of that year, Adolf Hitler was named Chancellor of Germany. Within six months, he had dismantled the parliamentary democracy and was ruling the nation with near-dictatorial power. And within another year, by the end of the summer of 1934, he had assumed total control.

In 1933, under Nazi pressure, an already existing federation of Protestant churches became the German Evangelical Church, a body that the Nazis intended to control and manipulate just as they hoped to co-opt the Catholic Church in Germany. There are two primary stories to be told concerning the interaction of the German Evangelical Church and the Hitler regime. One story concerns the church's response to the Nazi government's ever increasing harassment and persecution of the Jews. The other has to do with the church's effort to protect its interests and discern its duties in relation to the new regime. The stories are deeply interwoven, but not identical, and emphasis must rest on the latter, for that is precisely where the church placed its own emphasis.

These two stories should have been nearly identical. The Protestant churches should have been able to discern that the attack on the Jews in German society—through the street violence of Nazi hooligans, the media violence of Nazi propaganda, and the paper violence of Nazi bureaucrats—posed the primary threat to the interests and the integrity of established German Protestantism. What kind of Christianity stands by, fearful or complicit, and allows such evil to go unchallenged?

Unfortunately, not a single German church leader, with the arguable exception of Dietrich Bonhoeffer, saw that "the Jewish Question" was the defining issue of the era as the era actually unfolded, beginning in 1933. The leading clerics and theologians in German Protestantism who opposed Nazism in any way spent their time battling on two other fronts: the preservation of the institutional independence of the German Evangelical Church, and the maintenance of German Protestant theological integrity. The increasingly constricted civil status of Jews was viewed as a peripheral issue when compared to these more immediate problems—if it was noticed at all.

The "Jewish Question" at first intersected with these two other fronts primarily through Nazi efforts to turn Germans with some degree of "Jewish blood" into second-class citizens (before turning them into noncitizens, and finally into dead bodies). The "Aryan paragraph" legislation of April 1933 forced the dismissal of all "non-Aryan" civil servants from their posts. While the Aryan paragraph did not in these early days apply to clergy or theological faculty, some churchmen argued that the churches and theological schools should voluntarily and patriotically apply the paragraph to themselves—thus dismissing any ministers or professors whom the state would define as non-Aryan.

Of course, if a church or seminary dismissed a competent leader because of an unbiblical racial category defined by the state, grave issues of institutional independence and ecclesial integrity would be raised. Or if the state required church leaders or faculty members to swear an oath of allegiance to Hitler or if the state (or churchmen fiercely loyal to the state) required Christians of Jewish descent to attend separate churches, or to sit in separate sections, or finally to stop attending church at all; or if Christian doctrines would be altered so as to conform to the spirit of the age—all would raise critical institutional and theological issues.

These were in fact the very battles that preoccupied the most insightful of Germany's Protestant leaders during much of the Nazi era. The Confessing Church, that section of German Protestantism that for a time offered some opposition to Nazism, fought most of its battles precisely over the institutional independence and doctrinal purity of the church. A close reading of the well known Barmen Declaration of May 1934 clearly shows the centrality of these two themes. That resistance, as well as the ham-handedness of the so-called German Christians (Christians attempting to accommodate Nazism and Protestantism), led Hitler to wash his hands of Protestant church politics, eventually backing off from attempting a total co-optation of the church by the state. So the Confessing Church can fairly be said to have preserved more independence and integrity, at least for a time, than almost any other sector of German society was able to do as the Nazi steamroller "synchronized" all aspects of German life.

There were certainly extraordinary theological battles to be fought. Most casual students of recent church history are unaware of the heretical depths to which Nazified Protestantism sank. Some Protestant theologians went so far as to proclaim Hitler as God's "gift" and "miracle," and fundamental elements of Christian doctrine were compromised.

The nadir of Protestant Nazification is documented by Susannah Heschel in her chapter on the Institute for the Study and Eradication of Jewish influence on German Religious Life.[7] The Institute, which opened in 1939, was led by a New Testament scholar, Walter Grundmann, whose work is still quoted occasionally today. Grundmann, along with some other learned biblical scholars, made the argument that Jesus was not Jewish, but instead an "Aryan" who was Judaism's greatest critic and in fact sought its destruction. The Institute also published a New Testament (the Old Testament,

---

7. Heschel, "When Jesus Was an Aryan," 68–89.

illegitimate by definition, was simply abandoned), a catechism, and a hymnbook, all scrubbed clean of any "Jewish elements."

It was surely providential that in such a time German Protestantism was favored with a few leaders like Karl Barth, a man who knew heresy when he saw it and named it as such without hesitation. Thus Nazified Protestantism did not permanently corrupt Christian doctrine in Germany, despite the profound theological confusion and outright capitulation to Nazism of many distinguished clerics and theologians. For saying a clear no at this point, we can thank the Confessing Church.

And yet, one reason for any limited success the Confessing Church was able to achieve was its decision to remain largely silent about the ever-worsening Jewish plight in Germany. With rare exceptions, voices were raised on behalf of Jewish Christians but not, to coin a phrase, on behalf of Jewish Jews. Indeed, Gerlach argues that whatever unity the divided Confessing Church enjoyed would have been impossible if opposition to Nazi anti-Jewish policies had been made central and explicit.

This was the case for several reasons, Gerlach contends, all of them instructive. One was that even Confessing Church leaders were generally deeply in the grip of the same theological and cultural anti-Judaism that prevailed throughout German society. Further, Confessing Church leaders fell prey to what must now clearly be viewed as a misunderstanding of the relationship between church and state, according to which the state is viewed as fully autonomous in its sphere and patriotic Christians are called to submit loyally and uncritically to government and its policies. Finally, Gerlach says, Protestant academics and other leaders were too insulated, excessively focused on churchly self-interest and an ivory-tower confessional purity. Writing theological statements and arguing about church order came much more naturally to these men than expressing and acting on a real-world concern for victimized human beings.

There were, however, a few who mobilized individual and institutional efforts on behalf of all Jews in need. Marga Meusel, who served as director of the Protestant social welfare office in the Berlin area, pleaded as early as 1935 that the Confessing Church must resist Nazi racial distinctions and meet the material needs of increasingly impoverished Jews in Germany. Gerlach's lengthy quotation from the 1935 "Meusel Memorandum" is worth the price of the book. One example:

> We are seized with cold dread when there can be people in the Confessing Church who dare to believe that they are justified, even called, to proclaim to the Jews that God's judgment and grace are present in the current historical events and in the

suffering that we have brought on them. Since when does the evildoer have the right to pass off his crime as the will of God? . . . Let us take care that we do not hide the outrage of our sins behind the holy shrine of the will of God.[8]

Not surprisingly, Meusel channeled her outrage into determined efforts at meeting the practical needs of Jews, including rescue efforts when that time came. She was not alone. Gerlach offers extensive discussion of the Protestant relief efforts that took place both before and during the war. The most extensive operation was the so-called Gruber office in Berlin, established by the Confessing Church as its central relief operation.

Under the leadership of Pastor Heinrich Gruber this office undertook significant relief efforts, first legally and finally illegally, and ultimately, Gerlach says, at the cost of the lives of many of its fifty-five staff, many of them remarkably courageous women. The office helped with legal emigration efforts, offered social assistance and legal support, undertook education for Jewish children barred from public schools, provided food and medicine, and so on. Once the deadly threat of deportation and death loomed, the office turned to illegal efforts including passport and document forgery and all manner of rescue work. The office was shut down by the Nazis in late 1940, but this just sent the effort underground. Rescue continued till the very end of the war. Gruber's efforts, and those of other documented rescuers from the Confessing Church, have earned their designation as "Righteous Gentiles" by Yad Vashem, the Israeli Holocaust museum and memorial. And yet, like putting a finger into a leaking dike, the Gruber office and related efforts saved but a small number of lives amid the torrent of death that flooded Germany during the Holocaust. It was not enough to efface the failure of German Protestantism's all-too-silent witnesses.

Phayer, and Susan Zuccotti, explore essentially the same terrain, this time on the Catholic side. Kertzer traces Vatican attitudes toward Jews primarily from 1814 to 1939.[9] Phayer attempts to cover the overall approach of the Catholic Church toward the Jews from 1930 until Vatican II, and Zuccotti offers a detailed account of Pope Pius XII's response to anti-Jewish policies, and finally the Holocaust itself, as these events unfolded in Italy.[10] Guenter Lewy also offers a valuable review of the overall response of the Catholic Church to Nazism in a chapter in *Betrayal*.[11] Together the

8. Meusel, "Meusel Memorandum," 85–86.

9. Kertzer, *The Popes Against the Jews*.

10. Phayer, *The Catholic Church and the Holocaust*; Zuccotti, *Under His Very Windows*.

11. Lewy, "Piux XII, the Jews, and the German Catholic Church," 129–48.

discussions make a significant contribution to our understanding of what has become a highly controversial issue.

For these books do not enter a vacuum. The context in which they are offered is the so-called Pius XII debate, which shows few signs of slowing after several years of white-hot historiography and polemic. Stimulated afresh in 1999 with the release of John Cornwell's deeply flawed but widely publicized *Hitler's Pope*, the debate primarily concerns how to evaluate the wartime action and/or inaction of the worldwide leader of the Roman Catholic Church.[12] This debate cannot be regarded as resolved, or even resolvable, in part because the Vatican has refused to open its archives fully for historical inspection. Yet Phayer and Zuccotti, both of whom take stances largely critiquing Pius XII, believe that the documents currently available are sufficient to offer at least a provisional accounting. I will attempt here to draw distinctions between those issues that can be regarded as settled and those that remain most intensely disputed.

Kertzer's book offers a devastating description of Vatican attitudes and actions toward Jews for the 120 or so years that preceded the rise of fascist antisemitism in Europe. Drawing on many Vatican documents previously unavailable to researchers, and quoting them freely and to astonishing effect, Kertzer essentially demonstrates what his title suggests: that the popes were with rare exceptions simply "against the Jews" from 1814 until the Holocaust period itself.

As to why this was the case, Kertzer's argument tracks quite closely with that of Gerlach. The short answer is simply that Jews were viewed as the adversaries of a Christian civilization that was collapsing under the pressure of modernity. In its longing for a return to a vanishing world, the church—both Catholic and Protestant—heaped opprobrium on the Jews, who were seen as the primary beneficiaries of the new order. In its deep desire to return to "the good old days," the church both retrieved and manufactured a range of nasty anti-Jewish smears in hopes of winning the fight for Western (Christian) civilization.

Perhaps the most significant contribution of Kertzer's book is to challenge the distinction between theological anti-Judaism and racial antisemitism. Many Christians who have become aware of the painful history of Christian hatred of Jews have sought to defend the church by claiming that Nazi antisemitism was a modern brew that bore little resemblance to Christian anti-Jewish polemic, which was not racist but theological.

However, Kertzer shows from Catholic documents of the late nineteenth and early twentieth centuries that nearly every antisemitic theme the

---

12. Cornwell, *Hitler's Pope*.

Nazis used in the 1920s and 1930s could be found in the Catholic press (including journals and papers very close to the Vatican) either during the same period or just before. In Kertzer's summary, these included the following:

> There is a secret Jewish conspiracy; the Jews seek to conquer the world; Jews are an evil sect who seek to do Christians harm; Jews are by nature immoral; Jews care only for money and will do anything to get it; Jews control the press; Jews control the banks and are responsible for the ruination of untold numbers of Christian families; Jews are responsible for communism; Judaism commands its adherents to murder defenseless Christian children and drink their blood; Jews seek to destroy the Christian religion; Jews are unpatriotic, ever ready to sell their country out to the enemy... Jews must be segregated and their rights limited.[13]

Further, Kertzer is able to document the appearance of racial antisemitism—the idea that Jews are biologically inferior due to their inborn racial makeup—in the Catholic press. Reading the documents Kertzer so amply quotes, it seems that the only real differences between Catholic anti-Semitic literature of the period and that of "secular" antisemites was that the former rejected violence and murder, held out hope for conversion, and sought to protect the rights of ethnically Jewish Catholics. Those differences are not negligible, but there can be no doubt that Catholics—like their Protestant counterparts—contributed to the toxic brew of hatred that reached its logical conclusion in the Holocaust.

Phayer and Zuccotti show that Rome's stance during the war on "the Jewish Question" was deeply shaped not only by theology and this heritage of antisemitism but also by the unique political status of the Vatican. It is often forgotten today that the Vatican is actually a state and is treated as such in international law. The Vatican's self-understanding and role in the world are deeply affected by its political identity as a religious mini-state (which had once been a larger and more influential collection of Papal States), and this was especially true in the chaotic and frightening days of the 1930s and 1940s. The Vatican during this period was concerned with its own political interests as well as international Catholic interests; in a very real and deeply ingrained sense, it also viewed itself as the trustee of historic Christian civilization.

Pope Pius XII, who took office in 1939 on the eve of World War II, was profoundly steeped in a geopolitical understanding of the Vatican and

---

13. Kertzer, *The Popes Against the Jews*, 206.

the papacy. His ascent up the ranks of the Vatican hierarchy was undertaken through the Vatican Foreign Office, including twelve years as a papal nuncio in Germany (1917–29) and then as Vatican Secretary of State, the role which he held for over nine years until he was elected pope. Pius XII enjoyed the life of the diplomat and was perceived by many of his peers as consummately skilled in the work. Perhaps fatefully, he also came to love Germany and had many German aides.

Phayer argues that Pius XII's understanding of geopolitics and of himself as a diplomat tragically misshaped his priorities during World War II. For much of the war, Pius appears to have nurtured the hope of playing a pivotal diplomatic role in brokering peace between the warring parties and preserving a remnant of Christian Europe (the very role his predecessor Benedict XV undertook during World War I), and in general placed a strong emphasis on behind-the-scenes diplomacy. He believed his task was to remain neutral so that all parties could turn to him as an honest broker. The pope's ardent anti-communism, Phayer argues, also played a major part in his approach to decision making before and during World War II, leading him consistently to downplay the danger of German Nazism vis-à-vis that posed by Soviet communism—a claim that pro-Pius historians reject.

As leader of the worldwide Catholic Church, Pius XII prioritized protecting the Church's political interests and rights wherever he perceived them as threatened. Here he was in complete continuity with his predecessors. This, according to Phayer, made him reluctant to critique the anti-Jewish collaboration, and sometimes deadly indigenous antisemitism, of Catholic-led states such as Croatia, Slovakia, and Vichy France. It also contributed to his reticence to press German Catholics to resist Hitler. Phayer argues that he feared weakening the Catholic Church in Germany or provoking a crisis of conscience for German Catholics.

Finally, Phayer shows, as does Zuccotti, that when the war came to Italy, Pius XII was deeply concerned about the possible destruction of the Vatican and its treasures, and maneuvered carefully to preserve at least the appearance of neutrality and thus avoid giving the Nazis any pretense for overrunning Vatican City, the symbolic and temporal capital of Roman Catholicism. Pro-Pius historians emphasize that Hitler considered several plans to do exactly what Pius feared, including schemes involving the pope's abduction or assassination, and that Pius was warned about such deliberations.

Both Phayer and Zuccotti show that few people in the world had better information than the Pope did about the annihilation of European Jewry as it was happening. Both argue that the Pope never offered a clear public word of condemnation of this butchery. Pro-Pius historians argue to the contrary that on several occasions Pius decried mass killings on the basis of nationality and race, and that in doing so Pius was clearly speaking on behalf of the Jews while (admittedly) never naming them specifically—and that the Germans certainly understood what he was talking about at the time, as did the international press in its reports. Moreover, some historians argue that nothing in the Vatican's institutional history or the Pope's personal background served to foster the kind of very specific, morally outraged public protests the Pope's critics so ardently wish for. This was simply not the way the papacy operated.

According to Phayer, Pius did nothing to disseminate the information about the Holocaust that he did have, so that others might intervene even if he himself did not. He neither publicly nor privately directed Catholic clergy or laypeople to resist the Nazis and rescue Jews. Neither did he direct German, Croatian, French, Italian, Slovakian, or other Catholics to refuse to carry out mass killings or participate in any way in the killing apparatus. Zuccotti argues that the Pope appears to have permitted rescue to occur in his diocese, even in Vatican City, but not to have encouraged it either there or anywhere, even when directly asked his opinion. This issue continues to be bitterly disputed, as pro-Pius historians argue that the Pope at least encouraged rescue and perhaps can be said to have been a rescuer himself, given the indisputable presence of Jews in hiding on Vatican properties.

Phayer and Zuccotti both fault the engagement of the Pope and his representatives with Germany and collaborating nations. They argue that while papal representatives approached Nazi and collaborationist governments from time to time with protests against various particular anti-Jewish measures, these overtures were in general dilatory and half-hearted, almost always lacking the passion that would have been even remotely fitting to the gravity of events. Defenders of Pius read the historical record differently, commenting in particular on the Third Reich's perception of the Vatican as one of the staunchest public and diplomatic critics of Nazi anti-Jewish policy.

Phayer and Zuccotti offer inspiring tales of rescue efforts undertaken by thousands of Catholic laypeople and clerics in Italy. This record is commendable, and it is good to see the depth and breadth of Catholic rescue. Yet these authors differ from papal defenders in concluding that the rescuers acted without any explicit authorization or even exhortation from their leader, dismissing purported evidence to the contrary as not credible.

Phayer also depicts the Pope's postwar activities as blameworthy. He claims that the Pope sought clemency for some convicted German war criminals and proved uncooperative in extraditing war criminals actually hiding out on Vatican properties. He appointed Nazi and Croatian fascist sympathizers to Vatican positions, where they were able to aid and abet war criminals in escaping prosecution. Pius criticized the denazification process in Germany after the war, as well as the efforts of some Catholics to press for restitution and repentance by Germany and by Catholics in Germany. He refused to speak out on the continuing dangers of anti-Semitism when violence against Holocaust survivors was being perpetrated in largely Catholic Poland, and elsewhere, after the war. He opposed the birth of the state of Israel in 1948 and Jewish emigration to that state. And yet, pro-Pius historians remind us that during and after the war, and with a special outpouring at the time of his death in 1958, well known Jews praised Pius XII for his actions on behalf of the Jewish people in their darkest hour.

I can recall few instances where the opinion of reputable historians has been as deeply divided as it is in this case. The Pius XII debate, narrowly considered, will have to be considered unresolved. Yet these books do show, so lamentably, that the role of Christian antisemitism in helping lay the foundation for the Holocaust is clearer than ever.

If we conclude that both the Protestant and Catholic churches helped prepare the way for the Holocaust and failed to offer adequate resistance to that mass slaughter as it occurred, have we done anything other than add another count to the overwhelming case for human and even Christian moral failure—as if more evidence for the doctrine of sin were needed?

Perhaps we will have done something valuable if somehow we can cross the historical divide and consider whether we are doing any better today in responding to the moral challenges facing us in our own time. Hindsight is notoriously twenty/twenty. Getting it right at the actual moment of crisis is much more difficult, much more costly, and much more rare.

Consider two examples. In 1995, the Southern Baptist Convention publicly repudiated the racism that contributed to its founding in 1845 and undermined the moral integrity of its witness from that day forward. As one who helped draft that resolution, I was pleased to play a small role in identifying the evil of racism for what it had been in the life of our denomination.

And yet the resolution was written in 1995. It was fairly easy to repudiate racism in 1995. To do so even as recently as 1955 or 1965 was much more difficult, let alone 1855. Those white Southern Baptists and others who actually did repudiate racism in 1965 frequently paid a very heavy price for it. But the denomination as a whole certainly did not speak the right word at the right time. We did not read "the signs of the times" and remained largely captive to racism. Only our "radicals" broke with racism; despised then, and only now honored, their moral witness indicts us.

By temperament I gravitate to an irenic evangelicalism willing to live with many differences without breaking fellowship over them. And yet just such a spirit was precisely the wrong spirit when the churches of Germany, and the Vatican itself, faced off against Hitler and the Nazis. Sometimes the effort to find common ground, to make peace, to try to see the good in your adversary and the truth of what he is saying, is exactly wrong. Sometimes you have to say a clear No and dig in your heels. You can't always split the difference. But how do we know when we face just such a situation, and when, on the other hand, we are overreacting?

A few clues can be discerned from the failures of the church during the Nazi era. It is clear that Christians must define reality in terms of a faithful and clear-sighted reading of the biblical witness rather than allow the world's powers and principalities to set the terms by which we interpret events. The churches must guard against the kinds of mixed loyalties that leave us grasping for attention, approval, and even alliances with secular powers rather than striving for faithful obedience to Jesus alone as Lord. Church leaders must understand that their primary obligation is to bear both verbal and practical witness to the truth in their context rather than to protect narrowly understood ecclesial political interests. The churches must always be willing to confront the state when it radically violates its God-given mandate, even if that confrontation has the potential to produce martyrs among us. And Christian leaders must be willing to listen carefully to dissident prophetic voices whose discernment of the *kairos* may just be the right one.

To oppose Nazism with unmitigated passion as a vicious idolatry; to weep with sorrow over the humiliation and then the destruction of the Jews of Europe; to disobey Nazi laws and risk everything to "rescue those being led away to death"—these were the passions and the actions that the times demanded of the Christian churches from 1933 to 1945. We know that now. A very few knew it then. What will be known in 2050 about what we should have known and done in 2002?

5

Remembering Rwanda
Lessons from the Church's Complicity in Genocide

2004

APRIL MARKS THE TEN-YEAR anniversary of the beginning of the genocide in Rwanda, a catastrophic mass slaughter that claimed 850,000 lives in three months. Ten years later, Christian reflection must focus on the role Rwandan Christians played in the swiftest and in some ways most brutal genocide of the twentieth century.

Rwanda was the most heavily Christianized country in Africa. Some 90 percent of the people identified themselves as Christians. The Roman Catholic Church, to which 65 percent of the population belonged, played a huge role in Rwandan society. Christian churches, seminaries, schools, and other institutions were sprinkled throughout the land. And yet all of this Christianity did not prevent genocide, a genocide which leading church officials did little to resist, in which a large number of Christians participated, and in which, according to African Rights, more people "died in churches and parishes than anywhere else."

How could this be? Christianity should produce justice and love; it should certainly not produce genocide. So I believe and so I have taught.

But a study of the Holocaust, and now of the Rwandan genocide, has led me to realize that the presence of churches in a country guarantees nothing. The self-identification of people with the Christian faith guarantees nothing. All of the clerical garb and regalia, all of the structures of religious accountability, all of the Christian vocabulary and books, all of the schools and seminaries and parish houses and Bible studies, all of the religious titles and educational degrees—they guarantee nothing.

Careful examination of the role of the churches in Rwanda as well as in Nazi Germany reveals some heartbreaking truths.

First, it cannot be assumed that the Christian faith is taught in such a way as to emphasize love of neighbor (all neighbors) and respect for human life. No agency on earth has ever been able to control what is actually taught in a local church on a given Sunday morning. A variety of bastardized versions of the Christian message, including hateful ones, have been and continue to be communicated in congregations all over the world. This is true both in churches where authoritative (and sometimes authoritarian) church hierarchies supposedly have great power to control what happens in the local church, and in decentralized communions in which the local minister has the final say. Either way, the teaching of the Christian churches lands all over the map, from richly faithful to blandly mediocre to dreadfully immoral.

Second, it cannot be assumed that the people gathered to hear the Word proclaimed and to participate in the sacraments are serious about the Christian faith. People come to church for a wide variety of reasons. They bring widely varying levels of receptivity to the truth that leaders communicate from the pulpit and the altar. They bring widely varying moral and spiritual capacities. Jesus himself said that the seed of the gospel is scattered on all different kinds of ground; only one of the four kinds of soil that he mentions has the quality needed for fruitfulness (Mark 4). In light of Auschwitz and Rwanda, that sounds about right. Narrow is the road that leads to salvation; few there are who enter it.

Third, it cannot be assumed that all of the self-identified Christian people (baptized, born again, converted, members—whatever criteria or name you want to use) gathered in these churches are subject to the influence of the Holy Spirit. I cannot believe that what the Bible says about the work of the Spirit of God is erroneous. But what must be admitted is that there is quite a gap between the list of "Christians" on church rolls or in church pews and the much smaller list of Christians in whom the Spirit of God is working.

This is not a novel idea. The ancient concept of the true church within the visible church seems irrefutable in the shadow of Rwanda's killing fields and the crematories of Auschwitz.

Fourth, it cannot be assumed that Christian faith is the only or even the primary factor affecting the attitudes and behavior of those who claim

Christian identity. In fact, Christians, like everyone else, are subject to being blown about by ferocious ideological, economic, social, and political crosswinds.

In that light, the teachings of the Christian faith are often more like a candle flickering in a tornado than the sure anchor of the soul—the dominating factor in a Christian's thinking and behavior—that we often assume them to be. Or, to switch images, Christian teaching provides one set of inputs into human consciousness, but other inputs are always cycling through that consciousness as well.

Christians often speak of the terrific struggle of the soul before a profession of initial faith in Christ; but now we see that this terrific struggle of the soul for faith (and especially faithfulness) continues long after faith commences. The spiritual journey is never over, and the Christian is never free from the possibility of careening over the cliff into moral disaster, until he breathes his last breath.

We must move beyond the general to the particular. Certainly there were specific historical factors in Rwanda that contributed to the disastrous involvement and complicity of the churches in the 1994 genocide. The most significant appear to be the following:

The historic participation of the Rwandan churches, especially the Roman Catholic Church, in reinforcing ethnocentric thought and behavior both in public life and in the church itself. This weakened the church's ability to resist the quasi-fascist genocidal racism that emerged in a sector of Hutu society in the late 1980s and early 1990s and eventually led to genocide against their Tutsi compatriots.

The cozy relationship enjoyed by the leaders of the Rwandan Catholic Church and of several Protestant denominations with the Hutu government. This led church leaders to identify their interests with the interests of the then current government and its leaders. In the end, the outcome was a hesitation on the part of church leaders to stand up for innocent Tutsis (and moderate or resistant Hutus) and say a clear no to genocide.

The traditional teaching of the churches that the Bible mandates unquestioning submission to both churchly and governmental authority. This teaching left Christians very poorly prepared to resist the genocidal commands of local and national leaders.

The historic social power of the missionaries and churches that brought about the nearly universal "conversion" of Rwandans to Christianity. This nearly universal assent to Christianity, we can now see, was clearly more of a veneer than a living reality in people's hearts, as observers of Rwanda have noted.

It is striking that each of these problems was also apparent in the German churches (and throughout Europe) during the Hitler years.

German Christianity did not *produce* racist, pseudoscientific Nazi anti-Semitism any more than Rwandan Christianity produced racist, pseudo-scientific Hutu anti-Tutsism. But a misunderstanding of Christianity in Germany (and throughout Europe) that tied it to ethnic identity through historic antisemitism weakened the resistance of Christians to the allure of a much more vicious and hateful genocidal mentality when it emerged.

The cozy marriage of church and state that had existed throughout much of Europe was a prize that both Catholic and Protestant church leaders were loath to give up. In Germany, this left them susceptible to the false promises of a Hitler who at first promised a return to "positive Christianity" in Germany. Here was a conservative leader who would restore traditional German Christian values! It also left them indisposed to resist the unjust decrees and behaviors of the Nazi regime, for fear of weakening their already uncertain influence with the government as well as their institutional independence and social power.

The authoritarian understanding of power and the requirement to submit unquestioningly to it in all of its forms was, if anything, worse in Germany than in Rwanda. It certainly inhibited resistance to Nazism and to the Holocaust. Indeed, the same misunderstanding of Scripture as mandating total and unquestioning obedience to government (based on a misreading of Romans 13:1–7) contributed to submission to Nazi mandates among Christians in occupied Europe as well.

The Europe of the 1930s still bore the marks of the culture of Christendom that had dominated for over 1,500 years. Well over 90 percent of Europeans who lived through World War II identified themselves as Christians. When just about everyone is a "Christian," and all agree that they are living in a "Christian" culture, what is the meaning of Christianity? The observation of a *Commonweal* editorialist concerning Rwanda, that "the pervasive Catholic institutional and cultural presence ... proved little impediment to such mind-numbing savagery," applies equally well to Germany and German Christianity, both Protestant and Catholic.[1]

Plenty of evidence is in on this point: when a ruling elite decides to destroy a group of people in a society, most of the people who are not targeted will not resist, whatever their religious affiliation. To put it bluntly: politics usually matters more than religion does; or, politics co-opts religion and thus neutralizes it. To put it even more bluntly: people are sheep. Most will go along with what their elites tell them to think and do. Few have the

---

1. "Religion and Genocide," 6.

intellectual, spiritual or moral capacity to resist either the genocidal thinking of elites or the genocide itself once it begins.

But still we must affirm the mission and vocation of the churches. Churches are required to be agents of resistance to genocide or any other kind of social evil, as a basic expression of faithfulness to their God, their sacred Scriptures and their social responsibility.

Churches cannot, however, start preparing people for resistance only at the point when evil takes the stage. Training in resistance to evil should be a part of the daily teaching, preaching and training that occurs in every congregation. If the lessons of both Rwanda and the Holocaust are taken seriously, the implications are clear.

The churches should attempt to do everything they can to destroy racism where they find it in their congregations. Even "mild," subtle, unarticulated racist attitudes are poison. They are poison because they violate biblical norms. They are poison because they weaken or neutralize resistance to more virulent forms of political racism when these emerge.

The churches would do well to give up, once and for all, any hope of great social and political power, including a comfortable embrace by government leaders. The dream of Christian political dominance is alluring, but must be recognized as a demonic snare. And a cozy relationship with government almost always comes at far too high a price either for Christian integrity or for the victims of government injustice. Christians do nothing to protect the victims because we are too busy protecting our privileged position.

Churches need to teach that government powers, and all other structures of authority, are mandated by God to serve the well-being of people and communities. The mandate of government does not require Christians to offer unquestioning obedience. Government leaders and laws are to be respected, yes, but they are to be obeyed only insofar as they advance the common good and act in accordance with the dictates of justice. Otherwise they are to be cheerfully disobeyed, in the tradition of civil disobedience or even, in extreme cases, justified revolution.

The churches should reconsider what exactly we mean when we invite someone to "Christianity" or call someone among us a "Christian." In both Germany and Rwanda, we now see, Christianity was broad and wide but not deep, like the seed sown on rocky ground that has no root and so endures only for a while, till "trouble" comes (Mark 4:17, NIV). How can we read about this veneer-like faith and not shudder as we compare it to the broad, wide and often equally shallow thing that passes for Christianity in so much of our culture and in so many of our churches? What if we understood Christians to be only those who "hear the word, accept it, and produce a crop" (Mark 4:20)? What if we conclude that when Jesus said, "Not everyone who says to me 'Lord, Lord,' will enter the kingdom of heaven, but only he who does the will of the Father in heaven" (Matt 7:21), he knew exactly what he was talking about?

6

Can Christian Ethics Be Saved?

2004

PURPOSES AND OCCASIONS FOR THIS PAPER

Purposes

THIS IS A PAPER (a) mapping Christian ethics as an academic discipline, (b) defending this academic discipline, and (c) attempting to propose fruitful future directions for evangelical engagement in Christian ethics. Its primary audience is North American evangelicals, who are at this time especially in need of just such a topography, defense, and invitation to participate in Christian ethics.

Occasions

This paper is occasioned by several converging concerns.
   1. Evangelical skepticism about Christian ethics as an academic discipline
   The first occasion is the dismissal of Christian ethics as a viable discipline on the part of certain learned evangelical skeptics. For example, in the September/October 2001 issue of *Books and Culture*, theologian Stephen Webb opened an article provocatively entitled "Danger! Christian Ethics" with the following claims, among others:

- "Christian ethics is nothing more than simply being a good Christian."
- "Christian ethics becomes just another name for Christian theology."

- "What Christianity teaches about ethics is nothing different from or more than what Christianity teaches about Jesus Christ."
- "Christian ethics is not only an empty idea; it is also a dangerous one."
- "The study of religious ethics is one of the last strongholds of liberal Protestantism in the academy."[1]

This assortment of half-truths and untruths deserves a response on numerous levels. For now I will use it to indicate the fact that some scholars, such as Webb, and some of the institutions they serve are not convinced that a discipline called "Christian ethics" exists or that it ought to exist. Webb's claims reflect the broader marginalization of Christian ethics in the evangelical academy. I believe that this marginalization is a significant mistake, and hope to show why I believe that in this paper.

2. Popular evangelical ethical weakness in the practice of Christian ethics

Learned evangelical skepticism about Christian ethics as a discipline relates, I think, to popular evangelical weakness in ethical reflection and living. That is the second occasion for this paper. Capital E Ethics is an academic discipline; but little e ethics is an ecclesial discipline. Done well, Christian ethics the academic discipline serves Christian churches and Christian people in the formation of their way of life—their own Christian ethics. It is not hard to make the case that the North American evangelical scene is characterized by rampant moral incoherence, relativism, and acculturation. If evangelical intellectual life were characterized by the stronger academic practice of a convictionally evangelical Christian ethics, and if the evangelical public began to attend more closely to this work, perhaps the little e ethics of the evangelical world would improve. That hope animates not just this paper but all my efforts in Christian ethics.

3. The unsettled state of contemporary Christian ethics

The third occasion for this paper is an honest recognition of the unsettled state of contemporary North American Christian ethics. Among the best, and certainly the most visible, Christian ethicist these days is Stanley Hauerwas, who teaches at Duke Divinity School. In the preface to his recently released *With the Grain of the Universe*, the compilation of his 2000-2001 Gifford Lectures at St. Andrews, Hauerwas has the following to say:

> I never dreamed that I would be asked to give the Gifford Lectures. Theologians did not have a conspicuous role in the Gifford Lectures in the second half of the twentieth century. Moreover, I am not even a proper theologian but a representative of the even more disreputable field called Christian ethics, and it is not

1. Webb, Review of *Go and Do Likewise*, 21–22.

clear that I am a competent worker in that "field" because it is not apparent what constitutes competence in Christian ethics.[2]

With characteristic puckishness, Hauerwas here manages to describe his own primary field (and mine, and about 950 others of us) as "disreputable" — and to make the more significant claim that there is essentially no standard for competence in Christian ethics. Hauerwas is not saying (I hope) that there are no competent ethicists, but instead that there is no "center" defining what competence looks like in ethics. I would be interested to know if the situation is any less fluid and unsettled in theology, philosophy, or biblical studies as practiced in our postmodern context.

As one who has studied and practiced Christian ethics for some fifteen years now, I think that Hauerwas is not far wrong in his claim about the lack of clear standards of competence in Christian ethics as an academic discipline, though as usual his claim is overstated to grab the reader's attention. One occasion for this essay is to sketch how evangelicals should define such competence as we strengthen our involvement with this discipline and in turn perhaps strengthen the discipline itself.

4. The need to build bridges out of the evangelical subculture to the broader church

A fourth and final concern animating this chapter is my sense of both a personal and professional need to build bridges out of the evangelical subculture to the broader church and its associated academic apparatus.

At one level, this is merely personal. I am a Southern Baptist evangelical by conviction; yet I am also a practicing member of the Christian ethics guild. Living in two worlds, I have both a need and an interest to build bridges between them.

But the need for bridge-building is more than personal. I think that the rather stark divorce between the vast evangelical subculture and the leading professionals who write and teach Christian ethics is bad for both. In recent years I have noticed a growing interest on the part of the Christian ethics guild in dialogue and engagement with evangelicals. As I will attempt to show a bit later, evangelicals should rush through this open door, not only for the sake of the ethics guild and the churches it serves, but also for our own sake.

---

2. Hauerwas, *With the Grain of the Universe*, 9.

MAPPING THE DISCIPLINE OF CHRISTIAN ETHICS

Defining the Discipline

1. Mainstream definition of Christian ethics

When mainstream Christian ethicists say "the academic discipline of Christian ethics," what they normally mean is: that discipline practiced by those who (a) have earned a PhD or equivalent degree in Christian ethics, moral theology (the preferred Catholic term), or a closely related field; (b) identify themselves as Christian ethicists; (c) author scholarly and professional publications in the field; (d) teach Christian ethics in college, university, or seminary settings or engage in full-time professional work that is closely related to the field; and (e) find one of their primary professional/institutional homes in the organization called the Society of Christian Ethics (SCE). I adapt this definition from the Purpose Statement of the Society of Christian Ethics.

2. Christian Ethics A: historic Christian moral thought

Yet, as mainstream ethicist Edward L. Long of Drew University himself put it in his 1984 history of the Society of Christian Ethics:

> It is important not to equate the history of the Society [of Christian Ethics] with the history of an academic discipline. Christian ethics is as old as Christianity itself and even has roots in OT thought . . . A history of Christian ethics resembles a history of Christian thought and is integrally related to it.[3]

At one level, then, there is no discrete history of Christian ethics. It is simply the moral/ethical aspect of historic Christian thought. Let's call this historic Christian moral thought "Christian Ethics A" because it was here first—it can be witnessed in Scripture and every era of church history. Christian Ethics A is the church's reflection on its own moral life and on its engagement with society. It is a perennial task of the church.

3. Christian Ethics B: The teaching of "Social Christianity" in America

The precursor of modern North American Christian ethics can be found in the late nineteenth century. Both universities and seminaries began to offer classes in contemporary social problems in the 1880s and 1890s, at the very origins of the Social Gospel movement with its deep concern for the suffering and injustice created by unfettered laissez-faire industrial capitalism. The goal of the very first classes in Christian ethics was to help students translate Christian moral principles into action in a troubled and

---

3. Long, *Academic Bonding and Social Concern*, 160.

suffering world. The first and most influential of these classes was an 1883–84 course at Harvard taught by Professor Francis Greenwood Peabody. Long rightly points out that the "social passion" of these early practitioners of so-called "applied Christianity" or "social Christianity" has always been a central characteristic of the field which later came to be called Christian ethics.[4]

4. Christian Ethics C: The "mainstream" discipline of Christian ethics

Despite the steady existence of courses in Social Christianity or applied faith in the period between the late nineteenth century and World War II, it was not until the 1950s that the contemporary discipline of Christian ethics began to take shape. What eventually became known as the Society of Christian Ethics was founded in 1959 after several years of precursor activities. Over time its agenda has evolved to include various aspects of the entire moral tradition of the Christian faith (Christian Ethics A). Yet at its heart the discipline retains the "social passion" of the nineteenth century "Social Christianity" that was such an important part of its birth as a discipline.

5. Evangelical disengagement with the mainstream discipline of Christian ethics

North American evangelical disengagement from the mainstream discipline of Christian ethics has been obvious from its very origins. My review of the history of the discipline has convinced me that this disengagement clearly is linked to the context in which Christian ethics B was born—the Social Gospel. Though evangelicals were vigorously engaged with urban social reform efforts when that movement began, theological drift in the Social Gospel movement, as well as the related fundamentalist-modernist controversy of the 1920s, sheared evangelicals away from social engagement for a long season—a season unfortunately coinciding with the consolidation of mainstream Christian ethics as an academic discipline.

One of Carl Henry's signal postwar contributions was his effort to offer evangelical reflection on both "personal" and "social" Christian ethics. But his careful, even magisterial, works in this area did not signal either his own integration into mainstream Christian ethics or lead many other evangelical thinkers to beat a path in that direction. Academic evangelical treatments of Christian ethics, with certain important exceptions, have been undertaken by those not trained in mainstream Christian ethics (or in ethics at all). Thus, as I continue to map the discipline of Christian ethics, I map a discipline with which evangelicals have been largely disengaged.

---

4. Ibid., 160–61.

Diversity as characteristic of the discipline of Christian ethics

Perhaps the most obvious characteristic of the discipline of Christian ethics, defined now as Christian ethics C, the mainstream discipline, is its diversity. Even the SCE universe, which with 950 members is relatively small and chummy in comparison with the organized chaos that characterizes the American Academy of Religion, exhibits a striking diversity. This diversity can be mapped in several ways, and offers a nice snapshot of the field—a field which evangelicals need to get acquainted with—so here goes.

1. By Denomination

Christian ethicists are Catholic, Eastern Orthodox, and nearly every variety of Protestant: Anglican, Lutheran, Reformed, Anabaptist, Pentecostal/charismatic, and so on. Mainline Protestants have long played a leading role in mainstream Christian ethics but, contra Webb, Christian ethics today cannot accurately be reduced to a "bastion of liberal Protestantism." The Catholic voice in the SCE, just to name one example, is strong and quite well-represented at every level of leadership and activity. While there do exist some "religious ethicists" representing no particular confessional tradition, they are actually rather few in number. Most Christian ethicists, whatever denomination they represent, ground their work in a recognizable theological tradition to which they retain some measure of loyalty and whose sources and methods are visible in their work, even as they are also affected by dialogue with scholars outside their own particular faith tradition.

2. By Theological Stance

It is certainly fair to say that the discipline of Christian ethics has tended to lean to the center-left theologically while encompassing a wide range of views, from conservative to radical. In this way it has reflected similar trends in the broader religious studies academy. Yet it is clear to me after fifteen years of observation that the SCE has a theological groundedness that the AAR most certainly does not. Meanwhile, there is sufficient diversity of perspective within the Society to keep anyone from getting too comfortable. I happen to believe that engagement with reasonably diverse perspectives contributes to the sharpening and self-correction that is essential both to good scholarship and good discipleship.

An interesting example of the theological orientation of Christian ethics was the debate in 1980 (and again in the late 1990s) concerning whether to change the SCE to a kind of SRE—Society of Religious Ethics—that is, whether to drop the Christian identification of the SCE. Such a proposal has never prevailed in the SCE. Its recent failure has resulted in, among other things, the decision of Jewish ethicists to found a Society of Jewish Ethics. With very few exceptions, Christian ethicists want to do recognizably Christian ethics. The proposals of leading Christian ethicists never win universal approval, but they do have in common an explicit grounding in Christian faith. There is no interest in bare secular philosophical ethics and very little interest in a general human ethics, except perhaps by way of comparison with a thicker Christian ethics. It is certainly clear to me that confessionally explicit papers that would be difficult if not impossible to present in an AAR setting are welcomed in the SCE.

3. By Contextual Criteria

The last two decades have seen within Christian ethics the growth both of demographic diversity and ethical perspectives to match. The SCE was interested in "race relations" from its beginning, and in "women's rights" since the 1960s. But over time the guild has helped to nurture the training, development, and inclusion of a significant number of black, Hispanic, female, Asian-American, and other scholars from previously voiceless groups. Meanwhile, from these groups has begun the emergence of contextual social/theological ethics: feminist ethics, African-American ethics, womanist ethics, Latino/a ethics, etc. This effort at inclusiveness is consistent with the founding vision of Christian ethics and contributes greatly to the field's richness and diversity, and makes for a stark contrast with the overwhelmingly white and male face of most evangelical scholarship.

4. By Methodology

A major source of diversity within Christian ethics is by methodology. I have already noted the existence of contextual methodologies. These tend to emphasize engagement with biblical and theological themes and truths with careful attention to cultural and social location and personal or group experience. Sometimes these treatments drift badly from Christian orthodoxy but other times they do not.

Such approaches are complemented by a variety of methodological options of other types. Various philosophical, theological, biblical, and social scientific methodologies can be seen in Christian ethics. These methodological approaches are sometimes rooted deeply in long-standing confessional traditions; other times they represent the innovations of current thinkers. The fact of the matter is that there is no single "way" to do Christian ethics, despite various proposals that have been made over the years. This reality contributes greatly to the unsettled state of affairs in the discipline and often contributes to an overemphasis on methodological disputes at the expense of consideration of concrete moral norms.

5. By Issue Interest

One longstanding characteristic of the SCE is its focus on social issues. Indeed, in my training I frequently heard the term "social ethics" as the main term for denoting what I was learning to do, and that language remains significant in the SCE (it turns out that the original name of the SCE was the American Society of Christian Social Ethics). As we have seen, Christian ethics as a specialized discipline was born with industrialization and its ills. It came into its own in the mid-twentieth century in response to the convulsive social crises of those years: World War I, the Depression, totalitarianism, World War II, genocide, the Cold War and weapons of mass destruction, and the civil rights struggle. Given those roots, mainstream Christian ethics has tended to focus its gaze on pressing social issues like these, updating its issue set with the times. Thus today the issue mix includes economic globalization, the environment, family ethics, racial justice, bioethics, and so on. Varieties of professional ethics—business, ministerial, legal, medical, journalistic, etc.—have also won an important place in Christian ethics. Matters of public policy are always on the agenda. Thus a key source of the diversity in contemporary Christian ethics has to do with issue specialization. Bioethics, for example, is a vast enough concern to be its own field—which it is, actually—but other arenas of social concern all have been met by issue specialists to address them.

Of course, it is important to note that the mainstream guild offers radically diverse proposals for how Christians should respond to such issues. There is certainly a left-liberal contingent, perhaps most visible on issues of sexual ethics. And yet the strong Catholic presence, as well as more conservative voices within the mainline academy (and among the evangelicals already involved in the field) keeps the discipline from becoming merely a "bastion of liberal Protestantism" on these and other issues. Deepened evangelical engagement would only help balance the scales all the more.

A final note here: in what may be taken as a kind of a reaction to this focus on contemporary issues, other ethicists now specialize in perennial concerns and themes in ethics, such as character, ecclesiology and ethics, the history of ethics, liturgy/worship and ethics, covenantal ethics, moral psychology, and the interpretation of the Bible for ethics, or in the work of major moral thinkers of past and present. In the resurgence of interest in such themes one sees mainstream Christian ethics going back to Christian ethics A and doing work of great value to evangelicals if we would attend to it.

6. By Place of Service/type of work

Unlike what is normally the case for the other theological disciplines, Christian ethics places its practitioners in many places of service other than the classroom. The diversity of the discipline can, in part, be found in this vocational pluralism. Certainly Christian ethicists often inhabit academia. At its origins, Christian ethicists tended to cluster in seminary settings, but by now the secular university, church-related school, evangelical college, university divinity school, freestanding seminary, and so on, all find their way onto this map. But ethicists also can be found in churches, religious orders, denominational agencies, research institutes and thinktanks, government departments, parachurch lobbying, advocacy, and activist organizations, and in hospitals, health care bureaucracies, businesses, and the military. Whatever it is that this "disreputable" profession does, there appear to be quite a range of institutions that are interested in it.

7. By Ethics Tradition/Icon

Perhaps the most interesting way to map the discipline is by what might be called ethics tradition or key ethics icon. That is, since its founding it has been possible to identify traditions in Christian ethics associated with key figures either living or dead. Often these are then linked with particular divinity schools or universities where those traditions live on long after their originator has been gone from the scene. Some of the most significant of these ethics icons and the traditions associated with them would include:

a. The Reinhold Niebuhr/Union Seminary (New York) tradition—built around the great mid-century Protestant ethicist/theologian, with a strong emphasis on engagement with current national and international issues based on Protestant theology.

b. The H. Richard Niebuhr/Yale Divinity tradition—built around Reinhold's more retiring brother H. Richard, this tradition has always been more methodologically rigorous and—because it is less fixated on the current issues of the day—has tended to produce a more enduring literature in Christian ethics.

c. The James Gustafson/University of Chicago Divinity School tradition—Gustafson, one of the distinguished ethicists of the last generation, anchored a vigorous tradition in ethics at Chicago. The early Gustafson was a centrist Protestant of moderate Reformed leanings who engaged most of the important methodological disputes of his day with care and skill; the constructive work of the later Gustafson has been rather idiosyncratic, more theistic than Christian, but still fascinating.

d. The Stanley Hauerwas/Duke Divinity School tradition—The most recent powerhouse ethicist to make this rarefied list, Hauerwas has built at Duke a tradition of Christian ethics offering a kind of neo-sectarian

"Christ against culture" vision along with a strong emphasis on the retrieval of character and a focus on narrative.

These four streams of tradition hardly exhaust the list: one could also name a Dietrich Bonhoeffer tradition; a John Howard Yoder/Anabaptist tradition; an older Paul Ramsey/Princeton tradition now mainly abandoned; a feminist tradition that is quite collaborative but perhaps most closely identified with Beverly Harrison of Union Seminary; a strong sociology of religion/social ethics tradition at Emory University, associated with Jon Gunneman; multiple centers for a Catholic tradition in ethics, but especially Notre Dame, Boston College, and Georgetown; an African-American tradition in Christian ethics with Martin Luther King as a lodestone; the vigorous work in Christian ethics also being undertaken in several California institutions of various confessional traditions; and influential voices from Great Britain and the Continent.

8. General Trends in Christian Ethics: a Summary

While the existence of major schools of tradition centered around key figures still is a factor in mainstream Christian Ethics, the impact of these schools appears to be weakening in light of the increasing decentralization of the field. Dozens of schools offer doctorates in Christian ethics and the horizon is not dominated by the kinds of towering figures once common in an earlier era. Christian ethics appears to be irreducibly diverse but yet the field with few exceptions clings to its Christian identity and its outgrowth in a social passion to address grievous public wrongs. The range of diversity certainly makes it hard to identify obvious standards of competence in the field. This contributes to the unsettling sense that various ethicists make various proposals but a methodological center for the discipline is never quite found.[5] Even so, considerable sophisticated and very high-quality work happens nonetheless—much of it at some of the finest educational institutions in the world, and much of it remarkably relevant to evangelical life.

AN APOLOGIA FOR CHRISTIAN ETHICS

In light of all of the foregoing, I would like to offer a brief apologia to an evangelical audience for Christian ethics as an academic discipline. I want to claim that without attention to Christian ethics as an academic discipline, four very unwelcome things tend to happen in the Christian community;

---

5 Ibid., 164.

and thus that evangelical inattention to mainstream Christian ethics has contributed to the existence of these four problems in our midst today.

Without Christian ethics, the moral dimension of the Scriptures gets overlooked.

I usually define little e Christian ethics (that is, the work that all of us as Christians are called to do) as the Spirit-empowered effort of communities of Christian people to understand and to incarnate a way of life that conforms to God's will and advances God's kingdom. Christian ethics the academic discipline helps Christians do this work of moral discernment and moral living. Ethics has to do with who we as Christians fundamentally are (moral character), what kinds of decisions we make, and how we go about making them (moral decision making), what kinds of goals we embrace (moral intentions), how we see the world and its possibilities (moral vision), how we characteristically conduct ourselves (moral practices), how we interact with and seek to change society (moral activism)—and more. These various dimensions of Christian character and conduct are demonstrated and worked out in various areas of life: in individual life, in families, within the church, in the professions and the workplace, and in public life (culture, politics, law). For guidance in all of these areas, we desperately need biblical direction.

The Bible is indeed filled with moral content. But much of the time the moral dimension of the biblical message is overlooked or grossly misinterpreted. Christian ethics as a discipline helps Christians attend to and apply the moral commands, moral vision, morally significant narratives, and moral observations coursing through the Word of God. This discipline also calls our attention to the moral implications of core theological propositions of Scripture, such as the sovereignty of God or the goodness but fallenness of creation. Of course ethicists are not the only ones who do this work, and no claim to exclusivity is intended in any of what I say here. But it does seem to be the case that ethics calls the church to attend to aspects of Scripture and the doctrines emerging from Scripture that are otherwise overlooked. Evangelical engagement with Christian ethics would help ensure that attention to such biblical texts, themes, and principles.

Without Christian ethics, the moral tradition of the church gets overlooked.

The classic theological curriculum includes study in church history and the history of Christian thought. In my experience, the discipline of Christian ethics plays a key role in keeping alive the moral heritage of Christian thought. Just as there is a history of Christian theology that must be remembered and transmitted, there is also a history of Christian ethics.

The moral tradition of the Christian church has two dimensions—what Christians have believed about morality, and how Christians have behaved morally. It is important, for example, to know what Martin Luther or John Calvin had to say not just about election or the sacraments but also about family, government, and economic life. It is also important to know what role they played in the fierce religious and political battles of their time, and of the legacy of their moral thought and practice for Protestant social ethics and western culture to this day. The same holds true with every other major thinker in Christian history. Likewise, a morally sensitive history of the church as a whole deserves to be attempted.

One of the salutary developments of our time is the retrieval of the heritage of the church. Tom Oden's project in patristic biblical interpretation—the Ancient Christian Commentary series—makes a great example of this. On a much smaller scale, a branch of the ethics guild is doing similar archaeology in Christian moral thought. The most recent annual meeting of the SCE included papers on Calvin and the emotions, John Chrysostom's treatment of marriage, Luther on the self, Schliermacher on religious experience in theology and ethics, as well as discussions of Dorothy Day, Martin Luther King, Karl Barth, and the history of treatment of aboriginal peoples in North America. The more we dig around in the ancestral past, the more we discover riches beyond measure—as well as painful evidence of sins and missteps worth avoiding in the future.

Without Christian ethics, the church's treatment of contemporary social problems is weakened.

Stephen Webb says: "What Christianity teaches about ethics is nothing different from or more than what Christianity teaches about Jesus Christ."[6] At one level, this is a truthful statement. Glen Stassen and I have just completed an introductory text in Christian ethics based on Jesus' teachings, and InterVarsity Press tells us it has 180,000 words in it. So Jesus tells us quite a

---

6. Webb, Review of *Go and Do Likewise*, 21.

bit about Christian ethics. But of course many of those words are devoted to teasing out answers to such issues as whether an infertile couple should decide to pursue in vitro fertilization. Or what stance the church should take on poverty in American society. Or what to think and do about genetic engineering. Or what the church can do to prevent divorce and build successful marriages. The direction that Jesus offers to Christian ethics is a matter of considerable effort. It cannot simply be derived from christological formulations or, far worse, "what would Jesus do" slogans.

That effort involves interaction with other fields of study. Christian ethics—Christian social ethics, at least—is interdisciplinary. Most Christian ethics programs require training both in the classic theological/ethical canon and also in a social or natural science—sociology, economics, biology, genetics, political science. That's because Christian ethics is more than "just another name for Christian theology." It is the interaction of Christian theology with a fallen world on behalf of the church's efforts in moral discernment and moral action.

It may have been possible in the sixteenth century for the church's leading figures—Luther, Calvin, Zwingli, etc.—to do it all. They could be theologians, pastors, ethicists, biblical scholars. Given the scope, complexity, and rapidly changing nature of today's social problems, as well as the explosion of Christian scholarship, a measure of specialization is salutary today, even required. Ethicists tend to specialize in particular moral issues, and to work in an interdisciplinary fashion with social scientists dealing with the same issues. Somehow, again contra Webb, it will not quite do to say that "Christian ethics is nothing more than simply being a good Christian."

Without Christian ethics, the church loses an essential bearer of its internal and external prophetic witness.

Mainstream Christian ethics has always been taken by the example of the prophets and by the prophetic moral teachings of Jesus—perhaps the most neglected parts of the canon in evangelical life. Our discipline has always found its heartbeat at the intersection of God's love and human misery. The prophets called Israel to return to God, to keep the covenant once made with God; to do justice and love mercy, to protect and care for the widow, the orphan, and the alien, to live out God's compassion for the poor and victimized. And the prophets did not cease to bring a fiercely critical word from the Lord to the people of God, not because of disdain for God's people but instead out of the highest kind of love.

As a discipline, we have resisted the reduction of Christian faith to the affirmation of right doctrine. We have resisted the reduction of Christian morality to the recitation of right convictions. We have resisted the reduction of Christian spirituality to the generation of individual good feelings. We have sought to keep the poor and the victimized before the conscience of the church and the culture. And we have called the church away from triumphalism and toward a teachable humility fitting for God's elect-but-fallible people. This stance certainly challenges Webb's careless claim that Christian ethics is "an empty idea"—whether it is also "a dangerous one" perhaps depends on whether one welcomes a prophetic voice or does not.

SKETCHING A WAY FORWARD

I want to propose that rather than rejecting or marginalizing Christian ethics as an academic discipline, evangelicals need to heighten their efforts in the field, in four ways: training more ethicists, participating more heavily in the Society of Christian Ethics, producing first-rate scholarship in Christian ethics, and allowing the broad social passion of Christian ethics to be felt again within evangelicalism. Doing these things will have a positive impact both on evangelicals and on the discipline of Christian ethics.

Training more ethicists

The dearth of evangelical ethicists has left a gap in seminary and university faculties that is proving very difficult to fill. Even where these schools seek professionally trained ethicists they have difficulty finding people with both the appropriate training and evangelical theological convictions. This trend becomes self-reinforcing. The lack of ethics instruction and instructors at evangelical colleges and seminaries helps to limit the number of students who then pursue ethics at the graduate level. Those who do pursue graduate study in ethics are then less likely to be evangelicals or be in contact with evangelicals.

The same thing needs to happen in Christian ethics as has happened in philosophy, history, theology, and sociology of religion. Young scholars of excellent academic abilities and solid theological convictions need to be trained well and then sent to the best doctoral programs in ethics that can be found. As they do good work they will find employment in excellent universities and make their mark in the profession. Think of the philosopher Nicholas Wolterstorff, historian Joel Carpenter, and theologian Miroslav Volf. The door is open in ethics just as it is in these other fields if evangelicals are willing to walk through it. One hopeful sign was the recent addition of a young evangelical named Eric Gregory to the faculty of Princeton University. Gregory is a Yale doctoral student now appointed full time to the same university that not long ago hired Peter Singer. One of my fondest hopes is to eventually place a number of my finest students in ethics doctoral programs, and to see them eventually take their evangelical vision to places like Princeton. My understanding is that students at Princeton are already flocking to Gregory like weary desert travelers to an oasis.

Participating in the Ethics guild

The Society of Christian Ethics has an Evangelical Ethics Interest Group. I have served as co-leader of this group for some time, most recently with Christine Pohl of Asbury Seminary. Each year, a rather substantial number of ethicists surface for our late-night group session at the annual convention. Two years ago, when Dennis Hollinger (Messiah College) and I presented a paper on Evangelical ethics in the broader SCE setting, a large number of nonevangelicals showed up.

All of this is to say that the mainstream ethics guild both needs and welcomes the respectful but vigorous participation of evangelicals who teach and write about ethics. Within the 950-member Society, self-identified evangelicals are likely no more than 5 percent. But someone is teaching ethics at CCCU universities and in our dozens of seminaries and Bible colleges, and as far as I can tell few of these participate in the SCE. Involvement in the Society will both enrich evangelical teaching and have an impact on the direction of Christian ethics as a discipline.

Producing first-rate scholarship

The reason why folks like George Marsden, Alvin Plantinga, Miroslav Volf, and Nick Wolterstorff are taken seriously by nonevangelicals is simply that they produce good work. By the canons of the disciplines in which such scholars work, they are excellent. Their work demands attention. Even in a center-left leaning discipline, certain meritocratic standards still prevail. Excellent work is noticed. Often evangelicals convince themselves of a vast left-wing conspiracy against us when what is really going on is that our own ghettoization has kept us from reaching the level of excellence that might get our work noticed.

If and when evangelicals produce good scholarship in ethics, we are taken seriously. Richard Mouw, John Howard Yoder, Stephen Mott, Oliver

O'Donovan, James McClendon, Gilbert Meilaender, Glen Stassen, and Christine Pohl are examples of evangelical scholars representing a variety of traditions whose work has earned the attention of ethicists of all stripes. We need to produce more such work, and soon.

Allowing evangelicalism to be affected by the social passion of Christian ethics

Many fine scholars have documented both the rich early history of American evangelical social and political engagement and then its sudden abandonment in the 1920s after the fundamentalist-modernist controversy.

Evangelicals, partly under the influence of Carl Henry, wised up and reentered public ethical engagement, beginning in the 1970s. Unfortunately, especially at the popular and mass activist level, we have not always done our work well. But there is unlikely to be a second evangelical withdrawal from such social engagement. Evangelicals are in the public square to stay.

Yet few evangelicals (academic or otherwise) who engage public ethical issues do so in dialogue with the leading professionals of the field. Because the discipline of Christian ethics blossomed at the very time that evangelicals were withdrawn from public ethical engagement, we did not gain much of a foothold in that group in the 1950s and have remained alienated from it even after returning to the public square in the 1970s. One result of this estrangement has been some pretty shoddy ethical writing. Another has been a weakening of that passion for justice and righteousness that is so obviously biblical that evangelicals cannot forever neglect it.

But this is a new day. Evangelicals are back in the public square, and with plenty of moral passion in need of refinement and direction. And the Christian ethics guild is ready for interaction with evangelicals. For our own sake, we need to pursue that interaction.

CONCLUSION

Fading of the mainline

The mainline is fading, and everyone knows it, even the mainline. As early as 1984, in his history of the discipline of Christian ethics, Edward L. Long worried:

> If the institutional expressions of Christianity in our immediate milieu progressively decline in quality, even if they do survive,

> that also will undermine the possibility of doing Christian ethics well ... If robust Christian ethics can exist only within a context of vibrant faith and viable religious institutions, and if those very contexts are eroding right under our very noses, then business as usual for a society such as ours will not insure a promising future.[7]

My colleague George Guthrie has spoken to me of how evangelical scholars now dominate large sections of biblical scholarship simply because it is increasingly only evangelicals who still care enough about the biblical text to bother with it. In other words, the erosion that Long worried about has already deeply affected mainline involvement in biblical studies. The mainliners now desperately need evangelicals in their midst to keep their churches and academic enterprises alive.

Evangelical ethics as a welcome force for renewal

My experience of the mainstream ethics community is that in the midst of signs of their own decline they find evangelicals a refreshing, renewing, and hopeful presence in the discipline. An evangelical spirit in ethics (the right kind of evangelical spirit) reminds the discipline as a whole of its origins and founding passions. Our careful attention to a Scripture in which we still wholeheartedly believe, passionate grounding in a personal relationship with Christ, desire for excellence in the service of Christ as Lord, and kingdom vision for the transformation of the world, are like a breath of fresh air in a scholarly guild that once was characterized by more of this spirit as the foundation of its social passion—and at some level wishes it still was.[8]

I continue to think that one of the best definitions of evangelicalism is simply that it is a renewal movement within Protestant Christianity, calling fellow believers to what they once and truly believed. To renew we must engage rather than withdraw. To renew successfully might mean to make ourselves obsolete; that is, as a renewal movement. Instead we might just find ourselves reintegrated into a renewed church and scholarly guild both deeply affected by our biblical vision.

This dream, far broader in application than merely to Christian ethics, certainly applies to the discipline I serve and have been discussing in this chapter.

---

7 Long, *Academic Bonding and Social Concern*, 176.
8 Hollinger and Gushee, "Evangelical Ethics," 181–203.

7

Dietrich Bonhoeffer and the Evangelical Moment in American Public Life

2006

I WRITE NOT JUST as a religious scholar/activist, not just as a Christian scholar/activist, not just as a Protestant Christian scholar/activist, but as an American evangelical Baptist Protestant Christian scholar/activist.

While it is good to be clear about one's identity and context, I cannot speak for all who share that context. But I can reflect on what the witness of Dietrich Bonhoeffer means to me in these times. I can try to articulate the ways in which what I am trying to teach, write, and do these days reflects my long-standing effort to remain faithful to Bonhoeffer's demanding example—even as I am aware of the inherent danger of attempting to draw inspiration from Bonhoeffer for any context outside his own.

This leads to one especially important disclaimer: inevitably any effort to read Bonhoeffer for his contemporary significance involves making comparisons between interwar and wartime Germany on the one hand, and one's own context, on the other. If one sees similarities, parallels, and possible analogies, it is easy to be misread as *equating*, say, the United States with Nazi Germany, or US Christians with the *Deutsche Christen*. I am *not* attempting to offer such an equation. But I am attempting to think about the significance of Bonhoeffer (a man attempting to be faithful to his Christian calling in his own context) for my own efforts to be faithful to my Christian calling in my context.

The personal context that is most important for me to identify in this essay is my location as an American evangelical scholar-activist. I write in a time when it seems that all eyes are turned to evangelicals, who represent a massive slice of the American religious landscape, who have discovered and exercised their political power in quite visible ways in recent years, and in so doing have terrified many who do not share their/our convictions. This is the "evangelical moment" in American public life. I write during that moment and from within that community, simultaneously as an evangelical loyalist and as an internal critic. My exposition of key themes in Bonhoeffer's life and work must be understood within this context.

LOYALTY: CHRIST ABOVE ALL

Dietrich Bonhoeffer taught and modeled unrelenting loyalty to Jesus Christ. Like it or not, his was a Christ-centered theology and ethic. This theme works its way through his writings and his life.

This relentless commitment to Jesus Christ meant that all other loyalties were clearly distinguished from Christ, and relativized in relation to Christ. No human being, no nation, no ideology, no "race," no cause of any sort must be confused in any way with the person or mission of Jesus Christ. Nor can the cause of Jesus Christ be subsumed under some other, totalitarian scheme for organizing society. Note the paradox that this rigorous Christ-centeredness actually left him more concerned, not less, with the plight of his non-Christian fellow countrymen, especially the persecuted Jewish community, than most of his fellow church leaders. This shows us that it is not enough to be Christ-centered, which is a familiar enough slogan in the Christian community—it matters quite a bit what kind of Christ one is centering upon.

This clarity about his loyalties left Bonhoeffer far better prepared to resist the siren song of loyalty to race, *Volk*, nation, party, state, and Führer than were most German Christians. Moreover, the more that leaders either of the church or the state attempted to blur or blend or equate these loyalties, the more Bonhoeffer resisted. He was equipped with a theological alarm system, one might say, that alerted him to such dangerous syncretism and idolatry and kept him entirely clear of it. Karl Barth had the same alarm system, rooted in a similar Christocentrism. It was this spirit that animated the Barmen Declaration.

Today, for a variety of reasons, conservative American evangelicals regularly exhibit confusion about their loyalties. They (we—my people—though, again, I speak as a "connected critic" here) often conflate loyalty to Jesus Christ with loyalty to the United States of America. They weave together loyalty to Jesus Christ with loyalty to the president, the party, the troops, the flag, or the nation. They create labels, such as "traditional values," or "conservative values," or "family values," or "our Judeo-Christian heritage" that are themselves symbolic of a confusion, even syncretism, of identities and loyalties.

It is in part my own loyalty to Bonhoeffer's witness that drives me toward strong resistance to such confusion of loyalties.

COMMUNITY: THE CENTRALITY OF THE CHURCH

From his earliest academic work Bonhoeffer exhibited great interest in the church. If Christ is the "center," as he said, Christ takes form in the church, the community of saints. Bonhoeffer's robust ecclesiology was unusual in his day. The marriage of church and state in Europe had weakened and corrupted both. It had certainly co-opted the church to the interests of the state, which became painfully obvious during the Nazi years as the church's integrity was compromised by its loyalty to a radicalized state. Bonhoeffer's writings about the church ultimately amounted to an ecclesiological revolution. He lifted up the centrality of the church as the primary community/polity for Christian people, practiced and taught renewed ancient Christian practices of study, worship, and fellowship (thus linking the church to its historic heritage), and reminded the church of its allegiance to Christ alone. In the end, he supported the abandonment by the church of its cultural privileges and thus had moved towards at least the germinal stage of a post-Christendom ecclesiology.

Such a robust ecclesiology left Bonhoeffer far better prepared than most of his peers to resist the extremely corrupt form of Christendom that was represented by *Reichsbischof* Ludwig Müller and the German Christian Movement. Like others in the Confessing Church, he strongly rejected any tampering by the state with the internal life of the Christian churches. He sought to disentangle and clarify the identities marked "German" and "Christian" at a time when they were being purposefully entangled by Nazi leaders and their allies in the church. One way he did so was by pioneering a new model of seminary training in his work with the underground Confessing Church seminary at Finkenwalde.

I believe that even though evangelicals have created vast numbers of churches, some of them massive cathedrals of our own age, filled to the brim with people, we have not been particularly strong in our theology of the church. On the one hand, our pietistic individualism creates a "Jesus and me" ethos that often weakens any loyalty to the community of faith or any willingness to submit to a disciplined covenantal vision. Like Christians in Bonhoeffer's time, we retreat into a happy privatized faith. On the other hand, the moral mediocrity of this kind of church leaves us hopeless about the church as the center of God's redemptive enterprise in the world. And so we turn inward or heavenward in despair, or we turn to the state to enforce the values we can't seem to advance in our own churches. I believe that the weaker our ecclesiology, the stronger our tendency to confuse the identities "American" and "Christian" and to offer excessive loyalties to worldly powers.

Part of my own loyalty to Bonhoeffer is a strong emphasis on, and involvement in, a robust church, beginning with the local church. I have sought to be clear that the primary audience for Christian ethical reflection is the church, and the primary task of such reflection is to strengthen our faithful obedience to the concrete teachings and witness of Jesus Christ.

DESPAIR: RESPONDING TO CULTURAL DECLINE

Like all Germans, and many around the world, Dietrich Bonhoeffer was deeply troubled by World War I and the cultural and political crisis that afflicted his nation after the war. And yet he never demonstrated any susceptibility to what Fritz Stern called "the politics of cultural despair." I think it was because he believed in the interpretation of history offered by biblical revelation, which though realistic about human nature and history is never a counsel of despair.

It was this cultural despair—a toxic brew of reaction against secularism, anger related to the loss of World War I, distress over cultural disorientation and confusion, fears about the future of Germany, hatred of the victorious powers and of those who supposedly stabbed Germany in the back, and of course the search for scapegoats (mainly the Jews)—that motivated many Germans to adopt a reactionary, authoritarian, and nationalistic ethic that fueled their support for Hitler's rise to power. A broadly appealing narrative of national decline (or conspiratorial betrayal) was met by Hitler's narrative of national revenge leading to utopian unity in the Führer-state.

Conservative American evangelicals in recent decades have been deeply attracted to a parallel narrative of cultural despair. Normally the story begins with the rise of secularism in the 1960s, the abandonment of prayer in schools, and the *Roe* decision, all leading to an apocalyptic decline of American culture that must be arrested soon, before it is too late and "God withdraws his blessing" from America. While very few conservative evangelicals come into the vicinity of Hitler in hatefulness, elements similar to that kind of conservative-reactionary-nationalist narrative can be found in some Christian right rhetoric: anger at those who are causing American moral decline, fear about the future, hatred of the "secularists" now pre-eminent in American life, and the search for scapegoats. The solution on offer—a return to a strong Christian America through determined political action—also has its parallels with the era under consideration.

It is in part my own loyalty to Bonhoeffer's example that has led me to a rejection of the toxic politics of cultural despair and commitment to a hopeful vision of Christian cultural engagement in light of the sure advance of God's kingdom.

WITNESS: LIVING FOR CHRIST IN THE CULTURE

Dietrich Bonhoeffer was committed to Christian moral witness in contemporary culture. While refusing to identify Christian morality with any particular social or political program, he did seek to bring the teachings of Christ, indeed, the moral tradition of the church as a whole, to bear on a wide range of issues emergent in his day and time. Like most scholars who identify as Christian ethicists or public theologians, he sought to make a difference in his culture through faithful Christian witness. And his focus was not on a public witness that might protect the social privileges of the church, but instead on its solidarity with those in need.

The rise and appeal of the German Christian Movement is impossible to understand apart from the intense desire of at least some German Christians to regain greater influence on their own culture. Part of the appeal of the supposedly pro-Christian Nazis (in their early days) was that they promised to support "positive Christianity." They would bring back "traditional" (=Christian) values. They would reverse secularism and cultural confusion by restoring a manly Christianity to the center of German culture. Thus the SA brownshirts marched into the swastika-draped churches for their weddings and ritualizing occasions. Worried Christian traditionalists could think, with relief, "Good, at least the young people are back in church again, communism has been defeated, and the secularists are on the run."

Another way to say it is that Germany's Christian people were anxious to exercise influence in the culture and avoid social marginalization, and the sign of their renewed influence would be a re-establishment of their historic power and cultural privileges. They were thus susceptible to the false promises of the Nazis that Christianity would again receive such privileges, and were deceived by the appearance of influence in the form of young men wearing brown shirts occupying their pews. I believe it is apparent that conservative evangelical Christians in the US are also anxious to exercise influence in the culture and also concerned to avoid social marginalization over against secularism and other alternative ideologies. Thus they are also susceptible to false promises of political leaders who speak their language and throw symbolic crumbs in their direction, promising the political and legal privileging of Christian values if not Christian faith itself. The desire to make a difference in the culture is then exploited by those who mainly want our votes in order to make a difference in their election campaigns. The cynicism of politicians both then and now is really quite obvious.

It is partly my loyalty to Bonhoeffer's model (and awareness of the history of the German church in that era) that leaves me strongly resistant to this model of Christian influence on culture and strongly offended by the manipulation of religious language and symbols for political purposes. Instead, I seek to bear witness to Christian moral convictions while remaining fiercely independent of partisan loyalties and political manipulation.

RESISTANCE: PAYING THE PRICE TO SAY NO TO EVIL

It is certainly clear from *The Cost of Discipleship* that Dietrich Bonhoeffer understood that following Jesus will be costly. Jesus taught a particular way of life that stands in opposition to the practices of most worldly powers. To say yes to Jesus is to say no to these powers. Such resistance will be costly. It can involve the ultimate cost of laying down one's life.

And of course the enduring power of Bonhoeffer's example is that on this score his life reflected his teachings. From the very first time their lives intersected, he resisted Hitler and the pernicious influence of Nazism. He resisted in small ways at small cost and then in larger ways at larger costs and finally in a conspiracy that cost him his life.

The proper pattern is thus established: we follow Jesus, come what may. Having already renounced the ultimacy of any loyalty other than loyalty to Jesus, we are prepared to pursue the path of discipleship ("following after") where it leads. We do not seek confrontation with the powers, or suffering; we love life, and we are not looking for martyrdom. But having resolved our loyalty issue, and knowing what we know about Christ and about this sinful world, we are ready for whatever may come.

It is partly my loyalty to Bonhoeffer's model that has inspired me as an evangelical to take what I would call small steps of resistance in our own context. I am deeply grateful to have been able to find a community of fellow evangelicals who share this common vision. Sometimes the practices and policies that we resist, such as mass divorce despite its negative effects on children, the routine resort to abortion, or the endless manipulation of human embryos and genes, earn us scorn from the cultural left.

Other times, such as our refusal to affirm US militarism and especially the justice of the war in Iraq; our protesting of US torture of detainees; our working for just policies for the poor and the racially marginalized; and our pressure for protection of God's creation, we have garnered the angry attacks of powers on the American right.

But we interpret the discomfort that flows from our efforts to resist what we know to be wrong as part of the cost of discipleship. This too we have learned from Bonhoeffer, and from his Lord and ours, Jesus Christ.

8

Who Needs a Covenant?

2006

MARRIAGE IS A STRUCTURE of creation, divinely given, intended to meet some of our most significant needs as human beings. Because success in marriage requires the development of a range of important skills and virtues that help us to fulfill the creation purposes of marriage, most treatments of marriage emphasize the development of skills like communication, conflict resolution, and financial management.

There is another dimension to marriage, however, that is best addressed by using the biblical term "covenant." Recent days have seen a resurgence of the term "covenant marriage," both in Christian and secular circles. But this does not mean we understand the very rich meaning of the term. It certainly does not mean we are structuring our marriages as covenantal relationships.

Covenant is the structural principle of marriage. Just as God designed marriage to meet the needs of human beings for companionship, sex, and love, so also God gave marriage a covenantal structure. This covenantal structure is just as integral to the nature of marriage as the fulfillment of creation-based needs is to the purpose of marriage. There can be no successful marriage that is not both creation-fulfilling and covenantal, whether the couple realizes this or not.

The concepts of creation and covenant are deeply intertwined in biblical thought. Covenants are God's way of organizing, sustaining, and reclaiming relationships established in creation but damaged by sin. Our needs for companionship, sex, shared labor, and family partnership constitute the created ends or goods of marriage.

Covenant, on the other hand, emerges after sin enters the world. Covenant exists, not as an end in itself, but as a means to creational ends. As ethicist Margaret Farley has put it, "for the sake of our love . . . we almost always commit ourselves to certain frameworks for living out our love. The frameworks, then, take their whole meaning . . . from the love they are meant to serve."[1] Marriage has a covenantal character in order to safeguard the bond itself, which is prior to covenant but needs safeguarding due to our fallibility and faithlessness.

COVENANT AS SCRIPTURAL CONCEPT

The concept of covenant is dramatically introduced in the Bible as God's way of structuring his effort to redeem a primeval world already spinning out of control.

The first covenant in Scripture is the one God makes with Noah. Sickened at the wreck his creatures have made of the world, God determines "to destroy both them and the earth" (Gen 6:13b).[2] The floodwaters come and then recede. God makes a covenant with—and through—Noah. God will continue to relate to us—to every living creature—despite our rebellion and the misery we create for each other and for our Creator. God will continue to pursue his original intentions in creation, but will now do so by means of a covenant with the entire created order.

If we look closely at Genesis 9 we see eight key ingredients of most covenants in Scripture and of the Old Testament concept of covenant. First, *a covenant is initiated by someone, often the stronger party* (Gen 9:8). In this case, God establishes the covenant unilaterally; later divine-human covenant agreements often have a bilateral structure, though God always remains what might be described as the "senior partner" (see Gen 15:18).

A covenant establishes or ratifies a relationship between two or more parties. In short, *a covenant creates or restores community*. All parties to the covenant are explicitly named in the agreement, a public document to which all participants can be held accountable. *It spells out mutual responsibilities on the part of all parties*, in this case both God and humanity. People are called in the covenant with Noah to resume the creation mandate. God in turn promises to provide food, to demand accountability for life-taking, and to refrain from destroying the world again in a flood (Gen 9:1–11).

---

1. Farley, *Personal Commitments*, 124.
2. All scripture references in this chapter are from the NIV.

Covenant responsibilities commonly attest to both the *goals* of the covenant and the particular *rules* that apply to the covenant makers.[3]

Covenant involves the freely given verbal declaration of sacred promises or sworn oaths that publicly symbolize and even "perform" (speak into existence) the solemn commitments being made. In Genesis 9, these promises are made by God alone; in some biblical covenants the promises are explicitly made both by God and people.[4] *Furthermore, a covenant is marked by a sign or symbolic action to communicate its significance*—in this case, a rainbow (Gen 9:13). Other covenants have other signs attached to them, such as circumcision (Gen 17:10), Sabbath (Exod 31:16), and so on.

Covenants are declared to be lasting, enduring, or even "everlasting" (Gen 9:16, Gen 17:7, 1 Chr 16:17, Isa 24:5, and Ps 89:28)—God promises to "remember" the covenant always and to keep his end of the agreement faithfully. Covenant promises are binding; they restrict our future freedom of action on the basis of our present decision. *God is viewed both as the witness and guarantor of covenants*, so any breaking of covenant promises is a sin not only against a covenant partner but also against God. *Therefore, God will enforce dire consequences for breaking the covenant and offer great rewards for keeping it* (Gen 9:5). In this case the consequences include simply an "accounting"; often covenants include a graphic list of blessings and woes (Josh 24) or simply vivid threats of judgment and destruction.[5]

God could have responded to sin by annihilating his creatures. But God pulls back from this, and instead works to redeem us. The approach God uses to structure redemptive relationships is covenant making. Given the turn of humankind to evil, the only way to move us to right action is to organize redemption through covenants. Because we are untrustworthy and fickle, we need to make sacred agreements binding ourselves to promises of behaving in a certain way. We need to know what those promises are, the terms under which we are making them, and the consequences of their betrayal. We need symbols and rituals to remind us of all of this. We need the structure of covenants, so it is covenants we are given.

It is important to understand the similarities and differences between covenants and contracts, especially related to marriage. Both covenants and contracts are initiated by someone, establish or ratify a relationship, spell out mutual responsibilities, carry public status, and are a kind of promise that binds both parties to do certain things and refrain from doing other things.

---

3. Stackhouse, *Covenant and Commitments*, 145.
4. Hugenberger, *Marriage as a Covenant*, 11–12.
5. Stackhouse, *Covenant and Commitments*, 140–47.

However, while contracts emphasize the precise obligations each party is taking on, covenants place more focus on the *relationships* that are being established or ratified.[6] Contracts specify an exchange of money or services and terminate when the transaction is complete, while covenants establish a relationship that transcends any particular exchange of goods. Contracts always contain "escape" clauses to enable people to back away from what they judge to have been unwise commitments or failed agreements, while covenants promise open-ended and permanent fidelity to the promises being undertaken and the relationship being established. Finally, contracts are purely and simply human transactions, while covenants invoke the presence of God as guarantor and trustee—even when the covenant is undertaken at the human-to-human level.

MARRIAGE AS A COVENANT

There is considerable debate among biblical scholars as to whether the Old Testament actually defines marriage as a covenant.[7] The most important single text identifying human marriage as a covenant relationship is found in Malachi 2:10–16, especially verses 13–16:

> Another thing you do: You flood the LORD's altar with tears. You weep and wail because he no longer pays attention to your offerings or accepts them with pleasure from your hands. You ask, "Why?" It is because the LORD is acting as the witness between you and the wife of your youth, because you have broken faith with her, though she is your partner, the wife of your marriage covenant. Has not the LORD made them one? In flesh and spirit they are his. And why one? Because he was seeking godly offspring. So guard yourself in your spirit, and do not break faith with the wife of your youth. "I hate divorce," says the LORD God of Israel, "and I hate a man's covering himself with violence as well as with his garment," says the LORD Almighty. So guard yourself in your spirit, and do not break faith.

Malachi declares that Judah's men have been unfaithful to God by intermarrying with pagan women (2:11) and divorcing their own (Jewish) wives (2:14). It is possible that the offenses were related—some Jewish men may have been divorcing their Jewish wives *in order* to marry pagan women.[8] The threat posed by intermarriage with pagans is a central theme especially

---

6. Allen, "Covenant," 136.
7. Hugenberger, *Marriage as Covenant*.
8. Thatcher, *Marriage After Modernity*, 74.

in the postexilic books. Why God would be distressed at such practices is little debated. But why God should have a problem with "regular" divorce is much more controversial, given the provisions made for divorce elsewhere in the Old Testament (such as Deut 24:1–4).

Gordon Hugenberger argues that God is offended by Jewish men's divorce of their Jewish wives because the relationship between husband and wife within the covenant people Israel is in fact a covenant relationship. He shows that marriage was understood in Israel as a covenant relationship, including ratification by an accompanying oath and/or act ("oath-sign") in which God was invoked as a witness (Mal 2:14). In the case of marriage, besides solemn words that oath-sign was understood to be the sexual union of the couple. Malachi's allusion to Genesis and the "one flesh" relationship of marriage (Mal 2:15; Gen 2:24) connects here as well.

Malachi appears to have been unusually sensitive to the personal significance of the marriage covenant. He points to the solidarity of male and female in creation (Mal 2:15), alludes to the bond that develops between a man and woman over most of a lifetime spent together ("the wife of your youth," "your partner"—Mal 2:14; compare Prov 2:17), and seems to suggest the additional responsibility that develops upon the birth of children (Mal 2:15— "godly offspring"), in these ways summarizing the many binding moral obligations that marriage and family ties create. This vision of marriage means that men do a great injustice when they exploit their power over women to end their marriage covenants unjustifiably. Indeed, the section ends with a link drawn between divorce and violence, as if unjustifiable divorce is a kind of violence against its innocent victims.

Consider the number of ways that marriage is a covenant relationship like other covenant bonds in Scripture. *Marriage is a covenant because it is (and when it is) a freely entered agreement between two people.* It is initiated by someone, but it represents the culmination of a journey that fully involves both people. Contemporary marriage covenant agreements differ from biblical ones in that marriage in ancient Israel was not initiated (solely) by the individuals but was an agreement between families as well. But at its heart marriage is an agreement between two people to join their lives together.

Marriage is a covenant because it publicly ratifies a relationship between a man and a woman and subjects it to objective standards and social responsibilities. Marriage does not establish the personal relationship between a man and woman but it does ratify it, make it public, and establish its social legitimacy.

Marriage is a covenant because it spells out the mutual responsibilities and moral commitments that both parties are taking on in this new form of community. Earlier I claimed that biblical covenant stipulations commonly attested both to the *goals* of the covenant and the particular *rules* that apply to the covenant makers. The central goals God intends for us to seek in marriage are companionship, sexual expression, procreation, and family partnership. The central rules embedded in marriage's sacred promises are sexual exclusivity and permanence. Both goals and rules are situated in a broader context of mutual commitment reaffirmed by faithful conduct over time.[9]

Marriage is a covenant because it is sealed by various oath-signs that publicly symbolize and even "perform" the solemn commitments being made. The exchanged vows and rings, the promises publicly made, and consummation through sexual intercourse are the central acts that bring the marital relationship into existence.

Marriage is a covenant because it is a lifetime commitment. Marriage is treated in the Old Testament as a binding commitment that can be broken only for cause. This message is reinforced and strengthened in the New Testament. If the promise is not a lifetime promise, it is not a covenant and it is not marriage.

Marriage is a covenant because God is the witness and guarantor of its promises. This concept makes the most sense where the couple explicitly embraces God's role as witness and guarantor. But it can also be argued that God is the witness to every couple's marriage vows and, ultimately, the One who empowers the couple that manages to keep those vows for a lifetime.

Marriage is a covenant because there are dire consequences for breaking its terms and great rewards for keeping it. This is not only the case in the divine-human relationship, but at the human level as well. The blessings and curses of marital success and failure are visible all around us. They are built into marriage and do not require an intervening act of divine judgment.

COVENANT AND MARRIAGE TODAY

To speak of covenant at a wedding today is to acknowledge unattractive truths. It is to say that you can dress up this man and woman in the nicest clothes but underneath it all they are faithless sinners.

To speak of covenant is to be terribly unromantic about marital love. This man and woman may be desperately in love—today. But certainly tomorrow their bonds will be tested. To speak of covenant is to acknowledge that their love will be tried by fire, and to bind this couple to the promises they make today regardless of the inclinations of their hearts on some future

---

9. Nicholson, *God and His People*, 216.

tomorrow. As Mike Mason has put it, "In a very real way it is the vow which keeps the man rather than vice versa."[10]

Covenant functions as the structural principle of marriage because it takes faithless people and coerces them to keep faith. Covenant says: I will be sexually faithful even when my needs for sex are frustrated in my marriage. I will be emotionally and sexually faithful even when my companionship needs are frustrated. I will be faithful in my parental responsibilities even when I am tired of both you and the children. I will be faithful in my communication and forgiveness even when I never want to speak to you again. I will be faithful in sharing the work responsibilities of family life even when I can barely put one foot in front of the other. I will be faithful in sharing a home and a bed with you even when I want to flee.

Yet covenant is not all vinegar and sandpaper. The striking thing about marriage as a covenant is that it is, like every other divinely given structure, for our good.

Outside of the sturdy protective sheath provided by covenant, there is no safe context for the pursuit of the creational needs that are met in marriage. We want and need companionship, sexual intimacy, love, and family partnership. These are the benefits that marriage was designed to provide for us. But they cannot be reliably sought—let alone achieved—outside of a context of covenantal fidelity and permanence.

If I am involved in a trustworthy covenantal marital bond with another, I can relax enough to both give and receive love. I can try and fail and try again to develop communication and sexual skills. Our mutual confidence in the permanence and exclusivity of our bond allows us to give ourselves away, and only as we give ourselves away can we maximize our progress toward human intimacy as God intended it.

One of the most corrosive effects of our culture of divorce is a vicious cycle involving the deterioration of covenant sturdiness. Having been burned once by marriage, but still pursuing those God-given creational needs, a couple tries again in a remarriage. However, they are often less able to create a binding, lasting, and exclusive covenant the second time around, in part because they were so shattered by the failure of their first marriage.

They hesitate to give their hearts away because they are not sure that the investment is worth the risk—not sure, that is, that the covenant will hold. But precisely because they are unsure, they are less successful in achieving the goods of marriage. Thus the marriage never reaches a high level of satisfaction. Then one or both is inevitably tempted to betray or to end the tottering marriage covenant. Having done so before, it is easier

10. Mason, *The Mystery of Marriage*, 116.

to do it a second time. If the second marriage does end in divorce, and the individuals then pursue third marriages, the cycle is all the more likely to continue.

Under conditions of sin, covenant promise making is just as "natural" or "wired-in" an aspect of marriage as the fulfillment of creational needs. Theologically, it goes like this: because we are creatures with certain needs, we *seek* in marriage certain goods; because we are fallen creatures, we *need* covenants to bind us and keep us in our marriages.

The collapse of older moral certainties included a questioning of the concept of marital covenant. It became seen as archaic to make lifetime promises to anyone, about anything. Marriage began to be viewed by many as a purely voluntary relationship to be entered or exited freely, "as long as we both shall love."

The paradox is that such freedom is itself a kind of slavery. It allows the tyranny of the transient dissatisfaction to efface all commitments. The quest for true and unforced love has led only to weaker and weaker marriages, and finally to the near-collapse of the institution of marriage. The problem is not that a binding marital covenant is a tyranny, but that non-binding marital contracts undercut the very nature of marriage itself.

9

Evangelicals and Politics
Convictions, Controversies, Challenges
2006

INTRODUCTION

I UNDERSTAND MY PRIMARY task to be to take you inside the world of evangelical political reflection and engagement. Though I actually grew up Roman Catholic and attended the liberal Union Theological Seminary in New York, I am by now an evangelical insider, rooted deeply in red state mid-South America, a member of a Southern Baptist church (actually, an ordained minister), a teacher at a Tennessee Baptist university, and a columnist for the flagship *Christianity Today* magazine. Due to the blue state/red state, liberal/conservative boundary-crossing that has characterized my background, I am often called upon to interpret our divided internal "cultures" one to another. Trained to be fair-minded and judicious in my analysis and judgments (though not always successful in meeting the standards of my training), I seek to help bridge the culture wars divide that is tearing our nation apart.

As one deeply invested in American evangelicalism, most of my attention these days now goes to the internal conversation within evangelical life about our identity and mission, especially our social ethics and political engagement. My remarks today will focus extensively on problems I currently see with evangelical political engagement, and will address those from within the theological framework of evangelical Christianity. You might say that I am inviting you to listen in to what I am now saying to my fellow evangelicals.

But first, to lighten the mood a bit and give you a sense of my own experiences at the intersection of faith and politics, I want to tell you a few stories.

VIGNETTES

In 1979, I was a brand new seventeen-year-old "baby Christian" (as we used to call it), a fresh convert to evangelical Christianity in its Southern Baptist form. I lived in northern Virginia, land of the federal government, secret government agencies, and myriad lobbying groups. My father worked for the Congressional Research Service of the Library of Congress, doing energy and environmental policy analysis.

A woman in my church approached me that spring with a lucrative offer: would I be willing to appear briefly in a film that her organization was making? I would receive two hundred dollars for just a few hours work. With prom approaching, the money sounded awfully nice.

So it was that I found myself with dyed brown hair, dressed in a Soviet Army uniform, on the set of "Can Soviet Imperialism Be Stopped?" My job was to pour a bucket of red paint over a standing globe, beginning in the vicinity of West Germany. I need to report that I was excellent that day. I poured the paint just right, was handed the money after one take, and went on to the prom the very next night, dyed but flush with cash.

I didn't really understand at the time that I was making a propaganda film for one of the most hardline right-wing organizations in America, Howard Phillips' Conservative Caucus. This group still exists. Sadly, though, there is no mention of this great film on their website.

By 1986 I had graduated from William and Mary and come under the influence of the progressive wing of Protestant Christianity. I worked for a peace organization in Louisville while attending Southern Baptist Theological Seminary. (I am not making this up.) I supported the nuclear freeze campaign, which led to a particularly memorable moment one wintry evening in Chicago, circa 1987. Jesse Jackson was running for president. He was scheduled to speak to the freeze group on this frozen night. He came in late, sitting down right next to me on the front row. He tapped my shoe, saying "How ya' doin?" *Yes, Jesse Jackson sat next to me and tapped my left shoe.* The crowd shouted "Run, Jesse, Run."

From 1987 to 1989 I lived in New York City, where I pursued a doctorate in ethics at Union Seminary. I had gone there in part to broaden my horizons after lengthy immersion in Southern Baptist culture. I loved my ethics program at Union but culturally and theologically often felt like a stranger in a strange land.

One day the National Association of Evangelicals sent *Catholic* intellectual George Weigel to Union Seminary to talk to the school's few evangelicals. (This illustrates the paucity of their own intellectual resources at the time; they had to borrow a Catholic. It showed that the NAE had embraced the hard right line on the Cold War. And it also foreshadowed the eventual alliance between conservative Catholics and evangelicals.) We gathered in the Bonhoeffer Room, where Weigel tried to disabuse us of any peacenik inclinations or ideas of moral equivalence in relation to the Soviet Union or nuclear weapons. A few years later the Soviet Union was dead, ending that particular argument.

In 1990, I needed a job. Halfway through a doctoral program, with a child and another on the way, I interviewed for an editorial position with *The Other Side*, a radical evangelical magazine located across from an abandoned house in the depressed Germantown section of inner-city Philadelphia. Based on a deep commitment to economic justice, they were offering poverty-level wages to all their staff. During the interview one staff member helpfully told me that she trash-picked to supplement her income. I fled, vowing never to return. (Not exactly, but that's how I remember it.) A few months later I took a position with Ron Sider (author of the critically important book *Rich Christians in an Age of Hunger*) and his group Evangelicals for Social Action, living just around the corner from that abandoned house. I never did take up trash-picking. I did, however, find with ESA the kernel of a social-political vision that has never left me—pro-life, pro-justice, pro-peace, pro-poor, pro-creation care.

In 1992–1993 I was working at ESA, finishing my doctorate, and looking without much success for my first teaching post. Finally I got the chance to interview at Southern Seminary, my alma mater. I got the job. I was on campus the same day that Dr. R. Albert Mohler, Jr. was named president of Southern. The school swung sharply to the right. In just a few years, dozens of faculty left or were forced out. I myself left in 1996.

As an evangelical in an influential ethics post formerly held by a pro-choice professor, for a time I had numerous opportunities to enter the inner sanctum of the conservative Southern Baptist Convention, a hugely influential part of the Christian Right to this day. I drafted a 1994 SBC statement condemning the killing of abortion doctors, when that was a hot issue. I remember the drafting meeting, high up in an executive suite in Nashville, where most of the powers in the SBC gathered together to pick through the text that I had written. The denomination at the time was essentially dominated by about sixty men. The most influential fifteen of them were in that room with me. The next year I had a similar experience working with a top-level group on the SBC repudiation of its historic racism. It was thrilling. But such involvement soon ended. I was cut out of the loop because I publicly dissented from the SBC's boycott of the Disney Corporation.

Right, left, left, right . . . today I identify with what I call an emerging evangelical center, neither left nor right. It can be found in the editorial pages of *Christianity Today*, in the classrooms of most seriously Christian colleges, in the current vision of ESA, in the thoughtful scholarship/advocacy of the Center for Public Justice, in the "For the Health of the Nation" statement approved by the National Association of Evangelicals, and in the public affairs office of Rich Cizik, NAE's man in Washington. This evangelical center, I believe, offers the best way forward for us in the notoriously controversial engagement of our faith with American public life. I will say more about its vision later.

And yet it is not quite good enough to say we should move to the center from the right and the left. Any right-center-left language is political, borrowed from the world. We need a biblically grounded rethinking of our entire engagement with American culture. I daresay that comment is relevant to all religious engagement with politics in America.

UNCONTESTABLE FACTS

Little can be said about this issue without evoking controversy, but I would suggest that there are four uncontestable facts related to evangelicals and politics today:

1. *Conservative evangelical ("Christian Right") political activism is evoking a heated backlash.* This backlash comes from dissident evangelicals (Jim Wallis, Greg Boyd, Randall Balmer, Brian McLaren, George Hunter, Michael Horton, Ed Dobson/Cal Thomas, Jimmy Carter), from the non-evangelical Christian center and left (John Danforth, Mark Taylor, Barry Lynn, Robin Meyers, Becky Garrison), and from many other voices from the non-Christian left (Michael Lerner, Garry Wills, Thomas Frank). This backlash is in turn evoking a counter-backlash, with various defenses of the Christian Right now on offer. And of course, the Christian Right understands itself as a defensive movement; in other words, a reaction to prior challenges to traditional Christian values. So those in the Christian Right would reject any idea that the problem begins with them.

2. *Battles over evangelical involvement with politics are merging into the broader "culture wars" environment that is tearing our country apart.* It is increasingly difficult to distinguish a particularly Christian voice in the red state/blue state, right/left polarization of American public discourse. Conservatives like Ann Coulter, Rush Limbaugh, and Rammesh Ponuru do not speak as "Christian thinkers" but their arguments hit religious themes. The Left is only now finding its religious voice (through such thinkers as Michal Lerner, Jim Wallis, and others) but is (increasingly) trying to fire back with religious themes in this deeply religious nation—and the Democratic Party is paying close attention. The screeching tone of the argument (it's not a conversation) is contributing to the depressing, even dangerous polarization of American society and the loss of a sensible center—despite what ought to be soothing evidence that most average Americans aren't really culture warriors at all.

3. *Many sense that our culture is in crisis, but see the church as part of the problem rather than part of the solution.* Political divisions, hatred of the cultural "enemy," fiscal irresponsibility, growing income inequality, eroding international standing, government gridlock, business and political corruption, religio-ethnic balkanization, special-interest politics, endless political gamesmanship, the disappearance of statesmanship—these and many other problems threaten our nation. Yet the church seems unable to rise above these problems; instead it is enmeshed in the culture wars, in backlash upon backlash, conflict upon conflict.

4. *A growing number of visible evangelicals, including Billy Graham himself, are disillusioned with politics, especially with evangelical engagement in politics.* They sense that something has gone dramatically wrong, and they are attempting to call the church back to its core mission. I think they need to be heard. It's time for a complete rethinking of evangelical politics.

NON-NEGOTIABLE CONVICTIONS

This talk cannot do more than sketch such a rethinking. But it can suggest certain non-negotiable convictions. I suggest eight of these. Again, my words come from within the discourse of orthodox, evangelical Christianity. They are not intended to offend those who are not Christians; you have your own discourse, and hopefully can find striking points of overlap with mine.

1. *God is redeeming the world in and through Jesus Christ (2 Cor 5:19), not earthly politics.* The biblical narrative must be our narrative; its story of how the world is being redeemed must be our story and must govern our priorities and actions. The kingdom belongs to God, and it gains ground in the way God determines. There is no ultimate human redemption available through politics.

2. *The church's primary obligation is to follow Jesus (Matt 10:38–39).* As a community of Christ-followers, the church exists to worship God-in-Christ, to preach the Word, to make disciples, to serve the least of these, to love God with all we have and likewise love our neighbors as ourselves. We dare not drift from our core mission.

3. *Jesus Christ is Lord (Phil 2:9–11).* This most basic Christian affirmation means that all other loyalties are relative rather than absolute. "No one can serve two masters" (Matt 6:24) and no one dare confuse the one true God with other gods (Exod 20:3).[1] One implication of the lordship of Christ is fierce political independence. We do not belong to any political party, ideology, leader, or nation. The church becomes our primary community of loyalty, and the world as a whole our arena of moral concern, though that concern begins with where God has placed us. We assess earthly politics from within this unassailable structure of loyalty to Christ.

4. *Earthly politics in a sinful world is a necessary but grubby business.* It should be about the quest for the common good but is at the same time a constant struggle for power, characterized by the constant temptation to do whatever it takes to win. In these days it is filled with hatred. Christians are very easily manipulated and corrupted when they try to play this kind of power politics. As Jesus warned, "The people of this world are more shrewd in dealing with their own kind than are the people of the light" (Luke 16:8). If we play the world's game in the world's way we will lose every time.

5. *No nation is Christian.* Even where Christianity is or has been (culturally or legally) "established," no nation can be described as Christian. Sin is too deep for that. Biblical Israel struggled to be faithfully Jewish and the church itself struggles to be faithfully Christian. Speaking as a Baptist and out of my own tradition, I declare that we must abandon

---

1. All scripture references in this chapter are from the NIV.

the dream of Christendom in any form. This is not the political or social change strategy articulated in the New Testament.

6. *The church is called to "seek the peace and prosperity of the city" (Jer 29:7) in which it dwells.* This authorizes educational, cultural, moral, and carefully constrained political engagement. All such engagement must be aimed at the good of the whole, not just a narrowly understood "Christian" interest. It must be undertaken in the spirit of Christ and in a manner consonant with his example and teaching.

7. *The church's public moral witness must be as comprehensive as possible.* It should be focused on a vision of the human good, of "shalom" at every level of human experience in God's good creation. We should yearn to see "love and faithfulness meet together, righteousness and peace kiss" (Ps 85:10). We should seek to honor, protect, and advance abundant life (John 10:10), for all, at every stage, and in every condition. This might be called a vital Christian humanism, rooted in a global kingdom vision, and leading to a consistent ethic of life. It needs to be linked to a vibrant theology of God's creation and thus issue forth in a commitment to creation care (ecological stewardship) as well.

8. *The church's moral witness must first be practiced (embodied) in the church itself (Matt 7:21–27).* The church is a demonstration community, making plain that the teachings of Jesus are meant to be obeyed and that such obedience brings abundant life. Faithful, disciplined Christian moral practice-in-community is the most significant public moral witness we have available to us (John 13:34–35). Where we do not live what we teach we call the validity of the teaching itself into question; we also undermine profoundly the cogency of our public moral witness.

CONTROVERSIAL OBSERVATIONS

These non-negotiables are hard to contest, though some will do so. But their import becomes most apparent when they are applied to our current evangelical politics. Looking at the evangelical landscape, with its heavy involvement in Christian Right politics, its vocal but small evangelical left, and its nascent evangelical center, I would suggest that the following observations can be made.

1. *Evangelical Christians have fallen hard for politics.* We are in it up to our eyeballs. It seems to be the main thing we are now known for. It has distracted us from our primary mission and wounded our witness

in the world. We are at risk of becoming just another political party, or constituent part thereof. This shift is really only one generation old. It might win some elections. It is certainly already costing us access to people's hearts, who shut down their openness to our core message because they hate our politics.

2. *One could easily think that victory in politics has become our primary mission.* A recent story in the New York Times told of an Ohio pastor out and about in his neighborhood. Was he sharing the gospel? Inviting people to church? No, actually, he was registering voters. Is this really how pastors should be spending their time? Call me old-fashioned, but I think there's something quite wrong here. Perhaps we no longer believe that Jesus saves.

3. *The heated passions of politics have caused some Christians to abandon love.* This same pastor was interviewed about complaints that Ohio's new voter registration system discriminated against minorities and the poor. The pastor's response? "Quit your whining." Nice—if you want to score a point in the culture wars. Not nice, if you still care about "love, joy, peace, patience," and all those other fruits of the Spirit that are supposed to characterize our way of living (Gal 5:22–23, one of our cherished memory verses). Is this really the spirit we want to demonstrate to the world around us?

4. *Some of the politically engaged have been tempted to abandon Jesus for Machiavelli.* It is an enduring human temptation. If the cause is just, moral scruples in pursuing that cause are remarkably inconvenient. (Most evil is done for a transcendently "good" cause.) When in trouble, slime your opponent. Spread rumors and lies. After all, it's for "family values" or "justice." (Think about what happened to John McCain in the South Carolina primary in 2000, when cruel and malicious rumors were employed to hurt his standing with the voters of that Bible Belt state.) It is precisely such a temptation that the rigorous moral teaching of the New Testament is intended to train us against.

5. *The enormous money and power available in worldly politics are beginning to corrupt Christians in politics.* The recent moral downfall of visible politicians claiming Christian identity has deeply embarrassed the Christian witness in this country. The continuing embrace of such people as persecuted Christian martyrs is deeply offensive. I am thinking specifically of Ralph Reed and Tom DeLay and their enmeshment in the Abramoff affair. Both are still treated as Christian heroes by some of the more credulous.

6. *Evangelical Christians are being manipulated and used by politicians.* Since Ronald Reagan, (white) evangelicals have been a part of the Republican electorate. We have been treated as an important interest group, promised much, and given relatively little (despite howls of outrage from the left about our iron grip on power). We are (at least at the grassroots) rather naïve about politics, and too easily deceived by symbolic gestures that cost little, like invitations to the White House, presidential proclamations, and support for measures that everyone knows can't win. We get angry when our deeper goals are frustrated, and when the emptiness of the promises made to us gets exposed. And yet we keep coming back for more. To outsiders I can say that you should not be overly worried that evangelicals are actually dominating American politics. There is more smoke than fire there.

7. *Some evangelicals want a Christendom model of church-state relations.* The Left cries "theocracy!" at every sign of evangelical public witness, and this is surely wrong. Yet it is clear from conservative evangelical activism that some (not all) evangelical Christians have never fully assimilated the constitutional idea of religious disestablishment, of a free church in a free state. It's not just on the fringes with the Reconstructionists, a group that believes that the Old Testament law should be passed into American law, including the death penalty for sexual sins. It is apparent in much of our "God and Country" rhetoric, in the fascination with Calvinism and the Puritans that characterizes some within evangelicalism, and even in the rarefied work of certain elite theologians. And it seems especially apparent in the South, where I live, and where Protestant evangelical religion is more or less established to this day. I am not at all sure that the First Amendment would pass today if put to a vote in the old Confederacy.

8. *Our weak ecclesiology leaves us vulnerable.* Many have noted a general tendency in evangelical life toward a poorly developed theology of the church. This bears bitter fruit here. On the one hand, our pietistic individualism creates a "Jesus and me" ethos that often weakens any loyalty to the community of faith or any willingness to submit to a disciplined covenantal vision. On the other hand, the moral mediocrity of this kind of church leaves us hopeless about the church as the center of God's redemptive enterprise in the world. And so we turn to the state to enforce the values we can't seem to advance in our own churches. Meanwhile we probably still go to church, hoping for comfort, cool programs, and some really good singing.

9. *The backlash against evangelical politics is partly justified.* Certainly part of the backlash is rooted in a secular worldview that seeks a godless public square and, often, promotes values directly opposed to Christian ethical commitments. This gap is largely unbridgeable. But some of the backlash reflects resistance and reaction to the sub-Christian methods and spirit evangelicals often demonstrate. Anger evokes anger, caricature evokes caricature. Christians surely know how to do better than this.

10. *Evangelicals are deeply compromised by our complicity with state violence.* Whether we support just war theory or pacifism, Christians are called to resist the descent into violence so characteristic of the sinful human condition. Yet our witness for life is deeply compromised by our often uncritical support for US war-fighting, not to mention our apparent ambivalence about torture and our continued strong support for capital punishment. The just war theory means nothing if every war brings out the rally round the flag response from Christians. As long as we are unquestioning supporters of every war, and of whatever our troops do in every war, and of every policy dreamed up in every war, we cannot be faithful followers of Jesus Christ the reconciling Lord of the Universe. It is also hard to defend our claim that we are pro-life.

11. *Some evangelicals are also deeply compromised by their inability to critique American capitalism.* Many have observed that part of the Republican electoral strategy has been to weave together such disparate groups as libertarians, the Chamber of Commerce crowd, and the three-times-a-week churchgoers. The alignment of the latter two groups, in particular, has left evangelicals often unable to offer any critique whatsoever of the domestic or foreign practices of American business—even when those practices actually hurt the economic well-being of these selfsame evangelicals. It has also left us easily manipulated by the well-funded activism of businesses such as ExxonMobil when it comes to environmental issues like global warming. The good news here is that this business-evangelical marriage is being challenged strongly from within evangelicalism, with climate change being a major battleground.

12. *Our unflinching fealty to one political party or leader demonstrates a dangerous lack of prophetic distance.* A good test is this: do we have the capacity to say No to our favored party or politician? Can we imagine an occasion in which we might have to dissent? Would we be willing to lose our access to Karl Rove's or Nancy Pelosi's cell phone number if faithfulness to Jesus Christ required it? Are we okay with being

disinvited to the National Prayer Breakfast? You know you're in trouble when you find yourself saying yes to policies—like, say, torture—that you would once have never imagined supporting. When the "Christian agenda" happens to align entirely with any party's (evolving) agenda, we are serving some other master than Jesus Christ.

A CENTRIST AGENDA

Certainly in terms of political engagement, I think that a centrist agenda is preferable either to a political agenda emerging from the right or the left. The historic 2004 NAE "For the Health of the Nation"[2] statement offers the following moral commitments as central to an evangelical vision. I fully share in these seven principles:

1. "We work to protect religious freedom and liberty of conscience." Under this rubric the document strongly reaffirms the First Amendment, taking the "benevolent neutrality" line related to its interpretation. The document embraces a "gospel pluralism" that accepts the inevitability of differences in foundational religious beliefs and requires that people with varying beliefs have the same religious liberties.

2. "We work to nurture family life and protect children." The document affirms the centrality of the family as part of the divine plan, treats it as a lifetime relationship between one man and one woman, and catalogs threats to the well-being of the family both from within and from without. It offers a one-sentence rejection of same-sex marriage while more strongly emphasizing the damage caused by divorce and other corrosive threats to family integrity. It says that government does not have the primary responsibility for maintaining healthy family life but that it should do what it can to strengthen families within the limits of its mandate.

3. "We work to protect the sanctity of human life and to safeguard its nature." Rooting its stance in the *imago dei*, the document treats abortion, euthanasia, and unethical human experimentation as violations of human dignity. It expresses concern about biotechnological developments and our capacity to place limits on them for the sake of the uniqueness of human nature. It opposes human cloning and embryonic stem-cell research as well as genetic discrimination.

---

2. "For the Health of the Nation."

4. "We seek justice and compassion for the poor and the vulnerable." The NAE declaration here expresses concern not just for the poor but also women, children, the aged, persons with disabilities, immigrants, refugees, minorities, the persecuted, and prisoners. "God measures societies by how they treat the people at the bottom." It takes an equality of opportunity rather than equality of outcome stance on economic life, supports work-based social welfare programs where possible, and addresses global aid and trade policies and their effect on the poor. It calls for robust private and governmental support of effective international aid agencies. The document names the raft of social problems that affect the developing world and encourages systemic Christian and government intervention to change these conditions, such as the spread of HIV/AIDS, slavery and sex trafficking, extreme poverty, and political corruption.

5. "We work to protect human rights." Again grounding its stance in an *imago dei* religious ethic, the NAE statement declares the existence of God-given rights—and responsibilities. The list includes not just political and procedural rights but also the right to "food, nurture, shelter, and care." It calls on all governments to respect human rights and the American government to reward countries that do so and punish those that do not. The document emphasizes religious liberty, including the right to change one's religion. The document names America's own major rights violations, especially the mistreatment of Native Americans and African Americans, and calls on churches to "model good race relations" while pressing for efforts to "correct the lingering effects of our racist history."

6. "We seek peace and work to restrain violence." The NAE statement calls for the peaceful settlement of disputes in view of the coming peaceable kingdom. While embracing just war principles for guiding the use of force, it also calls for Christians to participate in practical peacemaking initiatives.

7. "We labor to protect God's creation." This seventh and final statement clearly places the NAE on record as supporting a Christian version of environmental concern. It embraces the principles of dominion, stewardship, and sustainability, as well as the government's "obligation to protect its citizens from the effects of environmental degradation." Among other measures, it calls for government to "encourage fuel efficiency, reduce pollution, encourage sustainable use of natural resources, and provide for the proper care of wildlife and their natural habitats."

BACK TO BASICS

While I resonate strongly with this kind of vision, I still find myself recoiling from the increasing centrality of politics in evangelicalism, and am instead driven back to the basics of orthodox, evangelical Christianity. Surely I will continue to engage in public moral witness along the lines suggested by biblical faith as I understand it. But the journey that began with a conversion experience in a Baptist church almost thirty years ago has circled round again to that starting point. The good folks of Providence Baptist Church—who loved a wretch like me and helped midwife my salvation—told me in 1978 that Christian existence looks something like this:

Christians read their Bibles every day, focusing especially on the teachings of Jesus.

Christians pray hard: for a lost and broken world, for their enemies, and for their own forgiveness and growth.

Christians are morally serious people, expected to live right for their Lord Jesus.

Christians are deeply committed to a local church, and serve there faithfully.

Christians are focused on preaching the gospel and winning the lost.

Christians serve the least of these in missions and ministry here and around the world.

Christian pastors shepherd their flocks more than fulltime; they don't do politics.

Christians are ready to give a reason for the hope (and conviction) that is in us, but always peaceably.

Christians exalt the love of God and love of neighbor as their highest responsibilities.

Christians look with joy for the return of Jesus Christ, when all shall be set right, and every tear is finally wiped away.

I think the challenge for evangelical Christians is simply to try to remember how to be Christians again, even while we remain engaged with the public life of our nation.

10

An Evangelical Declaration against Torture

Protecting Human Rights in an Age of Terror

2007

EXECUTIVE SUMMARY

1. *Introduction*: From a Christian perspective, every human life is sacred. As evangelical Christians, recognition of this transcendent moral dignity is non-negotiable in every area of life, including our assessment of public policies. This commitment has been tested in the war on terror, as a public debate has occurred over the moral legitimacy of torture and of cruel, inhuman, and degrading treatment of detainees held by our nation in the current conflict. We write this declaration to affirm our support for detainee human rights and our opposition to any resort to torture.

2. *Sanctity of Life*: We ground our commitment to human rights in the core Christian theological conviction that each and every human life is sacred. This theme wends its way throughout the Scriptures: in Creation, Law, the Incarnation, Jesus' teaching and ministry, the Cross, and his Resurrection. Concern for the sanctity of life leads us to vigilant sensitivity to how human beings are treated and whether or not their God-given rights are being respected.

3. *Human Rights*: Human rights, which function to protect human dignity and the sanctity of life, cannot be canceled and should not be overridden. Recognition of human rights creates obligations to act on behalf of others whose rights are being violated. Human rights place a shield around people who otherwise would find themselves at the mercy of those who are angry, aggrieved, and frightened. While human rights language can be misused, this demands its clarification rather than abandonment. Among the most significant human rights is the right to security of person, which includes the right not to be tortured.

4. *Christian History and Human Rights*: The concept of human rights is not a "secular" notion but instead finds expression in Christian sources long before the Enlightenment. More secularized versions of the human rights ethic that came to occupy such a large place in Western thought should be seen as derivative of earlier religious arguments. Twentieth-century assaults on human rights by totalitarian states led to a renewal of "rights talk" after World War II. Most branches of the Christian tradition, including evangelicalism, now embrace a human rights ethic.

5. *Ethical Implications*: Everyone bears an obligation to act in ways that recognize human rights. This responsibility takes different forms at different levels. Churches must teach their members to think biblically about morally difficult and emotionally intense public issues such as this one. Our own government must honor its constitutional and moral responsibilities to respect and protect human rights. The United States historically has been a leader in supporting international human rights efforts, but our moral vision has blurred since 9/11. We need to regain our moral clarity.

6. *Legal Structures*: International law contains numerous clear and unequivocal bans on torture and cruel, inhuman, and degrading treatment. These bans are wise and right and must be embraced without reservation once again by our own government. Likewise, United States law and military doctrine has banned the resort to torture or cruel and degrading treatment. Tragically, documented acts of torture and of inhumane and cruel behavior have occurred at various sites in the US war on terror, and current law opens procedural loopholes for more to continue. We commend the Pentagon's revised Army Field Manual for clearly banning such acts, and urge that this ban extend to every sector of the United States government without exception, including our intelligence agencies.

7. *Concluding Recommendations*: The abominable acts of 9/11, along with the continuing threat of terrorist attacks, create profound security challenges. However, these challenges must be met within a moral and legal framework consistent with our values and laws, among which is a commitment to human rights that we as evangelicals share with many others. In this light, we renounce the resort to torture or cruel, inhuman, and degrading treatment of detainees, call for the extension of procedural protections and human rights to all detainees, seek clear government-wide embrace of the Geneva Conventions, including those articles banning torture and cruel treatment of prisoners, and seek the reversal of any US government policy, law, or practice that violates the moral standards outlined in this declaration.

THE DECLARATION

1. Introduction

1.1 The sanctity of human life, a moral status irrevocably bestowed by the Creator upon each person and confirmed in the costly atoning sacrifice of Christ on the Cross, is desecrated each day in many ways around the globe. Because we are Christians who are commanded by our Lord Jesus Christ to love God with all of our being and to love our neighbors as ourselves (Matt 22:36–40), this mistreatment of human persons comes before us as a source of sorrow and a call to action.

1.2 *All* humans who are mistreated or tormented are *somebody's* brothers and sisters, sons and daughters, parents and grandparents. We must think of them as we would our own children or parents. They are, by Jesus' definition, our neighbors (Luke 10:25–37). They are "the least of these," and so in them and through them we encounter God himself (Matt 25:31–46). "When human lives are endangered, when human dignity is in jeopardy, national borders and sensitivities become irrelevant," Elie Wiesel declares. "Silence encourages the tormentor, never the tormented."[1]

1.3 However remote to us may be the victim of torture, abuse, or mistreatment, Christians must seek to develop the moral imagination to enter into the suffering of all who are victimized. Having personally witnessed the horrors of the Cambodian genocide of the 1970s, Robert A. Evans writes: "The motivation of basic human rights can never again

---

1. Wiesel, "Acceptance Speech for 1986 Nobel Peace Prize."

become a matter of statistics, or theory, or strategy, or legislation, or judicial decision. It will always be, for me, the violation of the dignity of other children of God."[2] Commitment to a transcendent moral vision of human dignity that is rooted in the concrete reality of particular suffering human beings motivates the signers of this statement as well.

1.4 The authors and signatories of this declaration are evangelical Christians and citizens of the United States. As Christians, we long to obey the moral demands of our faith as articulated in the Scriptures. We seek to serve Jesus Christ, who alone is Lord of our lives, of the church, of our nation, and of the world. As citizens, we bring our Christian convictions to bear on the most important matters that arise in the life of our democracy, for the health of our nation and its impact on the lives of people around the world. We know that we may not always succeed in shaping the laws and policies of the United States in the way we believe they should be shaped. But we must, on all occasions, attempt to bear faithful Christian moral witness.

1.5 The immediate occasion for this declaration is the intense debate that has occurred in our country since 2004 over the use of torture and cruel, inhuman, and degrading treatment of those who are detained by our nation and other nations in the "war on terror."[3] In 2005–2006 this debate evolved into a broader discussion of policies related to the legal standards that would be employed in detaining, trying, transferring, or punishing suspected terrorists in what is turning out to be a lengthy struggle against individuals and groups engaged in terrorist plots and acts against our nation.

1.6 This cluster of issues would not have arisen if not for the horrifying and heinous attacks of 9/11, which took nearly 3,000 lives and constituted a mass violation of the very moral standards we witness to in this declaration. The US response to these attacks, including intensified intelligence activities, the invasion of Afghanistan, and later the much-debated invasion of Iraq, has led to the apprehension of thousands of "enemy combatants," terrorists, suspected terrorists, and others. The question we now face is how we protect our society (and other

---

2. Evans and Evans, *Human Rights*, 3–4.

3. We use quotation marks for this term because we are not convinced of the precision or cogency of a war on "terror," which is at one level a tactic (terrorism) and at another level a feeling (terror). We do not use the term with quotation marks in order to downplay the significance of the terrorist acts that have been directed at other nations and our nation in the past two decades.

societies) from further terrorist acts within a framework of moral and legal norms. As American Christians, we are above all motivated by a desire that our nation's actions would be consistent with foundational Christian moral norms. We believe that a scrupulous commitment to human rights, among which is the right not to be tortured, is one of these Christian moral convictions.

2. The Sanctity of Human Life

"And God said, 'Let us make human beings in our image, in our likeness' . . . So God created human beings in his own image, in the image of God he created them; male and female he created them" (Gen 1:26a, 27).[4]

2.1 We ground our commitment to human rights, including the rights of suspected terrorists, in the core Christian belief that human life is sacred. Evangelicals join a vast array of other Christian groups and thinkers—Roman Catholics, mainline Protestants, Eastern Orthodox, and others—in a long history of reflection and activism on behalf of this critical yet threatened moral conviction.

2.2 The sanctity of life is the conviction that all human beings, in any and every state of consciousness or self-awareness, of any and every race, color, ethnicity, level of intelligence, religion, language, nationality, gender, character, behavior, physical ability/disability, potential, class, social status, etc., of any and every particular quality of relationship to the viewing subject, are to be perceived as sacred, as persons of equal and immeasurable worth and of inviolable dignity. Therefore they must be treated with the reverence and respect commensurate with this elevated moral status. This begins with a commitment to the preservation of their lives and protection of their basic rights. Understood in all of its fullness, it includes a commitment to the flourishing of every person's life.[5]

2.3 Christian belief in the sanctity of human life is rooted in themes that work their way through the entire biblical canon as well as much of Jewish, Christian, and Western moral thought. Rightly understood, the sanctity of life is a moral norm that both summarizes and transcends all other particular norms in Christian moral thought.

---

4. TNIV.
5. Gushee, *The Sacredness of Human Life*.

2.4 Scripture reveals that life is sacred. Humans, in particular, are given life by the breath of God (Gen 2:7) and are made in the image of God (Gen 1:26–28). The imago Dei serves as a common denominator for all of humanity. Every human being, therefore, deserves respect.

2.5 The sanctity of life is emphasized in legal and covenantal texts in Scripture. Murder is forbidden because human beings are made in the image of God; this theme is evident in the covenants both with Noah and with Moses (Gen 9:5–6; Exod 20:13). Everyone has a duty to conserve and respect human life (Gen 9:5; 4:8–10, 15), and to accept responsibility for the life of their fellow humans (Gen 4:9; Deut 21:1–9). Human life is sacred because it is "precious" to God (Ps 116:15) and must therefore be precious to us as well. The prophets remind Israel of the value of human life, especially life at its most vulnerable (Isa 1:17; Jer 7:6; Zech 7:10).

2.6 The Incarnation (John 1:1, 14) permanently and decisively elevates the value of human life. It reveals a God who is not dispassionate, but deeply moved by the brokenness of creation.[6] The Incarnation demonstrates the extraordinary value God places upon human life. It also signifies a mysterious bridging of the gap between God and humanity. Henceforth, the human experience in its joys and sorrows is inscribed upon the very Person of God in a new way. Furthermore, the Holy Spirit participates in human pathos with groans and sighs too deep for words. The cries of the tortured are in a very real sense, then, the cries of the Spirit.

2.7 Jesus Christ, God-made-flesh, taught the dignity of human life and practiced it in his treatment of those around him. He reaffirmed the biblical commands that are intended to protect human life. He diagnosed the vicious patterns of sinful behavior that lead us to violate God's commands, and the sickness of the heart and mind that lie behind that sinful behavior. He offered teachings amounting to transforming initiatives to enable us to obey God's will. This is most clearly illustrated in his single largest block of teaching, the Sermon on the Mount (Matt 5–7).

2.8 In his ministry, Jesus in all contexts treated persons as sacred in God's sight. This was especially apparent in the way he treated the marginalized: women, the sick, the dead, the poor, people of bad reputation, children, and enemies of Israel such as tax collectors, Roman soldiers, and Gentiles in general. He explicitly affirms the worth of human

---

6. Vere, "Sanctity of Human Life," 757–58.

beings in his teaching (Luke 12:24; Matt 6:26; 12:11–12). He taught peacemaking rather than violence, and on the Cross forgave those who assisted in killing him. He also stood with both the Law and the prophets before him in condemning injustice in its various forms: economic, political, military, and religious (Matt 23). The justice teachings of Jesus are closely related to a commitment to life's sanctity and serve as a fundamental building block of a Christian commitment to human rights.

2.9 For many centuries, Jesus' teaching about the "least of these" (Matt 25:31–46) has been especially significant for shaping a Christian moral vision of the sanctity of every human life. Not only does this familiar "sheep and goats" parable emphasize the centrality of practical deeds of service to the least, the last, and the lost, it also teaches us to see Jesus in the hungry, the stranger, the naked, the sick, and the imprisoned: "as you did it unto the least of these, you did it unto me" (Matt 25:40). This dramatic shift of moral vision has profound implications for how we as Christians think about our nation's imprisoned, sometimes hungry, sometimes sick, sometimes naked strangers.

2.10 Ultimately, it is the Cross of Jesus Christ that demonstrates how much God values human life. God-in-flesh dies, at human hands, for human beings who do not love him and are not worthy of his costly sacrifice. "While we were yet sinners, Christ died for us." Radical human equality is emphasized in the reason for this death, the universality of its scope, and the equality of its impact. At the Cross and in the Resurrection, by saying *no* to his Son's cry of dereliction, God says *yes* to all of derelict humanity.

2.11 Considered etymologically, a sacred thing is something that has already been sanctified, dedicated, consecrated, venerated, or hallowed. One might say, then, that our holy God has transferred his holiness onto us and therefore sanctified each person. This confers upon each of us a dignity that our attitudes, attributes, and activities neither deserve nor can nullify.[7]

2.12 In his *Gospel of Life*, Pope John Paul II asserts the sacred value of human life "from its very beginning until its end." He urges a fight against "the culture of death" and a holistic and comprehensive struggle to protect vulnerable humans, sacred in God's sight.

2.13 John Paul II is among those who have made the connection explicit: the concept of human rights is inextricably bound to the belief that

---

7. Gushee, *The Sacredness of Human Life*, 17–20.

human life is sacred and therefore must be held in the highest respect. "Upon the recognition of this right, every human community and the political community itself are founded."[8] Indeed, by focusing on human rights, we direct our attention and energy to those who need it most—those image-bearers whose dignity is being violated.[9] Human rights are not first of all about "my rights," but about the rights of the vulnerable and the violated. And they are about the responsibility, indeed obligation, to defend the weak. All people, all societies, and all nations have a responsibility to ensure human rights.

2.14 We believe that a commitment to human rights is strengthened profoundly by the kinds of theological commitments just articulated. They are certainly our convictions. We are very happy to work with persons of other faiths and no faith on behalf of human rights, but as evangelicals our convictions are rooted in God's love and the dignity it gives to all human beings.

3. Human Rights

"Defend the weak and the fatherless; uphold the cause of the poor and the oppressed. Rescue the weak and the needy" (Psalm 82:3–4a).[10]

3.1 Human rights *function* to protect the dignity of human life.[11] Because human rights guard what God has made sacred, they cannot be canceled by any other concern, nor can they be bracketed off as irrelevant in exigent circumstances. This is in contrast to the view that a right can be canceled or overridden. Human rights are a decisive factor in determining how all persons must be treated in all circumstances.[12] Rights correlate with duties—fundamentally, a duty to protect those whose God-given rights are about to be, or are being, violated.[13] Those who affirm a belief in human rights implicitly accept for themselves a range of moral obligations.[14] Affirmation of human rights and their corresponding duties is an important dimension of Christian belief, and also widely shared by persons of other faiths.

---

8. Pope John Paul II, *The Gospel of Life*, 2–4.
9. Stassen, "Foreword," 11.
10. TNIV.
11. Sundman, "Human Rights, Justification, and Christian Ethics," 41.
12. Ibid., 45.
13. Stassen, "Foreword," 12.
14. Marshall, *Crowned with Glory and Honor*, 34.

3.2 Human rights place a shield around people, even when (especially when) our hearts cry out for vengeance. It is precisely when we are most inclined to abandon a commitment to human rights that we most need to reaffirm that commitment.[15] The creation of a social order in which such legal and moral norms are honored even in the teeth of popular sentiment is both a high human achievement, and a fragile one.

3.3 Human rights apply to all humans. The rights people have are theirs by virtue of being human, made in God's image. Persons can never be stripped of their humanity, regardless of their actions or of others' actions toward them. In social contract theory human rights are called *unalienable* rights. Unalienable rights are absolute and completely inviolable; a person cannot legitimately cease to have those rights, whether through waiver, fault, or another's act.[16] This is not biblical vocabulary, but it does seem to us consistent with a biblical understanding of human rights. Consider the way in which even Cain was protected by the divine "mark," and legal provision to protect the rights of killers was made in the Old Testament through the cities of refuge and the processes of judgment required there (Num 35:9–34).

3.4 Some Christians reject human rights language because they have witnessed its abuse. They have heard numerous groups claim a right to engage in certain behaviors as expressions of their human rights. Many morally troublesome agendas are punctuated with "rights-talk," thereby cheapening those rights that are indeed both unalienable and threatened.[17] But the solution is not to abandon talk of rights. It is instead to clarify the range of legitimate rights-claims.

3.5 A variety of approaches can be taken to articulate and organize claims about human rights. An expansive approach argues that there are

---

15. An example from another context helps illustrate our point. In 2000, a young teenage girl in New Zealand was abducted by a neighbor. She was sexually violated, and then buried alive. She died a horrible death. The murderer was tried, convicted, and imprisoned for life according to the laws of New Zealand, but this did not satisfy the girl's stepfather. He was subsequently convicted for repeatedly hurling murderous threats at her killer. Hailed as a hero, the stepfather had overwhelming public opinion in his favor. One supporter said of the girl's killer, "When you commit that kind of crime, you give up your rights. That kind of person is not even human." A columnist for the *New Zealand Herald*, however, wrote in support of the judge's decision. Criticizing the public's lust for vengeance, he insisted that even the murderers of children "still have basic human rights and a decent society ensures those rights are upheld."

16. Sundman, "Human Rights, Justification, and Christian Ethics," 38, 44.

17. Glendon, *Rights Talk*.

three dimensions of human rights, and all must be equally valued by any society that respects any of them: the right to certain freedoms, especially including religious liberty, the right to participate in community, and the right to have basic needs met.[18]

3.6 If one takes a more constrained approach to human rights, such as the view which confines human rights to "negative rights," i.e., that which the state may not do to us, the issues under discussion in this declaration still fall well within the boundaries of legitimate human rights-claims.

3.7 Human life is expressed through physicality, and the well-being of persons is tied to their physical existence. Therefore, humans must have the right to security of person. This includes the right not to have one's life taken unjustly (equivalent to the right to life), the right not to have one's body mutilated, and the right not to be abused, maimed, tortured, molested, or starved (sometimes called the right to bodily integrity or the right to remain whole). The right not to be arbitrarily detained (an aspect of due process) and the *writ of habeus corpus* are also based specifically on the concept of bodily rights. In particular, the *writ of habeus corpus* is based on the right not to have the government arbitrarily detain one's body.

4. The Christian History of Human Rights

"Thus says the Lord: 'Do justice and righteousness, and deliver from the hand of the oppressor him who has been robbed. And do no wrong or violence to the resident alien, the fatherless, and the widow, nor shed innocent blood in this place" (Jer 22:3).[19]

4.1 Contrary to a common misunderstanding, one that has weakened Christian support for human rights, human rights are not an Enlightenment notion, and certainly not to be seen as an Enlightenment *fiction*. Rooted in Scripture, the concept of human rights was suggested as far back as the twelfth century, and can be traced into the modern period through a variety of routes, all of them versions of Christianity. Heirs to the English Christian traditions find especially important the work of Richard Overton, an English Christian thinker of the seventeenth century. In 1645, Overton wrote *The Arraignment of Mr. Persecution*, basing his argument on reason, experience, and Scripture.

18. Stassen, *Just Peacemaking*, 138, 159.
19. ESV.

The book was penned during a time of great oppression of religious nonconformists in England. Overton proclaimed the equal rights of Jews, Muslims, atheists, Catholics, Protestants, and all humankind.[20]

4.2 Thus human rights ideas developed in the English-speaking world during a movement for religious liberty among "free church" Puritans in England, and later among religious dissenters in North America like Roger Williams, and not first among Enlightenment rationalists.[21] The concept of human rights flourished in the seventeenth and eighteenth centuries with documents such as the American *Declaration of Independence* (1776), the French Assembly's *Declaration of the Rights of Man and of the Citizen* (1789), and Thomas Paine's *The Rights of Man* expressing the belief in "natural rights."[22] More secularized versions of human rights should be seen as derivatives of an earlier, explicitly Christian, articulation.

4.3 The late nineteenth century proved an inhospitable environment for belief in "natural rights" worldwide, in both philosophical and political arenas. However, the totalitarian assault on human dignity in the first half of the twentieth century, especially by Nazi Germany, Stalinist Russia, and Imperialist Japan, led to a reinterpretation of traditional natural-rights talk in the direction of "human rights."[23] Reacting to the devastation of the Nazi regime, and responding to the struggle by colonies for independence from their colonial masters, human rights gained worldwide momentum once again. Shortly after World War II, the United Nations Declaration of Human Rights was written, and then signed by the vast majority of nations.[24] The United States played a key role in drafting and advancing this UN Declaration. Many deeply committed Christians were involved in this process. Evangelicals struggled with the secular grounding of the Declaration's norms, but both then and now embrace its primary principles.

4.4 The Roman Catholic Church and the second Vatican Council (1962–1965) brought about another development in the maturation of the concept of human rights. Strongly affirming religious liberty after centuries of teaching otherwise, the Vatican II leaders, as with Overton, articulated strong concern for world peace and drew the connections

20. Marshall, *Crowned with Glory and Honor*, 148.
21. White, "Setting the Record Straight," 75–96.
22. Marshall, *Crowned with Glory and Honor*, 29.
23. Ibid., 29–30.
24. Stassen, "Foreword," 11–12.

between war and the violation of human rights.²⁵ A similar emphasis on human rights appears in many of the documents of the global ecumenical movement, as well as mainline Protestant theologians such as Reinhold Niebuhr. Meanwhile, the social movement of the 1950s and 1960s for African-American civil rights provided a powerful articulation of a heartfelt human rights ethic. It is hard to avoid the conclusion that an emphasis on human rights was very nearly a Christian consensus by the late twentieth century.

4.5 Yet talk of human rights evokes opposition as well. We have already noted theological and philosophical objections. But throughout history the primary opposition to a concept of human rights has emerged most intensely from privileged groups (religious, economic, political, ethnic, etc.) determined to maintain their unjust advantages or resist challenges to their mistreatment of those whom they dominated. Meanwhile, support for human rights has helped to spread democracy and in general to break the power of unjust social structures.²⁶

4.6 Love for one's neighbor should motivate the believer to act in the interests of those whose rights we are responsible to defend. Commitment to human rights can be seen as a systematic way to look out for the interests of others, and thus as an expression of Christian love. This is now the overwhelming consensus of the Christian community.

5. Ethical Implications of Human Rights

"Father to the fatherless, a defender of widows, is God in his holy dwelling. God sets the lonely in families, he leads out the prisoners with singing" (Ps 68:5–6).²⁷

Principles

5.1 It is vital for the future of any good society and for the development of democracy that we, as citizens of the United States and as Christians belonging to the Body of Christ, promote and protect the innate dignity of the human person and therefore honor human rights. In the last century we have witnessed far too many attempts to abolish

---

25. Stassen, *Just Peacemaking*, 156.
26. Stassen, "Foreword," 13.
27. TNIV.

that divine value in humanity, and to treat human beings in ways far worse than bestial. However, as Pope John Paul II stated, the sanctity of life is a value "which no individual, no majority and no State can ever create, modify or destroy, but must only acknowledge, respect and promote."[28]

5.2 Even when a person has done wrong, poses a threat, or has information necessary to prevent a terrorist attack, he or she is still a human being made in God's image, still a person of immeasurable worth. The crime we abhor, but we must distinguish the error from the person in error. A person might do inhuman acts, but is never inhuman.[29] This distinction is excruciatingly difficult to make, which is all the more reason why we must be vigilant in making it.

Responsibilities

INDIVIDUAL RESPONSIBILITY

5.3 As individuals we are responsible for protecting the dignity of others, as the Good Samaritan did when he went out of his way to minister to the victim he found along his path (Luke 10:25–37). The Lord brings justice, and governments have resources not available to individuals, but that does not release each of us from the obligation to make an urgent and concerted effort to raise every bearer of the image of God to the dignified level at which he or she was intended by the Creator.[30]

5.4 We live in a free society, a representative democracy, and while only a few may be direct perpetrators of human rights violations or even torture, we all share the responsibility because we are the citizens on whose behalf interrogators and military personnel are working. Whether we commit an offense against humanity, or simply sin by refusing to speak up for someone who is being victimized, as individuals and a society we are accountable for the indignities that are authorized and carried out by our nation.[31] We each have responsibility to exercise our right/obligation to participate in the deliberative processes of our democracy. Those who have greater social or political power have even greater moral responsibility to act.

---

28. Pope John Paul II, *The Gospel of Life*, 129.
29. Vatican II, "Gaudium et Spes," 929.
30. Marshall, "Human Rights," 313.
31. Evans and Evans, *Human Rights*, 3.

The Role of the Church

5.5 The churches have a very important responsibility to prepare their members to be faithful disciples of Christ who witness in and to the various contexts in which we find ourselves. Church leaders have a critical role in equipping Christians to think and respond biblically in all major areas of life, including the one we are considering here. One aspect of this discipling process is to help congregants prepare for the exercise of their citizenship responsibilities. Evangelicals alone make up one quarter of all voters in the United States. As evangelicals we are keenly aware of the gravity of our responsibility, and many of us have joined in articulating our own public ethical vision in a document released in 2004, and endorsed by all forty-three members of the Board of the National Association of Evangelicals, "For the Health of the Nation."[32]

The Role of the State

5.6 The government inevitably plays a central role in a nation's treatment of human beings and respect for human life. Unless human rights are embedded in a nation's constitutional documents, in its legislation, and in fair court procedures, and there is governmental respect for international laws that protect human rights, rights-claims can become mere abstractions that are not implemented in practice. In light of the sinfulness of humanity there is a need for the protection and restraint of laws.

5.7 Governments should be legally obligated to protect basic human rights. The US government certainly is so obligated.

5.8 It is striking that calls in the 1970s and 1980s for the US to advance global human rights initially assumed that human rights were an unquestioned part of our own constitutional order. The idea was to spread that vision around the world. Evangelicals have been deeply invested in that project. We have pressed for the rights of religious liberty, especially where religious minorities have been persecuted, for the rights of victims of sex trafficking, and for human rights in countries oppressed by dictatorships. Now we find ourselves having to turn our gaze homeward again, to the eroding human rights protections of our own practices.

32. "For the Health of the Nation," 363.

5.9 The goal of a nation that advances human rights for all is one that has been articulated by our current president and members of his administration. President George W. Bush has described the United States as being born from a "simple dream of dignity."[33] The American spirit, he has asserted, is "generous and strong and decent, not because we believe in ourselves, but because we hold beliefs beyond ourselves."[34]

5.10 This dream was not lost after 9/11. On October 31, 2001, Lorne W. Craner, Assistant Secretary for the Bureau of Democracy, Human Rights, and Labor, stated: "maintaining the focus on human rights and democracy worldwide is an integral part of our response to the attack [on 9/11] . . . We are proud to bear the mantle of leadership in international human rights in this century."[35] President Bush's speeches are full of belief in the dignity of every human life, regardless of political or national distinctions. "The American flag stands for more than our power and our interests," he has said. "Our founders dedicated this country to the cause of human dignity, the rights of every person, and the possibilities of every life."[36]

5.11 In light of these appealing words, it is clear to us that the terrorist attacks that jolted the nation in 2001 have blurred our national moral vision. National resolve, normally a virtue, can be misdirected, leading to the violation of human rights when it is allowed to overthrow our better selves. As the founding fathers intended, we have checks and balances within our Constitution's framework where Congress and the courts operate to check the presidency and thereby protect human rights. This is how it should be. Meanwhile, the United Nations Human Rights Charter and the great number of other human rights documents to which America has added its name serve as additional boundary-setters, so that the government does not act rashly or unjustly.

5.12 The current administration has at times used language that is rich with respect for human rights, even after 9/11. Today this language is less frequently heard, and our actions as a nation do not consistently reflect the values once articulated. Yet there is a structure of national and international principles and laws that can help us to regain our moral footing, and in some ways have already begun to do so.

33. Mertus, *Bait and Switch*, 57.
34. Ibid.
35. Ibid., 58.
36. Ibid.

6. Legal Structures regarding Human Rights

"A ruler who lacks understanding is a cruel oppressor, but he who hates unjust gain will prolong his days" (Prov 28:16).[37]

International Law

6.1 The Geneva Conventions, the Universal Declaration of Human Rights, and many other treaties outlining human rights are in place so each signatory nation is held accountable.

6.2 With a raging "war on terror," American policymakers and interrogators have faced the temptation of looking to torture, and to cruel, inhuman, or degrading treatment of their detainees in Iraq, Afghanistan, Guantánamo, and other US detention centers. Torture has often been a temptation (and far too many times a practice) in other countries facing perceived or actual security threats. Despite these abuses, the articles of the Geneva Convention and of the Universal Declaration on Human Rights are unambiguous.[38]

6.3 Article 3 of the 3rd Geneva Convention (1949) says:

> Persons taking no active part in hostilities... shall in all circumstances be treated humanely, without any adverse distinction founded on race, colour, religion or faith, sex, birth or wealth, or any other similar criteria. To this end the following acts are and shall remain prohibited at any time and in any place whatsoever with respect to the above-mentioned persons: violence to life and person, in particular, humiliating and degrading treatment; an impartial humanitarian body, such as the international committee of the Red Cross, may offer its services to the Parties in conflict.[39]

6.4 Article 5 of the same Geneva Convention states: "No one shall be subjected to torture or to cruel, inhuman, or degrading treatment or punishment." Article 9 reads: "No one shall be subjected to arbitrary arrest, detention, or exile."[40] The U.N. *International Covenant on Civil and Political Rights* (ICCPR—1966) states in article 7 that "no one shall

---

37. ESV.
38. Gushee, "Against Torture," 351.
39. Geneva Convention (III): Relative to the Treatment of Prisoners of War.
40. Ibid.

an evangelical declaration against torture 119

be subjected to torture or to cruel, inhuman or degrading treatment or punishment." Article 10 of the ICCPR also establishes a particular right to be treated in a humane and dignified manner for accused or detained persons deprived of their personal liberty.[41] This code of conduct is further clarified in the United Nations High Commission on Human Rights *Civil and Political Rights, Including the Questions of Torture and Detention* (2005). According to the Geneva Conventions, cruel, inhuman, or degrading treatment (CIDT), although falling short of torture, is still completely prohibited along with all forms of torture. "The overriding factor at the core of the prohibition of CIDT is the concept of [the] powerlessness of the victim."[42]

6.5 International treaties provide *no loopholes* for justifying torture or any form of degrading treatment. The ICCPR treaty says that although "in time of public emergency which threatens the life of the nation . . . the State Parties to the present Covenant may take measures derogating from their obligations under the present Covenant to the extent strictly required by the exigencies of the situation, . . . *no derogation from [article] 7 . . . may be made under this provision*."[43] The U.N. Convention Against Torture puts it this way: "No exceptional circumstances whatsoever, whether a state of war or a threat of war, internal political instability or any other public emergency, may be invoked as a justification for torture."[44]

6.6 The United States is a signatory to all of these international treaties. We have also historically incorporated their principles into military doctrine. However, these practices have come into question during the last five years. We believe that this has been a mistake, and we support a return to full adherence to the straightforward meaning of international conventions against torture.

US Law

6.7 The United States has often sought to position itself as being on the side of the oppressed, including soldiers imprisoned under unjust or

---

41. United Nations High Commission on Human Rights, *Civil and Political Rights*, 13.
42. Ibid.
43. *International Covenant on Civil and Political Rights*, UN General Assembly Resolution 2200A.
44. Gushee, "Five Reasons Torture Is Always Wrong."

cruel circumstances. During the American Revolution, our soldiers were mistreated by the British. Our nation has worked diligently since then to provide legal protection to any person in the custody of the enemy through laws of war.[45] The Geneva Conventions and the Additional Protocols of 1977 are the most recent version of this protection. In 1996, the United States adopted the War Crimes Act to make it possible for our courts to enforce the Conventions, and so the US had entered into enforceable compliance with these vital international safeguards.[46] It must be remembered that the United States has historically been a *leader* in pressing for such safeguards, not just a reluctant signatory.

6.8 Since human rights first became a prominent issue in the twentieth century, the United Nations and the United States have continued to make additions to former agreements, treaties, and statements in order to make them as comprehensive and relevant as possible. This is what a democracy should always be doing. Human rights have always been, and always will be, under attack. However, a liberal democracy works to guard against such violations of human rights through its laws. Its very identity depends upon the confidence that violations of human rights, such as torture, are prohibited.[47]

6.9 Between 9/11 and January 2006, tens of thousands had been detained in US detention centers.[48] The vast majority of these detainees were released without charge. It is important to remember that detention policies pertain to persons, most of whom will end up being charged with no crime and being viewed as no threat to our nation.

6.10 The boundaries of what is legally and morally permissible in war have been crossed in the current "war on terror." The evidence of acts of torture or cruel, inhuman, and degrading treatment against US detainees, especially in Iraq's Abu Ghraib prison, in Afghanistan's Bagram Air Base, in CIA black sites, and at the hands of other nations, has been documented by numerous researchers, including those serving the US government itself. Revelations of these outrages against human dignity led to intense pressure on the federal government to return to its earlier rejection of torture and to clarify its detention and interrogation policies.

45. Gushee and Kirkpatrick, "Rights of Detainees Must Not Be Violated."
46. Ibid.
47. Ignatieff, "Evil Under Interrogation."
48. Shrader, "US Detained 83,000."

6.11 Commendably, the US Army Field Manual, last revised in 1992, has recently undergone more changes in light of recent events. Specific cruel, inhuman, and degrading practices that had taken place at least sporadically from 2002–2006 are now overtly banned. In addition to the general language of the 1992 edition, which prohibited "acts of violence or intimidation, including physical or mental torture, threats [or] insults, . . . as a means of or aid to interrogation,"[49] there is now also more specific wording prohibiting military personnel from engaging in the behavior that put Abu Ghraib in the headlines. Beating prisoners, sexually humiliating them, threatening them with dogs, depriving them of food and water, performing mock executions, shocking them with electricity, burning them, causing other types of pain, and "waterboarding" are all explicitly banned.[50] The Pentagon is to be commended for this strong and positive revision of the Army Field Manual. It should become the policy of every agency of the United States government.[51]

6.12 Tragically, however, despite the military's commendable efforts to remove itself from any involvement with torture, the current administration has decided to retain morally questionable interrogation techniques among the options available to our intelligence agencies. For some time it did so without any form of public disclosure or oversight. In 2006 the administration moved its policies more fully into the light of day, pressing for legislation to authorize what it wanted to do.

6.13 The most recent legislation regarding these issues was signed into law in October 2006.[52] From a human rights perspective, the Military Commissions Act includes numerous problematic provisions, such as one in which CIA officials are not required to submit to congressional oversight, and are not held to the same standards as the US military.

49. Gushee, "Five Reasons Torture Is Always Wrong."
50. "Human Intelligence Collector Operations," US Army Field Manual 2-22.3.
51. The US has a moral obligation to train our military personnel in the best way to meet combat contingencies. That necessitates tough training in survival, escape, evasion, and rescue techniques. Also, history demonstrates that our enemies often do not observe standards of international law or the Geneva Convention. Therefore, part of military training involves sleep deprivation, exhaustive marches, food deprivation, and even some pain or discomfort. While this training is closely monitored to guard against abuses, it also must be sufficiently rigorous to arm the individual with physical, psychological, and mental coping skills to endure the unimaginable if taken as a prisoner of war. The signatories understand that this is part of military training and do not intend to condemn it.
52. *Military Commissions Act of 2006*. Many of the act's sections are codified at title 10 United States Code, section 948a and following.

CIA "black sites" may continue to exist, with interrogation rules established by the president but not specified publicly and now removed from the ability of either Congress or judicial authority to review.[53] This could prove to be a recipe for cruel, inhuman, and degrading treatment of detainees, without the Constitution's checks and balances so crucial for American justice.

6.14 Various procedural issues in the Military Commissions Act are also troubling. The new law does not allow terrorism suspects to challenge their detention or treatment through traditional *habeas corpus* petitions.[54] It permits prosecutors, under certain conditions, to use evidence collected through hearsay or through coercion to seek criminal convictions.[55] The legislation also rejects any right to a speedy trial,[56] and it empowers US officials to detain indefinitely anyone it determines to have "purposefully and materially" supported anti-US hostilities.[57] These provisions are deeply lamentable, in part because of their substance, and in part because they create the conditions in which further prisoner abuse is made more likely. They violate basic principles of due process that have been developed in Western judicial systems, including our own, for centuries. Anti-US "hostilities" is a vague term that a future administration can use against anyone perceived as its enemy.[58] We see this as fraught with danger to basic human rights.

7. Conclusion: Human Rights in an Age of Terror

"And the Lord said, 'What have you done? The voice of your brother's blood is crying to me from the ground'" (Gen 4:10).[59]

7.1 The terrorist attacks of 9/11 and the attacks that followed blatantly violated human rights in the most outrageous manner imaginable.

---

53. President George W. Bush, in a speech made at the signing of the *Military Commissions Act of 2006*.

54. Section 7 of the *Military Commissions Act of 2006*, title 28 *United States Code* section 2241.

55. Section 3 of the *Military Commissions Act of 2006*, title 10 *United States Code* section 948r and section 949a.

56. Section 3 of the *Military Commissions Act of 2006*, title 10 *United States Code* section 948b.

57. Section 3 of the *Military Commissions Act of 2006*, title 10 *United States Code* section 948a.

58. Ibid.

59. ESV.

an evangelical declaration against torture 123

We declare without hesitation that the terrorist attacks in New York, Washington, London, Madrid, Bali, and other locations around the globe were heinous assaults on human life. We condemn these worldwide terrorist activities and the radical ideologues that foment them.

7.2 It is certainly the responsibility of a nation's government to protect its people from such callous and cruel disregard of human life.[60] Our military and intelligence forces have worked diligently to prevent further attacks. But such efforts must not include measures that violate our own core values.

7.3 Our current circumstances and national security concerns do not present us with distinctively new temptations regarding the violation of human rights in relation to interrogation policies, torture, and the legal rights of detainees. Our nation's founders anticipated security threats in the eighteenth century; indeed, one could argue that they faced a far more threatening security environment than any that we have experienced since their age. Deterring evil ends without resorting to evil means are tasks in tension, but any liberal democracy must face dealing with this tension.

7.4 A significant challenge presented to us as we focus on deterring terrorism is not that terrorism is unprecedented, but that as it spreads and intensifies, terrorism is deeply frightening to people and unsettling to our way of life. The principle that we must "discharge duties to those who have violated their duties to us" seems even more difficult to bear.[61] It also makes it all the more necessary to be vigilant about guarding those moral boundaries.

7.5 Torture is but one of many violations of human rights. Sadly there are more. Even forty years ago, Vatican II was able to list the following such violations:

> The varieties of crime are numerous: all offenses against life itself, such as murder, genocide, abortion, euthanasia and willful suicide; all violations of the integrity of the human person, such as mutilation, physical and mental torture, undue psychological pressures, all offenses against human dignity, such as subhuman living conditions, arbitrary imprisonment, deportation, slavery, prostitution, the selling of women and children, degrading

---

60. The majority of the signatories of this document stand in the just war tradition. Those who are pacifists believe government should carry out its important responsibilities using non-lethal methods.

61. Ignatieff, "Evil Under Interrogation."

working conditions where men are treated as mere tools for profit rather than free and responsible persons: all these and the like are criminal: they poison civilization; and they debase the perpetrators more than the victims and militate against the honor of the creator.[62]

7.6 Slavery, human and sexual trafficking, genocide, prison rape, abortion, euthanasia, unethical human experimentation—these are some of the other human rights violations listed by the National Association of Evangelicals in its "For the Health of the Nation" statement of 2004.[63] As evangelicals, we are deeply concerned about all violations of human rights. We want to lead the way in honoring and defending human rights wherever they are threatened.

7.7 We gratefully acknowledge our brothers and sisters in other Christian traditions for their thoughtful and Spirit-led work in the area of human rights. In recent times, evangelicals have joined with others to articulate an increasingly vigorous human rights ethic. The Board of the National Association of Evangelicals, representing over 30 million evangelical Christians, in 2004 unanimously approved a statement of social responsibility, which declared that "because God created human beings in his image, we are endowed with rights and responsibilities. . . . Governments should be constitutionally obligated to protect basic human rights." Among those rights articulated in this statement is the right to live "without fear of torture."[64] Little did the NAE know how relevant that particular provision would soon become.

7.8 As evangelicals, we are first obligated to be faithful to Christ and his teaching. We are to be kingdom people, disciples who think biblically about all things. In this particular situation, discipleship requires a clear word from us to our nation and its leaders. We must continue to discuss the moral problems associated with our treatment of detainees both in recent years and still today. Indeed, all citizens in a liberal democracy must step up to the challenge we now face. The enormous burden of defending the human rights of United States citizens while also respecting those of the (suspected and actual) enemy is not one to be carried by our president alone.[65] As fellow Christians, fellow

---

62. Vatican II, 928.
63. "For the Health of the Nation," 363, 370.
64. Ibid., 373.
65. Haugen, "Silence on Suffering."

citizens, and fellow human beings, we let our leaders down by remaining silent.

7.9 When torture is employed by a state, that act communicates to the world and to one's own people that human lives are not sacred, that they are not reflections of the Creator, that they are expendable, exploitable, and disposable, and that their intrinsic value can be overridden by utilitarian arguments that trump that value.[66] These are claims that no one who confesses Christ as Lord can accept.

7.10 The most widely publicized acts of torture by the US came on the heels of the 9/11 attack. As our nation mobilized, the eyes of the Muslim world were on the US and how a Western civilization—in their eyes a Christian civilization—would respond to such barbarism. In this setting, that our actions were not bound by principles of human rights that we in the West profess was rightly seen by Muslims as hypocrisy and thus all the more damaging

7.11 Human rights must be protected for all humankind. A commitment to life's sacredness and to human rights is a seamless garment. It cannot be torn anywhere without compromising its integrity everywhere.

7.12 Therefore:

(a) We renounce the use of torture and cruel, inhuman, and degrading treatment by any branch of our government (or any other government)—even in the current circumstance of a war between the United States and various radical terrorist groups.

(b) We call for the extension of basic human rights and procedural protections to all persons held in United States custody now or in the future, wherever and by whomever they are held.

(c) We call for every agency of the United States government to join with the United States military and to state publicly its commitment to the terms of the Geneva Conventions related to the treatment of prisoners, especially Common Article 3.

(d) We call for the legislative or judicial reversal of those executive and legislative provisions that violate the moral and legal standards articulated in this declaration.

7.13 We make these renunciations and calls for action as Christians and as US citizens. Undoubtedly there are occasions where the demands of Christian discipleship and American citizenship conflict. This is not

---

66. Ignatieff, "Evil Under Interrogation."

one of them. Returning to the absolute commitment to human rights outlined here is right in terms of Christian convictions and right in terms of the interests of our nation. We commend these moral commitments to our fellow believers, and our fellow citizens, for such a time as this.[67]

---

67. Signatories: David Gushee, EHR Chair and Principal Drafter; Rich Cizik, National Association of Evangelicals; Carl H. Esbeck, University of Missouri-Columbia; Roberta Hestenes, World Vision; George Hunsinger, Princeton Theological Seminary; Cheryl Bridges Johns, Church of God Theological Seminary; Ron Mahurin, CCCU; Chuck Marvin, National Association of Evangelicals; Brian McLaren, Cedar Ridge Community Church; Stephen Charles Mott, United Methodist Church; David Neff, *Christianity Today*; Christine Pohl, Asbury Theological Seminary; Wyndy Corbin Reuschling, Ashland theological Seminary; Ron Sider, Palmer Theological Seminary; Glen Stassen, Fuller Theological Seminary; Clyde D. Taylor, US Ambassador; Nicholas Wolterstorff, Yale University.

11

Faith, Science, and Climate Change

2008

SETTING THE SCENE

IN OCTOBER 2006, I engaged in a lengthy face-to-face debate with E. Calvin Beisner of Knox Theological Seminary on the issue of climate change. I knew enough about Beisner's ideology, theology, and handling of data to know that he was a formidable adversary and also a slippery one. While the mainstream debate about the reality and primary causes of climate change was already over by the time of our encounter, it is still not quite over in the evangelical community. Triggered by the release of the Evangelical Climate Initiative in February 2006, which I helped to draft and then signed, a counterattack was waged by a group called the Interfaith Stewardship Alliance, led by Beisner. Our 2006 debate at Union University was an argument about the claims of the ECI statement. It was also a memorable encounter at the border of what in my new book (*The Future of Faith in American Politics*) I label as the evangelical right and center, and not one I would ever care to repeat.

I have been involved in evangelical environmentalism since 1993, when Ron Sider's Evangelicals for Social Action launched the Evangelical Environmental Network. At the time, evangelical environmentalism (or creation care) was clearly confined to the left wing of evangelicalism. It was not a significant enough issue within the evangelical community to attract that much attention (positive or negative) from the right or the inchoate center. Broad concerns about various environmental challenges, such as species loss or the ozone hole, failed to galvanize evangelicals in any serious way. The idea that an evangelical pastor might preach a sermon about the environment seemed almost laughably remote. And those interested in creation care had to constantly guard their flanks against the charge that environmental concern was a front for pantheism or New Age mysticism.

The climate issue has changed all of that. No single environmental concern has attracted such sustained international or (now) evangelical attention. The magisterial process undertaken by the Intergovernmental Panel on Climate Change over the past twenty years has finally proven impossible to ignore—though all but a small number of evangelicals did ignore it until just a few years ago. Now climate change is among the most heavily reported stories, and in my view one of the gravest human challenges, of the twenty-first century.

The hotly contested decision of Rich Cizik, then vice-president for governmental affairs of the National Association of Evangelicals, to take up the climate change issue was one of two major developments that have moved creation care from the evangelical left to the evangelical center. The other was the skillful work of the Evangelical Environmental Network's Jim Ball to engage a widening circle of evangelical leaders in addressing climate change along with other creation care issues. These events occurred in tandem with the explosion of national and international media attention to the climate change phenomenon. By now, creation care, and especially the overarching issue of climate, has become a predominant concern for both the evangelical left and center. Just about all of the major left and center leaders and groups are "on board" on creation care and climate, as can be seen by a review of the signatories of the ECI statement. But none of the evangelical right leaders are similarly on board, and few enough of leaders in what might be called the center-right. (An exception would be Timothy George, dean of Beeson Divinity School in Alabama). Thus it is fair to say that few contemporary moral/policy issues offer a more trenchant demarcation of the left/center vs. right boundary line in American evangelical Christianity. And the right appears deeply uncomfortable with this fact.

And so the right has developed a kind of offensive defensive. Often in tandem with conservative think tanks and politicians, and with the vocal help of Christian talk radio, auxiliary groups have formed on the evangelical right to address environmental issues—or defuse them. The most conspicuous of these is the Cornwall Alliance for the Stewardship of Creation, formerly known as the Interfaith Stewardship Alliance. In its new incarnation, this organization continues to be led by Cal Beisner, a longtime libertarian-conservative Christian writer on energy and environmental issues. Beisner had been laboring in the trenches of the conservative evangelical world for decades, but like other formerly anonymous evangelicals he has risen to a measure of national renown recently as the media has turned its gaze in the direction of evangelicalism. Beisner's niche has become his role as *the* anti-EEN, anti-ECI spokesman. It is almost as if the evangelical right has subcontracted its environmental portfolio to Beisner, who has not been hesitant to take it up. This may be because men like James Dobson feel that they lack the scientific competence to take up these complex issues for themselves. But one also wonders whether they are subtly seeking a kind of "plausible deniability" for their anti-creation care (especially anti-climate change) stance; if and when it collapses, they can blame Beisner—whose quotes they now use even as they rarely add their names to his declarations and official statements.

At the debate itself, Beisner was relatively gentlemanly. But afterwards, during the Q and A, I was astonished to encounter a questioner (a Baptist pastor from middle Tennessee) who attacked my theology, character, and ethics as a teacher for foisting the "myth" of climate change on my unsuspecting, gullible students. This man was deeply angry at a stance that he found impossible to interpret as anything other than a willful desire on my part to deceive those under my care. As I looked through the packet of materials he handed me, which mainly included copies of letters he had sent to Christian leaders all over Tennessee who had violated his view of the climate change issue, as well as occasional lawsuit threats, a vision of a life spent being chased around by this man floated through my mind. Fortunately, I left Tennessee and he has not found me in Georgia yet. (I think.)

I must admit that I have found myself deeply baffled by my encounters with the evangelical climate-change skeptics of the Christian right. I simply have had trouble understanding why grassroots conservative Christian culture has so readily embraced climate change skepticism as a Christian cause célèbre like abortion or sex in the media. Just spend a few hours on Christian talk radio someday and you will know what I mean. Here is one of the few places where the dwindling number of climate change-as-liberal-hoax voices can receive a regular hearing. How deeply dispiriting.

I was raised in the Washington D.C. area by an energy/environment policy wonk with an MIT degree who worked within the mainstream world of policy analysis at the Congressional Research Service. My father's job was to provide balanced, nonpartisan policy research for congressional staff and members. I learned at his feet such basic values as trust in the peer-review process as it exists in mainstream American science and the need for legislators to lead in making rational policy responses to clearly established scientific findings. I also learned about the power of self-interestedness, especially economic self-interest, as it affects policy advocacy and decision-making. My father used to say that every policy decision involves some combination of facts, values, and interests. So I can easily understand why, say, ExxonMobil would not be too interested in embracing climate-change science if it leads to costly congressionally mandated changes in their business practices. Their self-interest requires resistance—at least that is how they will look at it until they recalculate their self-interest. It may be, as some analysts have suggested, that this is really all the explanation needed for evangelical-right foot dragging on climate change—that it is purely a matter of internal alliances within the Republican bloc, and these include alliances with corporate interests that resist climate change efforts. This at least would make a straightforward kind of sense.

But my own encounters with Cal Beisner and his ilk lead me to the conclusion that there are forces indigenous to at least a large sector of evangelical Christianity that contribute to a kind of revanchist, die-hard climate-change skepticism and cannot be attributed to mere economic self-interest or internal conservative alliances. I am convinced that these are fundamentally theological and to some extent cultural forces, not economic or political, though these latter factors do play a major part. In the remainder of this talk, I would like to probe a bit further the sources of climate change skepticism and see where that leads us as we seek a better way forward. I will describe them as a kind of climate skeptic recipe consisting of a number of ingredients. I offer these as suggestions rather than authoritative pronouncements. They are based primarily on the kinds of encounters I have just described.

BEGIN WITH A LONGSTANDING DISDAIN FOR THE ("LEFTIST") ENVIRONMENTAL MOVEMENT

Undoubtedly one factor that contributes to conservative Christian resistance to climate science and climate-change efforts is an aversion to the environmental movement. All of us who have been involved in evangelical environmental efforts have been acutely aware that this ingrained resistance to the world(view) of the Sierra Club, World Wildlife Fund, and so on runs very deep in conservative evangelical circles. This has been so obvious a problem that for a long time it became de rigueur in evangelical environmental writings and speeches to begin with various efforts to distance the speaker from the tree-hugging greens of the left. But let's try to unpack the elements of this anti-enviro stance just a bit more systematically.

At least one major strand of the environmental movement was seen as (if not in reality being) rooted in a fundamental critique of Christianity and its worldview. The (in)famous 1967 article by Lynn White in *Science* which traced modern environmental problems to the dominion mandate of the Bible played a key role here. One response to that article and thesis is to conclude that one can either be committed to Genesis 1 or to the environmental movement, but not both. There are, of course, alternative options that are not nearly as stark. But perhaps Christians were not as accustomed in 1967 as we might be today to a thoroughgoing critique of Christian Scripture or Christian faith. Today Lynn White's article would seem relatively tame.

By extension, the surge of interest in Native American and Eastern religious traditions during the 1960s and 1970s appeared quite threatening to conservative evangelicals. If Christianity has been discredited as eco-unfriendly, then new (or, quite old) spiritual resources are needed. As various books and movements sought to retrieve alternative spiritualities to ground environmental concern (eco-spirituality), conservative Christians came to identify environmentalism with liberalism, pantheism, New Age spirituality, or Disney's Pocahontas talking to the spirits in the trees. It was not a long stretch to assume that environmentalists were animists, pagans, heretics, or all of the above, and that Christians needed to stay as far away from environmentalism as possible.

Another suggestion might be that ever since the first Earth Day (1970), environmentalism has been associated with the flower power ethos of the 1960s counterculture. If it is true that we have essentially been refighting the 1960s since they ended around 1975, then in a sense environmentalism gets free associated with sex, drugs, rock and roll, bell bottoms, and antiwar protests. And everyone knows that Bible-believing Christians were not found in such company.

A conversation not long ago with a former colleague who opposed me tooth and nail on the climate change issue offers one final lesson under this first heading. Just after a faculty luncheon one August day, this erstwhile colleague—a brilliant, deeply conservative young scientist with eight children and another on the way—approached me rather aggressively with these words: "You must look at my lifestyle and judge me to be in violation of God's will. Anyone with a large family like mine cannot be meeting your criteria of environmental stewardship. Isn't that right?" I was astonished. I try not to set myself up as the judge of someone else's entire life and had never thought to do so in relation to this colleague. But his comments open up a connection to another dimension of conservative Christian anti-environmentalism. To the extent that the environmental movement is seen as promoting birth control and/or population control and/or relatively small families, it does stand in stark contrast with that burgeoning strand of conservative Protestantism which has embraced the belief that the use of artificial birth control violates God's will. On the Catholic side, this is rooted in a natural law theology; on the Protestant side I find that it tends to be rooted in a high Calvinism. However it is rooted theologically, it does tend to lead to very, very large families—and is often correlated with resistance to at least some forms of environmentalism.

ADD DEEP DISTRUST OF MAINSTREAM SCIENCE, ITS LEADERS AND ACADEMIES, TRACEABLE TO THE STILL UNRESOLVED DEBATE OVER DARWIN AND EVOLUTION

The entire premise of this conference is that "a problematic relationship between faith and science . . . has persisted over the course of four hundred years" and that we need "a genuine conversation between science and religion which discerns the rightful place for both realms in the search for truth."[1] It has been amply apparent to me in the climate change debate that the poisoning of the well between faith and science continues to play a major role in undermining conservative Christian confidence in the trustworthiness of climate science.

A vignette from my debate with Cal Beisner might help. Right at the very end of our debate, in his closing statement, Beisner said something like this: "You rely heavily on the claims of what you call mainstream science. But isn't that the same mainstream science that gave us the theory of evolution? Why should we believe them on climate if they are so wrong on evolution?"[2]

And there you have it. The climate issue becomes a proxy for the endless refighting of the Scopes Trial. If you believe in evolution, you believe in climate change. Therefore you are a pagan. If you are a true Christian you reject evolution, and so climate change must be a myth just like evolution. Both have been brought to us by elite atheist scientists who cannot be trusted. These same scientists, such as Richard Dawkins, are the guys who are currently writing the atheistic books attacking Christian belief.

---

1. Conference Promotional Flyer. The conference referenced here was a gathering sponsored by the Christian Life Commission of the Baptist General Convention of Texas, in March 2008.

2. Beisner at Gushee-Beisner debate as recalled by the author.

I am not a scientist and I do not specialize in the ongoing fight over evolution, intelligent design, and creationism. I have a number of books on my shelf that attempt to reframe this fight and maybe even to heal the breach. I know that fine scholars are working on these issues, many from within the evangelical community. I have my own theological convictions about how the world began and how human beings got here. But I do not think that holding one or another particular conviction about evolution has anything to do with taking climate change science seriously. Still, one can easily see how a populist anti-science sentiment can be mobilized to fuel a populist anti-climate science sentiment.

It seems to do little good to talk about the amazing peer-review process involved in the work of the Intergovernmental Panel on Climate Change, the international scientific assemblage that has led the world community in analyzing climate issues for twenty years. If you are a student or a scholar, think of the grading or peer-review process on steroids. Imagine submitting a paper not to one professor or a few journal reviewers but in effect to the 2,500 best scientists on that particular subject from all around the world. Then, once it has passed through several layers of such review, imagine that paper having to survive a line-by-line editing process not just by these scientists but also by governmental representatives, some of whom are deeply self-interested in minimizing the seriousness of climate problems. What has resulted in four rounds of three reports offered every seven years or so by the IPCC has been state-of-the-art science framed with an inherent caution so as not to overhype any climate change finding or projection. This is one reason why some climate scientists actually think IPCC is too cautious and not expressing sufficient alarm—not the opposite concern, so commonly articulated on the right. It is not surprising that as this scientific process has continued, as the data set has grown and climate modeling has improved, the IPCC's findings have been refined. Mainly these refinements have led to increasing certainty about the reality of climate change, the centrality of human causation of climate change, and the likely effects of climate change based on various models related to how the world community will respond to what is going on. Every so often a particular finding (such as the relationship between climate change and the frequency of catastrophic weather events) is revised or changed. But this is about as significant as saying to someone standing on a railroad track that the train will strike us down at 12:24 rather than 12:18.

Inevitably in any scientific debate there are skeptics, some of whom have scientific credentials. Some of the climate change skeptics are honest scientists who simply read the data differently. Some are people who have spent their careers doubting the scientific consensus on various issues as a kind of temperamental proclivity. Others are or have been on the payroll of organizations that exist in order to cast doubt on climate science.

What is enough to drive at least this evangelical Christian to despair is the fact that when looking for insight on climate change, populist conservative Christians turn to this small fringe of skeptics rather than the thousands of scientists who take the majority position. Or they ignore the scientists altogether and jump up and down on the carcass of the Scopes Monkey Trial while quoting Bible verses.

At every level, Christians must do a better job of teaching good science to their young people. From the earliest exposure to God's creation in the home, to careful attention to even elementary school science teaching, to the kind of training we are offering our students in Christian colleges, to developing conscious and well-funded efforts to train up a generation of sophisticated evangelical research scientists, we have much work to do. Our weakness in science is one part of the "scandal of the evangelical mind,"[3] and on this issue it is hurting us profoundly.

BLEND IN A SIMILAR MISTRUST OF THE MAINSTREAM MASS MEDIA—IF THEY ARE HYPING AN ISSUE, IT SHOULD BE TREATED WITH SKEPTICISM

Attacking the "liberal" media is quite a popular sport in some conservative circles. Almost by definition, if an issue is treated as important in news outlets such as *Time*, *Newsweek*, CNN, or *The New York Times*, it is not to be trusted. This creates a kind of vicious circular logic—the more an issue is treated in these news sources, the more it is to be dismissed or mocked. The way a good conservative Christian can *know* that something is *not* true is if it appears regularly in *The New York Times*. A philosopher might call this the attainment of epistemological certainty through negative confirmation. Or something like that.

Having ruled out most of the nation's major newspapers and media outlets, this leaves a certain kind of Christian depending on Fox, Rush, and American Family Association radio. It is easy enough to say that this nicheing of news intake for Christians is a significant problem in its own right. And it does require that those of us who do gain occasional access to these climate-resistant news outlets need to do the best job we can when there.

3. Noll, *The Scandal of the Evangelical Mind*.

Of course, many of us have had experiences of attempting to do just that and getting ambushed by people interested more in scoring points than in dialogue. The broader challenge is to invite conservative Christians (and everyone else) to bust out of their ideological market niches and make a moral commitment to reading widely in a diverse range of national and international news sources. Ethics requires careful evaluation of data. Technical readers do this through technical journals. Non-specialists do it by reading general news sources, hopefully as diverse and balanced a diet as possible.

THROW IN LOYALTY TO A (REPUBLICAN) PRESIDENT OR PARTY WHICH TENDS TO BE SKEPTICAL OF ENVIRONMENTAL WORRIES OR COMMITMENTS

Political loyalties undoubtedly have played a role on the climate issue. Put rather bluntly, to the extent that environmentalism became a greater concern on the Democratic side than the Republican, to that very same extent conservative Christians were inclined to reject it—at least once the alignment between the Christian Right and the Republican Party had solidified (ca. 1980). If the Democrats are for it, and we know the Democrats are not God's Own Party, then by definition this cannot be a Christian concern, but instead quite the opposite. The heavy involvement of Al Gore in the climate-change debate has only intensified this problem. The resistance of the Bush administration to climate science, and serious climate action, inevitably has contributed to grassroots foot dragging among Republican Christians as well. Much can be explained by simple political loyalty. It is a powerful force, on all sides. I have been arguing that it is a force that must be resisted by a faith-based commitment to political independence.

COMBINE WITH LIBERTARIAN, FREE-MARKET ECONOMICS AND DISTRUST OF GOVERNMENT AND ITS INTERVENTIONS WITH THE MARKET

The climate debate actually consists of multiple debates. The first was whether climate change is real. That's done. The second is whether climate change is likely to be human-induced. The most recent IPCC concludes with "very high confidence" (90 percent or greater) that this is also true. In most sensible quarters, then, this debate has also concluded. The third debate has to do with the likely seriousness of the impacts of climate change. This involves a wide range of calculations and projections about all kinds of regions, problems, and possibilities for human response. The final debate concerns what policy measures and other human actions are most appropriate for responding to climate change, both at the level of adaptation and mitigation.

It is this latter debate that most exercises skeptics whose main concern appears to be an ideological commitment to a purist libertarianism in which the government intervenes little if at all with the functioning of market capitalism. To the extent that there are factual arguments here they have to do with the possible or likely effects of various kinds of government policies on American or global economic well-being. Libertarian skeptics usually argue that policy measures such as a mandated cap-and-trade system will damage the American economy and/or negatively impact the world's poor.

Undoubtedly congressional concern about the economic impact of climate legislation has been one factor slowing the passage of any kind of comprehensive bill. A variety of responses can be offered, such as the common argument among environmentalists that the transition to a green economy will actually create jobs for those inventors and entrepreneurs who get there ahead of the competition. Many major corporations, including energy giants like BP, have concluded that legislation is inevitable and they would rather position themselves as ahead-of-the-curve entrepreneurs and problem solvers rather than foot draggers.

Eventually legislation will be crafted that attempts to address such legitimate economic concerns. My puzzlement here really has to do with how a particular political-economic ideology—libertarianism—became entrenched in some very conservative Christian circles as *the Christian economic ethic*. I first noticed it when working for Ron Sider at Evangelicals for Social Action in the early 1990s, and seeing some of the very angry books that were published in a libertarian vein in response to his *Rich Christians in an Age of Hunger*. (He particularly delighted in showing me David Chilton's *Productive Christians in an Age of Guilt-Manipulators*.)[4]

It is my belief that economic ethics is one of the least developed strands of the overall field of Christian ethics and is particularly weak among evangelical Christians. There is much work to be done to arrive at a richly biblical and richly empirical Christian economic ethic. I edited one book on the theme and have some familiarity with the literature. But my overall sense is that Christians tend either to succumb to an unquestioning

---

4. Sider, *Rich Christians in an Age of Hunger*; Chilton, *Productive Christians in an Age of Guilt-Manipulators*.

laissez-faire capitalist theology or perhaps on the left to an anti-capitalist, anti-globalization economic populism. It is the former rather than the latter that is apparent among climate skeptics, and that economic ideology is definitely playing a role in fueling climate action skepticism.

ADD A DASH OF GENERAL HUMAN RELUCTANCE TO ACCEPT THE HARD-TO-COMPREHEND, UNPRECEDENTED NEWS THAT HUMAN BEINGS ARE ACTUALLY CHANGING THE CLIMATE

Certain truths are not just inconvenient, they are very hard to wrap our minds around. It is natural and inevitable that we normally respond to these surprising truths with reluctance and skepticism. I think that this general human tendency plays at least some role in climate skepticism, and has little to do with theology per se.

I remember when I was working on my doctoral dissertation on the Holocaust. I spent three years doing little but reading books about that terrible and deeply disturbing event. Sometimes I would wake up in the middle of the night after having dreamt about something terrible I had read that day. For a brief sleepy moment I would sometimes conclude that the whole thing had been a bad dream. But then I would once again reach the horrible realization that while I may have just awakened from a dream, what I had been dreaming about was actually true. It had actually happened. It was unbelievable, but it had to be believed, because it was true.

The idea that human beings can change the climate on this vast, beautiful planet seems unbelievable. It is not something most of us could even have imagined. But the data is in. It is unbelievable but true. One would think that a faith that centers on the only incarnate God-man, the only man to rise from the dead and ascend to heaven bodily, would have the resource to cope with truths that are both unbelievable and true.

MIX IN THE BELIEF THAT GOD ORDAINS ALL THAT HAPPENS ON THIS PLANET AND THEREFORE ALL IS IN HIS HANDS AND WE NEED FEAR NOTHING

Many in Baptist life in recent years have noted the resurgence of a version of scholastic Calvinism. Skeptics have been worried that this resurgent Calvinism might cut the nerve of missionary zeal. This may or may not be occurring. But there is little question that this kind of Calvinism does tend to cut the nerve of an acute sense of human moral responsibility.

In my debate with Cal Beisner he picked a particular Bible passage to attempt to demonstrate that we have little to fear. After the cataclysmic flood described in Genesis 7–8, God makes a covenant with Noah and all flesh. In Genesis 9:11, God says, "Never again will all life be cut off by the waters of a flood; never again will there be a flood to destroy the earth." Beisner quoted this verse, then turned to me and said that on this basis we need not fear the kind of coastal flooding projected as one major consequence of significant sea level rise caused by global warming.

I had never really encountered this kind of proof-texting before in relation to climate problems. The best response I could muster at the time was to say something like, "The text promises that God won't send a flood, not that we won't create one ourselves."

We are dealing with problems here at many levels. One is a biblical hermeneutics issue having to do with how we interpret specific kinds of biblical texts and genres and draw the applications of those texts to situations today. Applying the majestic words of the primeval history in Genesis 9 to a particular aspect of the climate problem in the way Beisner did that day violates the canons of biblical interpretation and application in more ways than one can name.

The deeper issue is a theology of divine sovereignty in which God ordains all that happens on the planet, from who will respond to the offer of salvation to whether we will flood ourselves after broiling the earth's climate—or incinerate ourselves with nuclear weapons. Thoughtful Christians need some very careful rethinking of what we mean by divine sovereignty and how we relate that to human responsibility. Orthodox Christians face the challenge of holding together a God who genuinely rules with humans who genuinely decide.

This is a classic conundrum in theology but its contours now have a very different shape in our own age. As theologians as diverse as Irving Greenberg, Dietrich Bonhoeffer, and Larry Rasmussen noted in the twentieth century, it is clear that the exponential increase in human technological capacity since the Industrial Revolution means that we are now co-creators (or co-destroyers?) in a way never before possible in human history. The human role has increased. We have what were once understood to be godlike powers. Among these is the power to affect the climate. And, as Bonhoeffer so earnestly warned us, we dare not wait for God as the *deus ex machina* who will descend from the rafters during the final act to rescue us from ourselves. God is sovereign in the sense that this world rightly belongs to God who is its creator and king. God is reclaiming the world in Jesus Christ.

But every day bears painful witness to the fact that this work is not yet done. Every abused and murdered child bears such witness. It is an obscenity to attribute such evils in any way to God. And it is hardly less an obscenity to lull Christians into a sense of complacency about God's creation on the grounds that whatever happens, God wills it, and we have nothing to fear.

ADD THE CONVICTION THAT THE BIBLE GIVES HUMAN BEINGS FREE REIN TO EXERCISE DOMINION AS WE SEE FIT

In my debate with Cal Beisner and in reading some of his work I was reminded that an older version of "dominion theology" still survives on the right. A particular reading of the "cultural mandate" of Genesis 1 leads to the belief that creation was made for humanity and that our relationship to the rest of the creatures is a relationship of rule. Pressed in a particularly extreme direction, this reading renders creation and other creatures as little more than raw material for humanity, which sits alone atop creation as its pinnacle and ruler.

Certainly it is possible to read Genesis 1 this way. But it is precisely this reading of Genesis 1 that Lynn White rightly attacked in 1967. This is a theology that made a whole lot more sense in a more primitive era in human history, when men and women were spreading across the earth in relatively small numbers, carving out of the wilderness new agricultural settlements, and experimenting with the earliest development of cities. Thousands of years later, when we are straining the capacity of the very creation to maintain its equilibrium, when we are destroying species at an alarming rate, and when our damage to creation is now seeping into damages to human well-being, this older reading of Genesis 1 simply cannot be sustained.

For forty years or more, creative efforts have been undertaken in Jewish and Christian theology to sift once again through the biblical record for resources leading to a better theology of creation and of humanity in creation. Genesis 1 has been read to emphasize the connections with rather than isolation of humanity from the rest of creation and the other creatures. Dominion has been redefined as stewardship, management, or creation care. The God-given limits of what human beings can do to other creatures has been emphasized, as for example these are taught in legal materials in the Old Testament. The Noah story has been reread as a parable for the human responsibility to care for an endangered creation, and the covenant with Noah has been rediscovered as a covenant between God and all creatures in all eras. The theology of redemption has been recast as a divine plan to reclaim the entire wounded creation (an appropriate move if one understands the reign of God robustly), and some are rediscovering an eschatological vision that involves, as Jesus said, "the renewal of all things" rather than the destruction of creation.

These exegetical, theological, and ethical developments involve some combination of discovering and mining previously ignored or overlooked materials in the Scriptures, together with a creative rethinking of sacred texts in light of new scientific discoveries and newly apparent threats to ecological well-being. For example, our connectedness to the rest of creation is more apparent than ever as we realize how much of our human genetic material is shared with other life forms on this planet, and as we discover to our horror that every toxin that we dump into our water, land, and air ends up in mother's milk eventually. These scientific facts then help us discover that Genesis can be just as easily read to emphasize our human connection with *humus* (soil) and other creatures created by the Creator as it can be read to emphasize our distinctiveness.

All of this, though, requires the Christian willingness and capacity to open our eyes to what is really going on in the world around us and to rethink our faith accordingly. We cannot function in a changing world that requires our best moral efforts with a construal of our faith that is frozen in amber. This kind of Christianity is a museum piece.

A better path is to use the God-given resources available through the best scientific research (for these are God-given), in conversation with the best biblical and theological work, in order to discern what it means to live for Jesus Christ today—in the world we are actually living in right now.

So much is at stake. However we assess the various sources of their view, the net result is that the climate skeptics are sowing sufficient doubt in the American evangelical mind (or reflecting the doubt that is already there) to block political movement to address climate change. Picture all of the red states on the famous electoral map, heavily Southern and Midwestern, most filled with evangelical Christians, most represented by evangelical-friendly congressmen and senators. Thus far these have not been hospitable locales for action on climate, either at the state or federal level. The 2008 elections may break the power of this foot dragging bloc. Already, though, it has slowed climate legislation by a decade or more. Those of us who are convinced that climate change is a major problem, and who work in red-state evangelical America, are in the fight of our lives on this one. We're trying to change the hearts and minds of our religious/political communities from the inside. Now let's get back to work.

12

Church-Based Hate
A Review of Mitchell Gold's *Crisis*
2008

"'FAG' RAN ACROSS MY chest in letters eight inches high," recalled Jared Horsford, a student at Texas Tech and one of forty gays and lesbians who tell their stories in this book.[1] "I stared in the mirror, bitter irony rolling through my mind about how illegible it was, bloody and backwards, in the bathroom mirror. I wouldn't make the same mistake a few months later when I carved 'I HATE YOU'—backwards this time—across the same skin."[2]

In high school, Jared was a basketball star, student government president, church youth group leader, and valedictorian. But Jared was also attracted to men rather than women. "So I fought. I got counseling; I fasted; I prayed; I dated a girl from church; I worked at a Christian summer camp."[3] But nothing worked. He spiraled between attending ex-gay meetings and engaging in anonymous gay sex. When his desires persisted, he "started feeling defeated because I wasn't getting 'healed' and [went] home and cut myself."[4]

Matt Comer, who came from a conservative Baptist family in North Carolina, began experiencing same-sex attraction in his pre-teen years. Matt's preacher said from the pulpit things like: "Put all the queers on a

1. Gold and Drucker, *Crisis*, 76.
2. Ibid.
3. Ibid., 77.
4. Ibid., 78.

ship, cut a hole in the side and send it out to sea."[5] The contrast between his sexuality and the beliefs of his church and family drove Matt to thoughts of suicide. But that same religious faith told him that suicide "would have sent me straight to the depths of hell, landing me in the same spot as being gay. So, I turned to begging and pleading."[6]

Lying on his bed at night, "crying and praying," Matt would ask God to spare him eternal damnation if he tried his very best not to feel attraction to men. But it didn't work. Finally Matt told the truth to his parents. "My mother said I was crazy and sick and told me I was going to hell."[7] Eventually, however, his mother changed her views. "Today," Matt writes, "she is my strength and my most avid supporter, and I know that she loves me no matter what."[8]

The coeditor of this collection, Mitchell Gold, grew up Jewish in Trenton, New Jersey in the 1960s. He spent his teenage years in a cloud of depression, loneliness, fear, and confusion. He tried to pass as straight but was unable to sustain the fiction. "I made a pact with myself: If I could not change and want to be with a woman by the time I was twenty-one, I would commit suicide."[9]

Like a number of others who tell their stories, he moved beyond suicidal thoughts into serious planning. Finally he received psychiatric care that helped him toward self-acceptance. "The number one reason I work toward equal rights for gay, lesbian, bisexual and transgender people is because I do not want kids to go through what I did."[10]

What exactly do such young people go through? Gold and coeditor Mindy Drucker offer not just stories but summaries of some key data. They include the following:

- Suicide is the third leading cause of death among fifteen- to twenty-four-year-olds, and for every kid who takes his or her own life, there are twenty more who try.

- Gay teens are four times more likely to attempt suicide than their heterosexual peers.

---

5. Ibid., 70.
6. Ibid.
7. Ibid., 72.
8. Ibid.
9. Ibid., 113.
10. Ibid., 115.

- Forty-five percent of gay men and 20 percent of lesbians surveyed had been victims of verbal and physical assaults in secondary school specifically because of their sexual orientation.
- Gay youth are at higher risk of being kicked out of their homes and turning to life on the streets for survival. Some engage in substance use and are more likely than heterosexual peers to start using tobacco, alcohol, and illegal drugs at an earlier age.
- Twenty-eight percent of gay students drop out of school, more than three times the national average for heterosexual students.[11]

All the stories in this volume focus on the particular problems faced by teenagers from religious families and congregations. Some of the stories are contemporary; others tell of long-ago hurts.

Jarrod Parker woke up one morning at Boy Scout camp (having apparently been drugged the night before) with the word "FAGGOT" written across his forehead, "a picture of a penis at the corner of my mouth," and further obscenities and pictures scrawled over his chest and back.[12] Jorge Valencia, who works at a teen crisis and suicide prevention hotline, recalls getting calls from youths whose parents had told them, "I would rather have a dead son than a gay son."[13] Rodney Powell, a black homosexual who marched during the civil rights movement, says: "I suffered more fear and numbing anxiety from my 'secret' as a teenager than I did from racism and segregation."[14]

Two of the stories are told by the parents of young adult children who died. Mary Lou Wallner lost her twenty-nine-year-old daughter Anna to suicide. Mary Lou was estranged from her daughter because of her inability to come to terms with her daughter's sexuality. Mary Lou writes that the last communication she had from her daughter was a letter that told her that "I was her mother only in a biological way, that I had done colossal damage to her soul with my shaming words, and that she did not want to, and did not have to, forgive me."[15] Mary Lou decided to "respect Anna's wishes and give her the space she was asking for."[16] The next communication she received was the news that Anna was dead.

11. Ibid., xx.
12. Ibid., 84.
13. Ibid., 119.
14. Ibid., 58.
15. Ibid., 302.
16. Ibid.

"What do I wish I'd done? What would I do now? Grab my toothpaste, credit card and car keys, jump in the car, drive to where she lives and tell her I love her no matter what. I did not do that, and now I never can."[17] Mary Lou Wallner and her husband now run an organization whose goal is to unite parents with their gay children.

Elke Kennedy was awakened at 4:30 in the morning with a call from a South Carolina hospital, where her twenty-year-old son Sean had been brought:

> When I finally got to see my son, my knees buckled. He was lying flat on his back, stitches on his upper lip, blood on his hair and neck, hooked up to a respirator. As I stood there holding his hand, he felt so cold. I wanted to hug him, to keep him warm. I kissed him, telling him I was there and that I loved him so much and to please wake up. I remember praying. A doctor came in and explained that the tests had revealed Sean had severe brain damage and his injuries were not survivable.[18]

What had happened to Sean? As he was leaving a bar, a man named Stephen Moller got out of the car and called Sean a faggot, "Then he punched Sean so hard he broke Sean's facial bones and separated his brain from his brain stem. Sean fell backward onto the pavement, and his brain ricocheted in his head."[19]

Sean died. Stephen Moller will apparently spend less than a year in jail.

Gold and his organization "Faith in America" believe that religious hostility is at the basis of violence against gays. If the problem is religion, then religion must change.

Religious groups have a First Amendment right to teach their convictions about homosexuality. By law, if they want to teach that homosexuality is wrong, that is their business. Gay advocates usually recognize this right while asking that traditional religious communities not bring such convictions into the public arena.

Gold takes a more confrontational tack. He believes that the heart of the issue is precisely what religious groups teach within their own walls and what religious families teach within their own homes. He pleads for an end to the "misuse of religion to harm gay people."

As an evangelical Christian whose career has been spent in the South, I must begin my response by saying this: It is scandalous that the most physically and psychologically dangerous place to be (or even appear to be)

17. Ibid.
18. Ibid., 308.
19. Ibid., 309.

gay or lesbian in America is in the most religiously conservative families, congregations, and regions of this country. Most often these are Christian contexts. Many of the worst stories in this volume come from the Bible Belt. This marks an appalling Christian moral failure.

In contrast to the love and mercy that Jesus exemplified, Christian communities offer young lesbians and gays hate and rejection. Sometimes that rejection is declared directly from the pulpit. But even when church leaders attempt to be more careful, to "hate the sin but love the sinner" in that hackneyed formulation, the love gets lost. Perhaps we need to focus on refining our ability to love; maybe we are not actually capable of compartmentalizing hate.

Christ's command that we love our neighbors, especially the most despised and rejected, means we must respond immediately to the crisis outlined in this book. Such love requires that we be vigilant about the impact not only of individual and congregational words and actions, but also that we consider seriously the broader ramifications of Christian activism that seeks to oppose all social advances for gay and lesbian people. Many Christians act as if opposing gays and lesbians is fundamental to the church's mission, which leads many gay and lesbian people to perceive Christianity as their mortal enemy. Is this how we want to be perceived?

Reading of the murder of Sean Kennedy in Greenville, South Carolina helps cement a conclusion for me: there is very likely a gap between what traditionalist church leaders may intend to say when they discuss biblical references to homosexuality or the issue of gay marriage and what those listening to them actually hear. Such discussions may inflame the less discerning in the pews and lead them toward hateful and contemptuous attitudes and behavior. We must be extraordinarily careful, especially in a polarized cultural climate.

We who are Christians must love our homosexual neighbors. We must treat them as we would want to be treated. We must remember that as we do to them, we do to Jesus (Matt 25:31ff.). We must oppose their harassment and bullying in schools, churches and clubs—everywhere. We must rebuke any Christian who speaks or acts hatefully toward gays and lesbians. We must teach Christian parents of gay children to communicate unconditional love and under no circumstances evict them from either their hearts or their homes, no matter what they believe about the moral significance of homosexual inclination. We must seek opportunities in the church to build relationships with those who so often have received Christian hatred.

Crisis tells the sad stories of dozens of young people who, like the biblical Esau, cried for a blessing from their parents, friends, and churches. How often they have not received it. How often they have been left broken, rejected as human beings—at the hands of Christians and in the name of the Bible. Obviously we must extend such basic acceptance, such human and Christian love.

But after reading these stories, it seems to me that Christians have something not just to give but to request from God and from the gays and lesbians among us. We need forgiveness.

13

What the Torture Debate Reveals about American Evangelical Christianity

2008

INTRODUCTION

THIS IS A PAPER about how American evangelical Christians responded in the days after American abuses of prisoners (euphemized as "detainees") held in the so-called war on terror were first disclosed. That disclosure began with the spring 2004 release of the degrading and obscene photos from Abu Ghraib prison in Iraq. The gradual leaking and forced publication of government documents over the ensuing four years, as well as journalistic efforts to reconstruct events and talk to those involved, revealed that decisive policy shifts by the United States government had occurred that led directly to the abuses at Abu Ghraib and elsewhere. Meanwhile, aided and abetted by the Bush Administration's evasive and unpersuasive half-denials of its own policies, a morally corrosive national debate about the morality of torture erupted. The Bush Administration officially denied that it tortured, and so did not officially enter the debate. But this did not prevent Christians and others from debating whether torture *per se* might in fact be morally permissible—with all too many believing even today that it can be justified at least some of the time. In a September 2008 poll of evangelicals sponsored by Faith in Public Life and Mercer University, 57 percent of southern evangelicals said that torture can be often (20 percent) or sometimes (37 percent) justified "in order to gain important information."[1]

1. Gushee, Zimmer, and Zimmer, *Religious Faith, Torture, and Our National Soul*, appendix.

My paper emerges from personal experience quite directly. I have been a participant in the events that I will describe, and cannot pretend to any kind of dispassion or distance. In 2006, the National Religious Campaign Against Torture (NRCAT) approached me, ethics colleague Glen Stassen of Fuller Seminary, evangelical scholar-activist Ron Sider of Palmer Seminary, and Rich Cizik (then Vice President for Governmental Affairs of the National Association of Evangelicals), to ask for our joint efforts to mobilize the evangelical community and to join their campaign to reverse Bush Administration detainee policies and end torture. For the last thirty months I have led the project that followed. Under the name of Evangelicals for Human Rights, we have partnered with NRCAT and a host of other human rights organizations to resist these policies and press for their reversal.

The election of Barack Obama and his promise (as yet only a promise) of decisive changes in American detainee policy along the lines we have pursued may mean that our efforts will come to a largely successful conclusion—this time. Thus it may be that this paper represents a kind of retrospective on lessons learned in a fight now about to be concluded. Even if this happy state of affairs turns out to be the case, there are indeed lessons to be learned—for it was indeed a fight, and even if we win the policy outcomes we seek, it is clear that very many evangelical Christians have directly supported or indirectly acquiesced to policies of cruelty and torture and would continue to do so if given the opportunity. Along the way, those who have opposed our efforts to reverse these policies have left written evidence of their views for scholars and historians to examine. I will cite some of this material in this chapter.

To signal my key conclusions in advance: the evidence shows that white evangelical Christians in the United States demonstrated during the torture debate the existence of profound theological and ethical confusions and that we/they often failed the test of fidelity to Jesus Christ. The torture debate revealed and widened fractures within our community that will probably prove irreparable. The split between those who excused torture, justified torture, or redefined-in-order-to-accept torture and those who refused to do any such thing, is deep and abiding. From my own perspective as an evangelical in the anti-torture camp, this issue represents something of a *status confessionis*; it was a Barmen moment for American evangelicals, when it became clear where one's ultimate loyalties truly could be found. There can be no return to the *status quo ante*.

This chapter will establish an analytical framework for these events by looking back to research I and others have undertaken related to "righteous Gentiles," those non-Jews, most of them Christians, who resisted the Nazi onslaught on the Jewish people during World War II by rescuing Jews from death. It will then narrate events and describe the two major documents emerging in the evangelical community in response to the torture debate. Next I will look at the major criticisms offered of our anti-torture efforts from within the evangelical community. A conclusion will reflect further on lessons learned.

THE RIGHTEOUS GENTILES PARADIGM

My own understanding of how individuals and societies, including people of faith, respond to the encroachment of government wrongdoing has been shaped profoundly by studying the righteous Gentiles. In my doctoral dissertation I examined the ways in which Europe's Christians responded to the Holocaust.[2] I wanted to know how the resources of Christian faith functioned (or failed to function) when Europe's Gentiles/Christians (beginning in Germany) discovered that their Jewish neighbors were being persecuted, deported, and annihilated by Nazi Germany. I was especially interested in learning about those who rescued Jews—those persons the Jewish community, drawing on its own tradition, decided to honor so beautifully as the "Righteous Gentiles of the Holocaust."

OBSTACLES TO RESISTANCE

Among the many things I learned from that study is that when governments misuse their massive power to violate the basic human rights of those caught in their grip, they have numerous built-in advantages over those forces of resistance that might come to be arrayed against them or on behalf of their victims.

They have an *informational advantage*, as only the government (actually, a relatively small number of persons within the government) actually know in detail what its policies are and how and where those policies are being implemented. Even in a society with a free press and a political opposition there will always be a time lag between the development and implementation of secret government policies and the public discovery of those policies. Thus any resistance will always be playing catch up, and operating on the basis of less than complete information—often information purposefully distorted by the government.

Governments also have an *authority advantage*, in that the presupposition of most ordinary citizens is that the government has both the right

---

2. Gushee, *The Righteous Gentiles of the Holocaust*.

and the obligation to undertake the policies it deems necessary to protect national security or advance the common good, and that citizens should trust government with that power.

Governments have an *intimidation advantage*, in that, if they choose, they can impose considerable costs on any individuals or groups within the society who might decide to resist their policies. In Nazi Germany, and Nazi-occupied Europe, such intimidation was a major factor inhibiting resistance. Most people are not terribly brave.

Finally, resisters have a *resistance-process disadvantage*. The process of moving into resistance—or into any active rendering of help to someone in need, even help that is minimally costly to the helper—is actually more cumbersome and elaborate than most of us imagine.

The resistance/helping process begins with *noticing that something is wrong or someone needs help*. This requires not only access to information, but also a character quality of basic attentiveness to realities outside the self, in particular, attentiveness to the injustices and miseries suffered by others, so that if information is available it will actually be noticed. This can be blocked by perpetrators who purposefully hide the wrong and the wronged, and by the self-centeredness or particular distractions and stresses faced by the potential helper.

Beyond noticing, the potential helper/resister must be able to *discern the significance* of what is noticed. At one level this is a moral judgment, rooted in the observer's worldview, character, moral values, and capacity for moral discernment, but many factors feed into that judgment. This perception of significance can be blocked by all kinds of factors, including, for example, perceptions of the worthiness of the persons needing help.

Once having discerned the significance of an event, an observer or potential helper must still somehow *shake off the inertia* created by their engagement with other people, problems, projects, interests, or concerns. They were headed in one direction and circumstances now suggest they must do something different. This directional shift rarely happens quickly.

One critical factor affecting whether that inertia is shaken is a sense of *personal responsibility to act*. I can notice a car accident and discern that it is a significant one, without then accepting that I have a *personal* responsibility to do something in response to it. There is a gap between the sense that "someone should do something here" to "I must do something here." Especially where there is no context for relationship between the victims and potential helpers, this sense of personal responsibility can be quite attenuated. If the victim is perceived in advance as a stranger, alien, or enemy, the development of a sense of personal responsibility to aid that victim will be even less likely.

Once sensing a personal responsibility to act or help, still further steps are required. The ones sensing that responsibility must believe that they have the capacity to act in a constructive way. This sense of *efficacy*, which many lack in the most basic aspects of everyday life, must then be coupled with the capacity to *develop a plan* of action. There is yet one more step from developing such a plan of action to *actually executing it*. Resisters soon learned during the Holocaust that against such massive state-sponsored evil they needed not only such an implemented personal plan of resistance but also the resources available through *networks of resistance*. These then needed to be discovered, or developed. It is easy to see that many ordinary human beings lack the needed efficacy, strategic sense, follow-through, and networking skills.

Finally, resistance must be *sustained* over whatever length of time is required to aid the victims and end the wrong being done to them. In the case of Christians resisting Nazis in Germany or in occupied Europe, this took as long as twelve years (as many as four to six years in occupied areas). Many began rescuing Jews but could not sustain the effort due to the fear of discovery by the Nazis, the costs of rescue, or both. Those of us who have extended ourselves in less demanding ways to friends or family members will understand the limits of human energy and courage even in causes that we believe in and with people that we love deeply.

For all of these reasons, it was sadly predictable that civilian resistance and rescue of Jews was able to help save only a relatively small number of Jews, perhaps 250,000 out of seven million. The great majority of European Christians proved to be *bystanders*, neither helping the Nazis nor helping the Jews. A relatively small number of perpetrators killed a large number of victims, against the backdrop of a massive number of bystanders, with resistance offered by a small number of rescuers—perhaps one-half of 1 percent of the Christian population.

These structural factors inhibiting resistance most often prove far more powerful than the resources provided by religious faith. Those of us who are hopeful about the impact of our weekly preaching and teaching in church or synagogue will be sobered or even driven to despair by these hard facts. We will never give up our belief in the significance of what we do. But we dare not forget what we are up against.

TORTURE, RESISTANCE, AND EVANGELICAL CHRISTIANS

In drawing on events in the Nazi era I am not saying that Nazi genocide and American prisoner abuses are morally equivalent. But I do contend that the same basic pattern has characterized the *response* of American evangelical Christians to the use of torture and cruelty by our government in these years. Probably a similar analysis could be undertaken of the sluggish religious, Christian, or evangelical response to a number of issues in this or other nations, historically or today. Let me consider certain relevant parallels.

Informational Advantage and Time Lag

First there was the government's information advantage and thus a predictable time lag in developing any kind of response. There was a gap of more than two years between the development of now clearly documented secret new government interrogation policies in late 2001/early 2002 and the coincidental discovery of the abuses at Abu Ghraib in 2004.[3] Once again, government had a head start over those who would check its behavior, and has retained an *informational advantage* as the Bush Administration has sought to keep its paper trail as hidden as possible.

After Abu Ghraib's unveiling, evangelical Christian leaders (in key pastorates, parachurch organizations, denominational offices, and academia) remained almost universally silent. Undoubtedly most accepted the government's contention that the abuses at Abu Ghraib were the unfortunate acts of a few bad apples frolicking on the night shift—as they were originally described by the Bush Administration.[4] They had no way of knowing then—and still show little sign of accepting now—that at least some of the acts of cruelty, torture, and degradation that took place at Abu Ghraib (and elsewhere) were explicitly authorized by officials within the Bush Administration. This claim, long central to the anti-torture movement, has now been so widely verified by documentary evidence that it cannot be denied.[5]

George Hunsinger, the insightful theologian-activist from Princeton Seminary, deserves great credit for moving in 2005 to plan the Princeton Seminary torture conference (which took place in January 2006) and then for bringing to birth the National Religious Campaign Against Torture

---

3. Mayer, *The Dark Side*, 86.
4. Carter, "A Few Bad Apples?"
5. "Report on Detainee Treatment."

(NRCAT) in 2006. Even here, though, the time lag factor is evident, as we see a gap of four years from the development of torture policies to the formation of a religious resistance organization. Still, by early 2006 the religious counterattack on detainee abuse had begun.

The Beginnings of Evangelical Resistance to Bush Policies

The first evangelical effort to deal with torture as a moral problem, as far as I know, was launched by our community's flagship magazine *Christianity Today* (CT) in late 2005 when its editors asked me to write a cover story on the morality of torture. It is most interesting to note that requests from evangelicals serving in American military and intelligence services for moral guidance in dealing with their troubling orders helped to motivate CT to seek out this article. Afterwards, I actually heard from a former Guantanamo prosecutor, Marine Lieutenant Colonel Stuart Couch, about his experiences and appreciation for my article in his quest for moral clarity about the moral choices he was facing at Guantanamo. Couch became well-known for his faith-based moral revulsion to US detainee policies.[6]

My article, which came out in February 2006, argued unequivocally that torture is "always wrong." It can be seen as launching the evangelical anti-torture movement.[7] I gave five reasons why torture is wrong: because it violates human dignity and the *imago dei*, mistreats the powerless and thus violates government's mandate to do justice especially toward the most vulnerable, trusts government too much (giving it a power no government should have), invites the dehumanization of not just the tortured but the torturer, and erodes the character of the nation that tortures. My original draft added a sixth reason, that torture brings negative consequences that far exceed any purported positive benefits, but this was cut.[8]

As I look back on this initial article, I regret a lack of significant Christocentric argumentation. I ended the article with reference to Jesus the tortured, crucified Savior. But in an effort to speak to an evangelical community that is often quite suspicious of "sectarian" appeals to the model of Jesus and the radical demands of discipleship and very much attracted to arguments based on government's mandate to use the sword to protect the innocent, I avoided grounding my argument in Jesus Christ in any thoroughgoing or explicit way. I am now persuaded that while there were good tactical reasons for this approach, it is precisely our inadequate Christocentrism

6. Bravin, "The Conscience of the Colonel," A1.
7. Gushee, "Five Reasons Why Torture Is Always Wrong," 33–37.
8. Gushee, "Against Torture: An Evangelical Perspective," 349–64.

and Christomorphism that lie at the heart of our theological and ethical weakness as a religious community. Jesus Christ must be moved from the margins to the center of American evangelical ethics and public theology.

The Evangelical Declaration Against Torture

Evangelicals for Human Rights (EHR) was midwifed by NRCAT in the summer of 2006. We established as our initial task the drafting of a substantive group statement against torture, involving key leaders throughout our community. We decided to aim for the approval of our statement by the National Association of Evangelicals (NAE), America's leading umbrella organization that can be said to represent the diffuse but massive evangelical community. The lengthy document, eventually named "An Evangelical Declaration Against Torture: Protecting Human Rights in an Age of Terror," was released and simultaneously approved overwhelmingly by the board of the NAE in March 2007.[9] I served as the principal drafter of this document.

The argument of this essay is more elaborate than that in my original CT article. We made the choice to dig a deeper theological foundation for opposition to torture by grounding that stance in a thoroughgoing commitment to the sanctity of human life, which is then rooted with reference to a range of sources across the canon and to recent Catholic articulations of a comprehensive understanding of life's sanctity (section 2). Then we affixed an articulation and defense of a Christian commitment to human rights on both the foundation of the sanctity of life and on a long history of Christian commitment to such rights (sections 3–4).

We next moved to assign individual, ecclesial, and governmental responsibilities for the defense of human rights (section 5). We zeroed in on our policy goals by turning to international and domestic treaties, conventions, and laws that protect human rights and, in particular, offer complete bans on torture (section 6). Internationally, these include the Geneva Conventions, the UN Convention Against Torture, and the UN International Covenant on Civil and Political Rights. Domestically, we cited the fifth, eighth, and fourteenth amendments, the 1996 War Crimes Act, and the US Army Field Manual.

We suggested that the United States government had violated our nation's long history of leadership on behalf of human rights by systematically weakening such protections for detainees held in the war on terror (section 6.7–6.14). We concluded by renouncing any use of torture or cruel, inhuman, and degrading treatment of prisoners held by the United States, and

---

9. Chapter 10 in this volume.

calling "for the legislative or judicial reversal of those executive and legislative provisions" that violate the terms of the Geneva Conventions and basic human rights and procedural protections (7.12). We wait in hope today for the fulfillment of this call made now almost two years ago.

For those who knew the white evangelical community, the approval of this statement by the National Association of Evangelicals, and the endorsement of the statement by hundreds of leaders within our community, came as a considerable shock. Some were happily shocked. Others were far less happy. Historians and sociologists of American evangelicalism will one day examine the signatories on this statement for insights about the significance of who joined and who did not.

My own observation is that the signers and drafters included key representatives of almost every part of the white evangelical community, and leaders from Hispanic and African-American evangelicalism. But it did not include signatures from any leading officials and organizations of the Christian Right: Focus on the Family, Christian Coalition, Family Research Council, American Family Association, Prison Fellowship, etc. It was rejected bitterly by the Institute for Religion and Democracy, whose representative on the NAE board cast the lone dissenting vote. It did not include any leading figures in the Southern Baptist Convention, the nation's largest Protestant denomination. And it was from these groups that the counterattacks soon came.

At a superficial political level, the split between those who signed and those who did not can be viewed along political-ideological lines. The evangelical political right did not sign; the evangelical political center and left did. The same right vs. center and left breakdown has been visible on other recent issues, most notably climate change. This pattern helped inspire me to write my most recent book, *The Future of Faith in American Politics*, which suggests that there is an emerging evangelical center that is competing with the right for the hearts and minds of American evangelicals.[10] The fracture between these parts of the evangelical community is obvious and may be irreparable.

But of course the limits of these categories are quite profound. Entrusting the government with the power to torture those it detains is hardly "conservative" in any understanding of democratic political theory rooted in a commitment to limited government. Enabling government officials to evade statutory law by presidential fiat cannot be seen as conservative in terms of commitment to democratic or American principles. Deeper

---

10. Gushee, *The Future of Faith in American Politics*.

realities are at work, both politically and in terms of the dynamics of the Christian community.

Evangelical Opposition and Defenses of Bush Policies

The opposition that our coalition against torture has received from within the evangelical community has been astonishing, and at times astonishingly harsh. These critics do not accept that the government has authorized any wrongdoing in its policies or treatment of prisoners. We are deemed to be wrong for our stance against these policies—factually, theologically, morally, politically wrong. The following main lines of argumentation have been offered as counterattacks to our work against Bush counterterrorism policies:

(1) Those who oppose Bush counterterror and detainee policies are politically motivated "leftists."[11]

(2) Those who oppose these policies are pacifists-in-disguise who do not support the legitimate use of force to defend our country.[12]

(3) Torture is a much worse problem around the world, and especially on the part of the very terrorists we are capturing. That is where those worried about it should focus their attention. Failure to pay proper attention to such problems reveals that opponents are at least anti-Bush, if not anti-American.[13]

(4) The evangelical anti-torture movement is divisive within the Christian community and should be dropped on grounds of Christian unity; besides, there are far more important concerns facing us.[14]

(5) The struggle against Islamist terrorism is a new kind of war requiring new means.[15]

(6) Terrorists are not protected by international law and its conventions.[16]

(7) Those in the anti-torture movement have failed to define torture adequately.[17]

11. Tooley, "The Evangelical Left's Nazi Obsession."
12. Ibid.
13. Ibid.
14. Heimbach cited in Roach, "Ethicist: NAE Torture Declaration 'Irrational.'"
15. Mayer, *The Dark Side*, 34; Mohler, "Torture and the War on Terror."
16. Pavlischek, "Human Rights and Justice."
17. Ibid.

(8) Just war theory permits considerable coercion in defense of national security, the protection of which is government's primary responsibility.[18]

(9) Any argument made about torture that is not offered within just war theory's canons of argumentation is by definition invalid. Our work approaching torture via a sanctity-of-life argument is overly emotive and even irrational.[19]

(10) Some argue that torture (narrowly defined) should be banned and not employed; others argue that it should be banned in principle but possibly applied in emergency circumstances with later accountability.[20]

The Problem of Evangelical Authoritarianism

In the space of this paper I cannot attempt a comprehensive response to all of these criticisms. My purpose here is rather to offer reflections on what they reveal about American evangelicalism. I will seek to do so with reference to the categories discussed earlier in relation to the obstacles hindering resistance to misuse of government authority in the case of anti-Nazi resistance during World War II.

I believe that evangelicals consistently prove susceptible to what I earlier called government's *authority advantage*. The latter is especially strong in our particular faith community for several reasons. One is that many white evangelicals have been schooled on Reformation-era readings of the biblical text Romans 13:1–7 that tend toward a high degree of respect for, trust in, and subordination under, government authority, especially in its exercise of the "sword," that is, state violence.

This is related to a broader evangelical authoritarianism also apparent in understandings of family and church life. The pattern is that all authorities are viewed as having been put into place by God, as answerable primarily or only to God, and as existing fundamentally to secure order through coercion. This sets up at least an intrinsic bias against challenging the decisions of those in authority, of instituting legal and moral systems that check centralized power, or of establishing anything like a true "last resort" bias against the use of coercion or violence.

It seems to me that evangelicals are among the last bearers of a Christian approach to structures of authority and especially government power

18. Ibid.
19. Heimbach cited in Roach, "Ethicist: NAE Torture Declaration 'Irrational.'"
20. Mohler, "Torture and the War on Terror."

that is characterized by deep pessimism about uncoerced human nature, an understanding of government's primary role to be securing the state from dangerous enemies, a strong belief in the perennial need for government's use of "the sword," or coercive power, and a tendency to defer to government leaders in their privileged and demanding decision-making related to the use of such power. One might say that evangelicals are still reading Luther, Calvin, and the just war/just force tradition without reference to lessons that might have been learned in the intervening 500 years.

My "side" is often derided for referring to the Nazi era, as if we have been equating George W. Bush with Adolf Hitler.[21] That has not been our purpose, and one might think intelligent readers might recognize the intended limits of historical analogies and examples. But the Nazi era does provide relevant insights related to the shadow side of every claim made by the older Protestant traditions on the use of coercive power by governments. It is hard to study the Hitler regime, or any other evil regime of the twentieth century, without seeing the dangers of a militarized national-security state, a state all too ready to wield the sword, and a state in which deference to or intimidation by government leaders resulted in mass violations of human rights.

The Christian ethical tradition is not, and must not be, set in stone. It did not end with Luther's essay on secular authority or Calvin's treatment of Romans 13. There are other ways of addressing issues of state power and violence, and just war/just force theories themselves have undergone considerable development under the impact of our world's recent horrors.[22] Here, ironically, evangelicals who claim a high commitment to biblical authority actually prove unwilling to hear a fresh word from Scripture or perhaps fresh winds of the Spirit. Nothing seems capable of penetrating their encrusted commitment to the authority of a particular ethical tradition related to the use of force by government. It also leads them to deride any other methodology for addressing an ethical issue like torture other than the refined casuistry associated with their version of just war theory.

Another authority-related factor specific to events of recent years is that the particular administration that altered longstanding American policies on torture has been Republican, conservative, and has been led by the "evangelical" president, George W. Bush, a favorite of white evangelicals even now.

Many of the criticisms leveled at our efforts against these detainee policies can be traced to this fundamental question of loyalty. Charging

---

21. Tooley, "The Evangelical Left's Nazi Obsession."
22. Chapter 3 in this volume.

us with being politically motivated, or of being leftists, is a way for our adversaries to try to dismiss even the possibility that a conscience-driven resistance to a Bush Administration policy could be anything other than a partisan strategy. It helps our case that many who have been most opposed to these policies are veterans of Republican administrations and even of this particular administration, which is one reason why we know about internal administration deliberations even now—those who opposed the policies sometimes contacted the press. But the existence of Republican opposition to Bush policies has not been persuasive for some of our critics. The inability of some evangelical Christians to disentangle loyalty to Christ from loyalty to the Republican Party or the president signals a profound corruption of fidelity to Christ.

The Problem of Noticing and Discerning Significance

In terms of the dynamics of the resistance process, white evangelicals proved especially unable to notice the transition to policies of torture and especially the moral significance of that transition. For conservative white evangelicals, a generation of treating Christian public witness as focused entirely on the "life and family" issues such as abortion and homosexuality systematically hid other moral issues from view. It has taken a major fight within evangelicalism for the evangelical center-left to gain much ground with the claim that a broad human dignity and common good agenda is more biblical than a narrow abortion and homosexuality agenda. Every time proponents of a broader agenda think the issue is settled, we hit another setback, as in the recent forced removal of Rich Cizik as Vice President of NAE.[23]

This helps to account for the criticisms we have received related to our efforts supposedly distracting evangelicals from more important issues and dividing the church. For many leading conservative evangelicals, attention to any issue other than abortion and homosexuality is by definition a distraction from the core moral values agenda of "the church." It is also defined as "divisive," which essentially means that it prevents evangelical unity around the agenda defined by the Right as appropriate for evangelicals. Those of us who have worked on both issues can easily recall receiving the exact same criticism when working on climate change.

Overcoming this systematic evangelical self-blinding to issues beyond "family values," narrowly understood, and pushing evangelicals to a broader moral vision are important projects for many progressive evangelicals. Part of that broader theological-ethical work, as I see it, must be to offer a richly

23. Pulliam, "Richard Cizik Resigns."

biblical and theological account of the sanctity of all human life, a moral norm that remains at least rhetorically important to millions of evangelicals (and Catholics). Articulating a broad understanding of life's sanctity is both morally constructive and strategically fruitful for strengthening evangelical public theology and ethics.[24] It is the approach we adopted in the "Evangelical Declaration Against Torture" with some success.

Perhaps this focus on life's majestic dignity before God also can root an organically evangelical strengthening of commitment to human rights. Despite a biblical record full of the demand for justice and the affirmation of human dignity, despite the commitment to justice and human rights of the Radical Reformers, despite the nineteenth-century evangelical reform groups that fought for abolition, women's rights, and the rights of workers, despite the civil rights movement anchored in the highly evangelical black churches, and despite a flowering of contemporary grassroots evangelical advocacy efforts for justice, many white evangelicals still have no feel for justice or human rights as biblical norms. This has left us with weak antennae for sensing injustices, and weak motivation for protesting injustices, in society—or for that matter, in our own churches. What an incredible tragedy that evangelicals lost touch with their own tradition and with the broader Christian tradition, and with such horrifying implications. Part of the new reformation needed among us is a deep entrenchment of a human rights ethic so that it can never be displaced under the pressure of partisanship or security concerns.

Intimidation and the Bystander Phenomenon

I argued earlier that government has an intimidation advantage, due to its great power over the lives of its citizens. Certainly it has become clear by now that intimidation was used to stifle dissent from within the Bush Administration to its detainee policies.[25] But it also became clear in evangelical life during these years that the evangelical power structure also has an intimidation advantage. Good standing among conservative white evangelicals has been to some extent tied to loyalty to the Republican Party and, from 2001–2009, loyalty to the good friend of evangelicals in the White House. Those who dissent from such loyalty in any significant way have risked their standing among the evangelical power structure. Nothing that I personally have done in the last eight years has enraged politically conservative evangelicals more than my criticisms of Bush Administration policy, leaving me

24. Gushee, *The Sacredness of Human Life*.
25. Mayer, *The Dark Side*.

to wonder whether political loyalty rather than, say, commitment to biblical truth, has come to function as the ultimate test of (conservative) evangelical identity.

This power of intimidation became most obvious to me in the process of pressing for signatures on our declaration against torture, and on later documents. Often my team discovered highly placed evangelicals who expressed support for our efforts but calculated that they dare not go public (or not go public more than once) on this particular issue due to the problems it would create for them. I came once again to see the relevance of the categories discovered and developed in the work on the righteous Gentiles. One of those categories is the sympathetic bystander, who wants to do something to help but ultimately is too frightened to do anything. I have encountered many such bystanders in recent years. Remember that these were not Republican political appointees, but parachurch executives, mission agency leaders, Christian university administrators, academics, and pastors. They were intimidated by the fierce political loyalties in their particular organizations, or in the broader evangelical world in which they wanted to retain good standing.

The Perceived Worthiness of the Victims of Injustice

I noted earlier that a perception of the relative worthiness of the victims of injustice affects whether potential rescuers become actual ones. This is closely related to whether the potential helper has any context for knowing or caring about those whom government is mistreating. Christians were most likely to rescue Jews in Nazi Europe if they had Jewish friends whose fate mattered to them. This made Jews not strangers or aliens but friends and "neighbors," worthy and valuable human beings.

It is clear to me from the nature of conservative evangelical discourse about Islam and terrorism that many evangelicals after 9/11 perceived Islam as an intrinsically dangerous or even demonic religion and Muslims as the enemy of both America and Christianity, as the international cultural Other. In the environment of post-9/11 fear, anger, and grief it was hard to find many evangelicals who could generate much sympathy for suspected Muslim terrorists; they readily acceded to the weakening of human rights protections against people who were so deeply alien to them. Some derided concerns about the mistreatment of detainees as wimpy multiculturalism.[26]

All too few evangelicals had any preexisting context of ongoing friendships with Muslims, and conversations between leaders of the two faiths at

---

26. Tooley, "The Evangelical Left's Nazi Obsession."

the national and international levels were rare. Dealing with the "otherness" of Christians and Muslims from each other is the extremely important goal of those Muslims and Christians who are attempting the urgent work of dialogue and mutual friendship, such as in the "Common Word" process begun by Muslim leaders working now in partnership with leaders at Yale Divinity School.[27] Clearly, much work must be done for evangelicals to come to see the Muslims indefinitely detained at Guantanamo and elsewhere as their neighbors.

CONCLUSION

Both at the leadership and the grassroots level, evangelicals were slow to notice government abuses of prisoners or to sustain attention to these problems once forced to notice. We were and remain confused and divided in our moral judgments of practices such as waterboarding, stress positions, and sexual humiliation. Many who did notice, and felt uncomfortable with what they were hearing, felt little or no personal responsibility to do anything about it or were afraid to get involved due to negative ramifications for their careers. The issue—shamefully—did not have an appreciable effect on how evangelicals voted in 2004 and was not treated as a "moral values" issue. When a group of evangelicals mobilized against torture in 2006, we made considerable headway but also gained intense resistance from within our own community, with opponents who simply could not believe that criticism of a Bush Administration policy could be morally rather than politically motivated. Once again our instinctive political conservatism and authoritarianism, and our narrow understanding of "moral values," betrayed us.

But it seems to me that the acquiescence and silence of many leading evangelicals to torture has helped finally to discredit these evangelical leaders. If our faith's leaders can't figure out that psychologically and sometimes physically destroying people (often innocent people) is immoral, we need some new leaders. I think that shifts happening in the evangelical community right now bear witness that new leadership is in fact emerging, especially among younger evangelicals. But the road is long and rocky.

What did the torture debate reveal about American evangelical Christianity? That government has incredible power to do wrong and must be watched vigilantly and resisted forcefully when it strays, and that American evangelicals are not well prepared to do that, at least not when the president comes from our favored party. It revealed that evangelicals have gaps and

---

27. www.acommonword.com

weaknesses in our public theology, and in our public leaders, that proved fateful in limiting our resistance to the government injustice of state torture. It demonstrated that our combination of an archaic and an acculturated social ethic in relation to government's use of coercive power is hugely dangerous.

But this sad debate also shows that we have resources in our theology, and in some of our leaders, that can help us do better. The most important of these resources is a passionate commitment to the person and work of Jesus Christ. Some evangelicals, at least, operated from the recognition that the gracious Savior whose forgiveness we claim is also the sovereign Lord who demands our entire lives, who taught justice and mercy, who requires our setting aside of all ideologies, loyalties, and fears that hinder our faithfulness to his will, and demands our embodied love for the enemy, the alien, and the abandoned of the earth.

When the actions of these last seven years are finally and fully reviewed and weighed; when, as is anticipated, Bush administration officials face accountability for their actions even up to the point of criminal sanctions;[28] one can dare to hope that evangelical Christians who defended these cruel and abusive policies will face their own kind of accountability.

---

28. Horton, "Justice After Bush," 49–60.

14

Scripture, Government, and the World's Poor

2010

INTRODUCTION

THIS ESSAY OFFERS A sketch of a biblical theology regarding the normative role of government in addressing global poverty.

First, we will talk about not just government in general but the United States government in particular. That introduces certain contextual realities that will affect the approach that we take. Second, we will talk not just about the role of government in addressing global poverty but specifically about the role of the government in global foreign assistance. Third, we will talk about the role of Christian citizens and churches in advocating for the United States government to be involved in global foreign assistance. It is our view that this movement from abstractness to concreteness will produce both a more realistic and a more significant treatment of this critically important subject.

The difficulty of developing a Christian moral vision for global governmental foreign assistance is aptly captured in these insightful comments from Douglas Hicks and Mark Valeri, in their book *Global Neighbors*:

> Our traditional Christian moral norms about economic life presuppose face-to-face economic interaction. *Commutative* justice involves fairness in the person-to-person exchange of goods;

distributive justice involves very tangible laws about aiding impoverished persons within one's own community. Even when the apostle Paul speaks about aiding other Christian communities, he is able to speak in detail on a first-person basis about visiting and corresponding with those persons. *Traditional Christian morality in economic life is based on interpersonal relations among neighbors, but our contemporary global economy is based on impersonal exchanges around the world.*[1]

Hicks and Valeri are correct in pointing to two great difficulties here. One is that biblical moral exhortations related to economic ethics were addressed primarily within specific faith communities to direct the behavior of those communities. The second is that these biblical exhortations generally involved territories no bigger than the tiny land of Israel or the budding faith communities of the Greco-Roman world. We face significant challenges in properly employing biblical economic ethics to apply to the United States government and to a political economic context in which every local economic exchange simultaneously participates in the vast web of the global economy.

But these challenges cannot be evaded. Our approach will begin by considering briefly what we understand global foreign assistance to mean. Part II prepares for the normative discussion of US foreign assistance by describing the many ways the United States government already relates to and impacts the world's poor. In Part III we sketch a biblical theology of the role of government. Finally, Part IV explores a theology of Christian citizenship and the role of advocacy within citizenship.

PART I: THE NATURE AND GOALS OF GLOBAL FOREIGN ASSISTANCE PROGRAMS

We will define global foreign assistance here as *efforts undertaken by national governments to foster economic development and alleviate poverty in other nations.* In this sense, such foreign assistance can be distinguished from the efforts undertaken by nongovernmental organizations (NGOs), and from multinational efforts to alleviate poverty, such as those undertaken by the United Nations.

Global foreign assistance involves both responses to short-term *humanitarian* crises and efforts to advance long-term economic *development*. A repertoire of best practices employed in both short-term and long-term foreign assistance can be identified and is always under reconsideration

1. Hicks and Valeri, *Global Neighbors*, xix.

based on successes or failures. For long-term foreign assistance, this repertoire includes such measures as debt forgiveness, efforts to increase agricultural productivity, programs to encourage entrepreneurship and job creation, women's empowerment projects, healthcare advances, educational assistance, and so on.

In 1970, the United Nations General Assembly approved a resolution affirming that wealthier industrialized nations should give .7 percent of their GNP to fight poverty.[2] This has remained a kind of global standard. It seems like a tiny amount but is always hotly contested, not least in our own nation. For 2007, .7 percent of GDP in the United States would have amounted to $102 billion. By contrast, our nation's actual foreign assistance budget in 2007 was $28.9 billion. Though still larger than any other country's assistance budget, this figure was less than one-third of that target, not all of it devoted clearly to poverty alleviation and much of it deeply affected by immediate political and security concerns. (The United States also provided $13 billion in military aid to other countries in 2007.) The foreign aid levels proposed in legislation before the Senate (S.1524) would cost $2 per American from 2010–2014. This does help to contextualize our essay—we are asking about the theological rationale for whether and how our government should invest .7% of our Gross National Product on global foreign assistance.

The primary goal of global foreign assistance, advocates agree, should be poverty reduction via economic development. Global foreign assistance advocates ask self-interested nations to devote a (tiny) percentage of their national wealth to the altruistic task of helping the poor of other nations. This poses the interesting theoretical problem of why intrinsically self-interested nations would ever spend a penny toward the poor of other nations. But advocates of US foreign assistance readily respond that "development and poverty reduction abroad are . . . both moral imperatives and prerequisites for sustained US national security."[3] The economic self-interest of the United States is also benefited by the expansion of markets and economic opportunities abroad as nations rise from poverty and are integrated into the global economy.

The text of Senate bill 1524[4] (section three, lines 17–23), claims that "(1) Poverty, hunger, lack of opportunity, gender inequality, and environmental degradation are recognized as significant contributors to (A) socioeconomic and political instability; and (B) the exacerbation of disease

---

2. UN General Assembly Resolution 2626, October 1970.
3. "New Day, New Way," i.
4. Foreign Assistance Revitalization and Accountability Act of 2009.

pandemics and other global health threats." In other words, this very solid foreign assistance bill links global poverty to the self-interest of the United States in avoiding the exposure of its people to global health problems and in preventing the disruption and destabilizing of the international order.

The international moral reputation of the United States constitutes one aspect of our profile in the world. A better moral reputation wins more friends and weakens more enemies of our nation than does a worse moral reputation. Assuming that the perception of altruism on the part of our nation toward the world's poor will enhance our international moral reputation, US foreign assistance can also be situated clearly within national self-interest.

To summarize our claims so far: Our topic is the Christian theological ethics of US foreign assistance. US foreign assistance involves our nation's relatively small amount of funding of efforts to assist the world's poor, on the basis of a mixture of altruistic concern for suffering people and realistic calculations about the impact of global poverty and of our nation's perceived generosity on the national interests of the United States. We are asking about a biblical theology related to this reality.

PART II: HOW THE UNITED STATES GOVERNMENT IMPACTS THE WORLD'S POOR EVERY DAY

Given the massive economic and political power of the United States, and given the fact of economic globalization, the United States and its government impact the world's poor every day. Any adequate ethical discussion of global foreign assistance requires that we face this fact. Once we do, the question becomes not *whether* the United States should seek to have an impact on global poverty, but how Christian citizens might press our government to have the *least bad or best available* impact on the world's poor. We cannot hide behind theoretical abstractions that are belied by the facts. What follows is a brief non-specialist exposition of ways that our government's policies already affect the poor of the two-thirds world.

Globalization connects everybody

Whatever one's definition of globalization—as primarily economic or political or cultural—or one's opinion of it—as primarily healthy or harmful or homogenizing—the world is increasingly interconnected. In a trend that has been accelerating inexorably at least since the days of western colonialism, globalization connects everybody. As Cavanagh and Mander put it:

> The fusion of politics and economics has gone beyond national boundaries, and national governments are increasingly integrated into a transnational system of power distribution of which transnational corporations and supranational organisms like the World Trade Organization are other significant components.[5]

Coming to terms with globalization requires overcoming a certain kind of innocence in relation either to Christian theological ethics or to the role of the United States in the world. There is no available Edenic Garden in which the United States could remain isolated from the world, which includes the world's poor. Therefore there is little point in asking a theological question about a world that does not exist, a world in which the United States is not already impacting the world's poor each day. The following are several primary examples of the nature of our government's daily impact on global economic life and therefore the life of the poor.

The International Economic Regime

Since World War II, international economic relations have been heavily influenced if not dominated by the United States. The World Bank and International Monetary Fund help to set the terms of global trade and are led by the United States and the other wealthy nations. The policies of these organizations tend to favor an understanding of "free trade" as well as development policies that benefit the interests of the United States and its powerful allies. As disillusioned former World Bank Chief Economist Joseph Stiglitz has written, "The institutions [IMF and World Bank] are dominated not just by the wealthiest industrial countries but by commercial and financial interests in those countries, and the policies of the institutions naturally reflect this."[6]

Agricultural Subsidies and Tariffs

In the 1980s and 1990s the World Bank and IMF pressured two-thirds world countries to lower tariffs and cut domestic farm support programs

---

5. Cavanagh and Mander, *Alternatives to Economic Globalization*, 265.
6. Stiglitz, *Globalization and Its Discontents*, 19.

as part of economic liberalization. Meanwhile, under the pressure of entrenched political constituencies the United States government continues to pay massive agricultural subsidies to its own farmers, many of them large agribusinesses, and keeps agricultural tariffs high. The subsidies allow the US to export goods cheaply and the tariffs raise the prices of goods coming especially from developing countries.

Cotton makes for an interesting example of these problems. Between 2003 and 2005, cotton was the second highest US-subsidized commodity at $7 billion.[7] According to Oxfam International, a complete removal of US cotton subsidies would increase the worldwide price of cotton by 6–14 percent.[8] In African countries, these US cotton subsidies mean a loss of more than $350 million in potential revenue.[9] In countries where people survive on less than $1 per day, $350 million is no small amount. Our cotton subsidy policies hurt the poorest of the world.

World Trade Organization Policies

Or consider the World Trade Organization (WTO), which was formed in 1994 and replaced the old GATT trade contract. Under the rules of the WTO, no member of the WTO can maintain measures that restrict or distort trade. Basically, this eliminates a country's ability to ensure national interests by shaping foreign investment. In other words, all 153 countries of the WTO are at the mercy of trade rules that the WTO deems appropriate. Many critical observers conclude that these rules benefit the already wealthy nations such as the United States, and the world's most powerful businesses, and certainly harm poorer nations and people.

One example of a problematic WTO policy is TRIPs, or Trade-Related Intellectual Property Rights. Under the auspices of promoting and protecting creativity, and with strong US support, the WTO added this intellectual property protection to its mandate. Under TRIPs, seed patenting laws have meant that corporations can lay claim to their genetically engineered seeds as "intellectual property rights." This is problematic because seeds are not inanimate; they are alive and cannot be contained in one specific field. Monsanto actually hires detectives to find farmers who might be engaging in the traditional practice of seed-saving.[10] This is relevant to our discus-

7. "Top Commodity and Conservation Programs in United States, program years 2003–2005."
8. "Burkina Faso: Cotton Story."
9. "Bumper subsidy crop for US cotton producers: African farmers suffer."
10. Cavanagh and Mander, *Alternatives to Economic Globalization*, 116.

sion because TRIPs are beginning to impact people in the two-thirds world. Pharmaceutical companies are patenting seed varieties and plant properties that have been used for centuries in India.[11] In addition, TRIPs make it difficult for two-thirds world countries to copy drug formulas and make their own cheaper versions of life-saving drugs.[12] Recent efforts to revise the TRIPs rules on behalf of poorer nations have frequently been undercut in bilateral trade agreements involving the United States, which have actually added additional requirements under US pressure.[13]

These kinds of inequities in international economic relations lead Joseph Stiglitz to say the following:

> Undoubtedly, some pain was necessary [for economic development]; but in my judgment, the level of pain in developing countries created in the process of globalization and development as it has been guided by the IMF and the international economic organizations has been far greater than necessary. The backlash against globalization draws its force not only from the perceived damage done to developing countries by policies driven by ideology but also from the inequities in the global trading system.[14]

Multinational Corporations

As of 2000, of the one hundred largest economies in the world, only forty nine were countries, while fifty-one were corporations.[15] In the same year, United States corporations made up the majority of the top two hundred economies, with a total of eighty two, over 40 percent.[16] There is much that can be said here, but at least this: corporations of this size and strength have the power to affect the world's poor in countless ways, and the United States government has a vested national interest in advancing its most powerful corporations.

---

11. Ibid., 117.
12. Munoz, "More than Aid: Partnership for Development," 5.
13. Ibid., 5–6.
14. Stiglitz, *Globalization and Its Discontents*, xv.
15. Anderson and Cavanagh, "Top 200: The Rise of Corporate Global Power," 3.
16. Ibid.

The US Military Presence

The United States has by far the most powerful, expensive, and far-flung military in the world. With an official military budget of $513 billion dollars in fiscal year 2009,[17] with US troops in 152 countries,[18] with a navy sailing in all of the world's oceans, the US affects the world's poor every day through the use of our military to advance our nation's perceived foreign policy goals and economic interests.

Consider this fact: of the twenty poorest countries in the world, the United States has troops or military basing rights in sixteen of those countries.[19] The purpose of the US military in those countries is manifestly not to alleviate poverty. While foreign policy and counterterrorism strategy may at times call for economic development efforts, this is not why our troops are based in the world's poorest nations, and foreign assistance advocates argue that these efforts often undercut actual poverty alleviation and economic development strategies in the long term.

Let us summarize our claims in this section. Our theoretical question is whether we can develop a biblical rationale for government foreign assistance to help the world's poor. The factual claim we have developed and sought to illustrate in this section is that the United States government daily affects the world's poor through its domestic economic policies, its trade policies, its impact on global economic organizations, and its military activities around the world, and that these impacts are often though not always negative. A number of other impacts could have been mentioned, such as the impact of our carbon consumption on global climate and therefore on the world's most environmentally vulnerable populations. All of this has been to show that the right question is not if the government should (seek to) affect the lot of the world's poor, but instead how Christian citizens can wield their advocacy efforts to *improve* the way the US government in fact does affect the world's poor.

PART III: TOWARD A THEOLOGY OF GOVERNMENT— AND BENEVOLENT EMPIRE?

We turn now to a consideration of biblical resources for a theology of government and its responsibilities. This topic could sprawl indefinitely, but its scope can be narrowed by recalling both the context we have been

17. "DoD Releases Fiscal 2010 Budget Proposal."
18. "Active Duty Military Personnel Strengths by Regional Area."
19. "Human Development Indicators," 231–32.

considering and the assignment we are undertaking in this chapter. Our question is whether or not theological resources can be identified for a biblical theology of a national government *serving the well-being of those most needy people who dwell outside its national borders*. In particular, we are looking for a biblical theology for the United States government serving the economic and survival needs of the poorest outside our national borders.

This task challenges the biblical resources available in the Old Testament canon that are most often cited in constructing a theology of government. Israel and later Judah were buffer states far more often trampled upon by great powers to their south and north than in any position to offer assistance to anyone beyond their own rough borders.

Psalm 72

However, it is interesting to consider the implicit moral exhortations offered to the king in Psalm 72.[20] We want to suggest that this psalm be linked to the reign of Solomon and consider the implications of that possibility. While the extent of Solomon's territorial reach may be idealized here (8–11), scholars agree that the nation of Israel never controlled more territory than during his reign. Certainly, then, Solomon's actions would have had an effect on the poor of many peoples, including but not limited to the Jewish people. Let's read Psalm 72 in this context.

Psalm 72 is a prayer of support for and implicit exhortation to the (new) king, calling him to be a covenant-keeping Jewish monarch who will serve, in Ron Sider's words, as "a channel of God's justice."[21] The psalm is indeed a prayer, requesting of God that the key characteristics of God's own holy character and rule—justice and righteousness (*mishpat* and *tsedeqah*) be granted to the king. The psalm celebrates not just the kingship of a new Davidic ruler but the kingship of God as well.[22]

From the very beginning, in v. 2, the psalmist emphasizes the importance of caring for the poor on the part of the king. This defines what it means to "judge your people with righteousness" (v. 2a). It is demonstrated by such acts as "defend[ing] the cause of the poor. . .giv[ing] deliverance to the needy, and crush[ing] the oppressor" (v. 4).[23]

Throughout this critically important psalm, national prosperity and royal success are linked and interwoven with the king's care for the poor.

---

20. Weiser, *The Psalms*, 502.
21. Sider, "For the Common Good," 24–29.
22. Weiser, *The Psalms*, 503.
23. All Scripture citations in this chapter are NRSV unless otherwise noted.

Verse 3 prays that the mountains will yield "prosperity" (NRSV); the Hebrew word here is actually *shalom*, which as we know means not just peace as absence of war but also as *bountiful harvest peaceably enjoyed*.[24] Verse 5 apparently prays for a reign of indefinite duration, verses 8–11 for a reign of broad territorial scope and unquestioned international power. These prayers are immediately grounded in a kingship that "delivers the needy when they call, the poor and those who have no helper" (v. 12).

> He has pity on the weak and the needy,
> and saves the lives of the needy.
> From oppression and violence he redeems their life;
> and precious is their blood in his sight (Ps 72:13–14).

It is not too much to say that for this coronation psalm the success and even the justification of the king's rule are measured by his care for the needy and oppressed. The blessings that this prayer seeks for this king are grand, but they are tightly connected to his care for the poor. James Limburg does not overstate the case when he suggests that "the quality of the king's rule will be judged by the quality of life of the poorest citizens."[25] Patrick Miller argues that "the very grounds for worldwide acknowledgement of the king's rule are found in the fact that he helps the poor and needy and redeems them from oppression and violence." This point is more or less taken for granted in the very structure of the psalm (see the "casual for" in v. 12).[26]

This kingly activity on behalf of the poor blesses Israel but—in fulfillment of Israel's ancient calling (Gen 12:2)—also blesses other nations. Perhaps because of the extent of this particular king's rule, it is not just "your poor" (v. 2b) in Israel whose needs are met but also "all nations" who are blessed in him and through his benevolent rule, which is itself a channel of God's justice. The language of the psalm broadens quickly from what appears to be a focus on Israel's people to all people who are delivered from injustice by this king's reign.

Patrick Miller suggests that this psalm and other similar texts points to another benefit for Israel of such benevolent rule. True security for Israel comes through a reign of justice and care for the poor—not just the poor of Israel but also of all peoples affected by Israel—rather than merely crafty foreign allegiances or overwhelming military might.[27]

---

24. Limburg, *Psalms*, 241.
25. Ibid., 242.
26. Miller, "The Prophetic Critique of the Kings," 93.
27. Ibid.

Here we appear to have a very rare moment in which an Israelite king or series of kings (a dynasty) of Israel also has power over other peoples. This coronation prayer does not simply celebrate this moment of great power for Israel or her king, but instead ties the moral legitimacy of this power to the activities of the king on behalf of the poor. And the poor in question are not only the domestic poor but the international poor. International respect and support for the king, and security and prosperity for the nation of Israel, are linked to the king's care for the poor and needy wherever his power reaches. Benevolent care for the international poor will mean that "all nations will be blessed in him." They will "pronounce him blessed," (RSV, v. 19), which means they will hope for and look with favor upon this king and his nation, and in their joy they shall ultimately give praise and glory to God (vv. 18–19).

We suggest that direct applications to our own US context are readily visible in Psalm 72. To the extent that the United States and its government exercises its great global power as a blessing to "save the lives of the poor and needy," we please the God of justice and righteousness, serve as a channel of God's righteous kingdom and rule, save and improve the lives of millions of people, enhance our moral standing in the eyes of other peoples, and therefore bring peace both to others and ourselves.

Jeremiah 21–22

Preaching in the late sixth century BCE as the weakened and barely surviving kingdom of Judah was staggering toward its demise, the prophet Jeremiah offers a moral vision of kingly rule very similar to what we see in Psalm 72. These texts in Jeremiah 21–22, however, are primarily framed as intense prophetic denunciations of kingly power gone terribly wrong.

Jeremiah anticipates the coming devastation of Jerusalem and the destruction of the last rulers in the Davidic line. They have gone wrong because they have failed to "act with justice and righteousness, and deliver from the hand of the oppressor anyone who has been robbed" (22:3a). They have failed to "do no wrong or violence to the alien, the orphan, and the widow" (22:3b). Instead, these kings, especially Jehoiakim, have used their power to undertake elaborate royal building projects using forced or uncompensated labor just because they can get away with it (22:13–14). Jeremiah says that what makes a king a real king is doing "justice and righteousness" and "judg[ing] the cause of the poor and needy" (22:15–16), not cedar and vermilion.

Instead, King Jehoiakim has violated his responsibilities as "king in order to enhance his own prestige by his conspicuous consumption."[28] The result is that destruction will come upon Jerusalem that no military weaponry or diplomatic strategy can prevent. No grand heritage of God's special relationship with Israel will lead to divine mercy this time.

Without identifying the United States with biblical Israel, we suggest that Jeremiah 21–22 offers applications to our context that are just as legitimate as those seen earlier with Psalm 72. To the extent that our nation or its leaders use their power to exploit the poor, the needy, or the powerless affected by our global actions, or even fail to use their power to protect the poor, needy, and powerless within our reach, we harm innocent people, attract global enemies, and invite the judgment of God.

Cyrus as Benevolent Emperor?

Any contextually serious treatment of the contemporary US relationship with the poor of the world requires direct consideration of the concept of empire. If we define an empire minimally as "an extensive territory or enterprise under single domination or control," then it is fair to define the United States as at least a quasi-empire, geographically, economically, politically, and militarily speaking. This is not to demonize the United States but to attempt to describe the great power of our country with accuracy.

Our final textual considerations will relate even more directly to this theme of empire, though the discussion of Psalm 72 already hinted at this direction.

In general, the history of ancient Israel was the sad tale of a people threatened or trampled upon by one ancient near eastern empire after another. The Solomonic moment in which Israel acted as its own kind of mini-empire was over in the blink of an eye.

The Old Testament offers little love for these empires whose tyrants came Israel's way. Pharoah, Tiglath-Peleser, Nebuchadnezzar, Belshazzar, Artaxerxes, and Darius do not come off as heroes in the biblical text. They are almost uniformly treated as cruel and bloodthirsty imperial tyrants, drunk on their own absolute power.

However, there is one Old Testament-era emperor who receives kinder treatment and who occasionally surfaces in contemporary treatments of the possibility of the United States functioning as a kind of benevolent empire in the world. That ruler, of course, is Cyrus of ancient Persia. Interestingly enough, Cyrus and his officials purposefully pursued this image of liberator

28. Ibid., 93.

and built on the near eastern tradition of portraying good rulers as "gatherers of the dispersed."[29]

After the calamitous destruction of Jerusalem in 587 BC and the forced dispersion of the Jews under Babylonian tyranny, the emergence of a Persian ruler who would allow the Jewish people to return home and to worship their own God without interference was treated by Isaiah as deliverance sent from God: "I stirred up from the north, and he has come, from the rising of the sun he was summoned by name. He shall trample on rulers as on mortar, as the potter treads clay" (Isa 41:25). The language is even more elaborate in 45:1-7, where Cyrus is referred to by God as God's "anointed," translatable as "Messiah," and his victories are claimed as coming from the hand of God, even though "you do not know me" (45:4,5).[30] Ronald Clements argues that in this portion of Isaiah, Cyrus displays the characteristics of the normative ruler we have considered in Psalm 72.[31] Cyrus' decree is of course also celebrated and partly quoted/reconstructed in both 2 Chronicles 36 and in Ezra 1.

Hailing Cyrus as a model of a good and benevolent ruler is tricky. From Isaiah to the Greek historian Herodotus to Machiavelli, Cyrus is lauded as a great ruler. The fact that Machiavelli supports Cyrus and praises his expansion of Persian territory should make us wary of using Cyrus as a model. Cyrus was an imperial ruler and an expansionist who dominated a vast part of the ancient world. The fact that he preferred a wiser and freer occupation policy cannot obscure our view of the more basic facts. Even a benevolent world conqueror is a world conqueror.

The application to the US relationship with the poor of the world is similarly tricky. We could at least say that given the staggering global power of the United States, given the fact of economic and military power at least approaching imperial reach, our nation's leaders should seek to function as benevolently as possible. We should look more like Cyrus than any other emperor depicted in Scriptures. Better Isaiah 45 than, say, Revelation 13's depiction of the cruelties of Rome.[32] But this is not to say that the concentration of that kind of power in the hands of any one nation is a good thing in itself.

---

29. Miller and Hayes, *A History of Ancient Israel and Judah*, 505.
30. Tucker, "The Book of Isaiah 1-39," 394.
31. Clements, "Psalm 72 and Isaiah 40-66," 339.
32. Monera, "The Christian's Relationship to the State," 124.

PART IV: ROMANS 13 AND CHRISTIAN CITIZENSHIP

No treatment of a biblical theology of government can be complete without considering Romans 13. But the issues associated with this hugely important text have to do not just with the text itself but with its long use and abuse, primarily in historic Christendom.

Let's begin by saying that Romans 13 is written by a Jewish Christian convert named Paul, who was a Roman citizen and whose context was imperial Rome. The intended readers of this letter were themselves located in the capital city of the empire, some of them apparently in the royal household itself. This was a city from which Jews had not long before been expelled and in which Christians were soon to be murdered by imperial fiat.

Essentially, in this passage, Paul is telling Roman Christians that even though they are followers of Jesus Christ—the legitimate ruler of this world—they cannot become anarchists in relation to human authority structures. They must still submit to their earthly rulers, who are charged with ensuring God's justice and order. But contrary to the Roman emperor-cult, these rulers are not divine. They are established by God and are therefore answerable to God. Paul is essentially demoting these "arrogant, self-divinizing rulers"[33] even as he is calling for respect for their function in the world. Many Christians died in the first 300 years of the church's history on the basis of their unwillingness to offer worship to these rulers.

The history of Christian exegesis of Romans 13 has far too often emphasized the punitive role of government through its exercise of the "sword" (13:4b). The text has far too long been used as justification for the endless resort to force by government and unflinching participation of Christians in any and all such uses of force.

Too often the prior calling of government to act as "God's servant (*diakonoi*) for your good" (13:4a) is missed. This broad calling of the state to advance the "good" opens the door for consideration of the constructive task of the state to serve the good of one especially needy part of the population—the poor. Paul is here implicitly charging the leaders of the Roman state to advance the good of that vast array of peoples under Rome's authority, most of whom were in fact poor. It is hard to imagine that a leader so steeped in Hebrew Scripture would be indifferent to the Old Testament's many demands that righteous rulers must act on behalf of the poor.

The use of Romans 13 as the *locus classicus* for a Christian theology of government has tended to obscure the role of Christians as citizens. Our attention has been directed by our theologians to the activities of a state above

---

33. Wright, "The Letter to the Romans," 719.

us, sent from God even further above us. This hierarchical or top-down rendering is a legacy of the era of monarchy. Monarchies don't have citizens, they have subjects.

Of course even in a monarchy or other form of undemocratic government Christians can and sometimes do call governments to their God-given task. Even when Christians were merely subjects we could and sometimes did cite biblical texts like Psalm 72 and Romans 13 to call government authorities to care for the poor and advance the common good. Even today in parts of the world in which Christians lack full citizenship and participation rights this is exactly what Christians do. It is part of our public witness.

But in a liberal democracy such as our own—thanks be to God—we are more than subjects. We are citizens. And the theory of government in a liberal democracy is that government's actions flow upward from the will of the people rather than downwards from the will of the monarch. Many evangelical Christians have never really made the theological transition to citizenship in a representative democracy. We speak of government as if 1776 and 1789 never happened.

In a representative democracy, if a significant portion of a nation's citizens desire that the power and resources of government be deployed in a way that helps rather than harms the world's poor, then those elected and appointed to serve in government will have to take that desire seriously. Whatever becomes important to citizens becomes important to any citizen who would like to be chosen or retained as the people's representative.

If the United States is indeed a kind of global military-political-economic empire right now, that is not exceptional. Empires have come and gone on the planet for millennia. If this empire has a large number of professed Christians, this would also not be exceptional. But if the United States were to become an empire whose professed Christians pressed insistently for generous global foreign assistance on behalf of the world's poorest, this would indeed be exceptional, and exceptionally good news. It is entirely legitimate for this nation's Christian citizens to exercise their advocacy rights and responsibilities toward this end.

We can see from the work of creative and effective advocates that many in this nation still respond in exceptional ways to appeals to Christian compassion. This is why the ONE campaign has had so much exposure and so much success. Celebrities, like Bono, still have the power to inflame our moral imagination and to appeal to the language of faith. Bono spoke at the

National Prayer Breakfast in 2006 and used biblically saturated language to urge the American government to adjust its federal budget. He used phrases like "good news to the poor," and "Jubilee," and quoted the beatitudes.[34]

The ONE campaign, along with our New Evangelical Partnership and other partners, was able to have success earlier this year in pressing the US government and others to respond to Haiti's current crisis by cancelling much of its foreign debt and giving rather than lending money to Haiti now. Here Christian citizens used their advocacy power to press the government to act on behalf of some of the world's poorest people. Doug Hicks is right: "What is required is a large bloc of citizens willing to express a moral and political commitment to end extreme poverty."[35] Government leaders will have no choice but to respond.

We are the government. We do not need to have a pre-democratic theology of the state that disconnects us from our responsibilities as citizens. Government is the community collectively acting. We as Christians are a part of the community collective acting. We must move beyond an authoritarian, top-down understanding of government and an individualistic understanding of citizenship.

As well, our economic system is not value-free. It is a human creation, created by us, regulated poorly or well by our government, and influenced by our priorities. Right now our primary economic values are profit, efficiency and growth.[36] But these can be challenged or reformed as citizens, including Christian citizens, choose to challenge and reform them.

Many conservative Christians join their libertarian non-Christian friends in arguing for strictly limited government and the lowest possible taxes. These impulses would not generally support an expansion of US global foreign assistance. To this we say that such a cramped view of government's role is convenient when you are in power in society, when the rules benefit you, and you don't need anything. Such a view has rarely been adopted by those not benefited by existing power structures. There's a reason why, for example, African-Americans have long favored a much more activist federal government than most white evangelicals do. History tells the tale.

Advocacy is inevitable because we do not act in a vacuum. To not act is still to act. Our nation, our government, and our economy interact with the poor of the world every day. Much of this interaction does not redound to the benefit of these poorest of our brothers and sisters. To care about

---

34. Hicks, "Global Poverty and Bono's Celebrity Activism," 47–48.
35. Ibid., 60.
36. Peters, "Economic Justice Requires More than the Kindness of Strangers," 106.

what happens to the poor of the world, and to call on government to undertake policies that bend on their behalf rather than further crushing them, is a "natural outflow of our pastoral concern for the social good under the sovereignty of the God who loves all persons."[37] Perhaps it is not too much to hope that God's mission in the world is advanced as we do precisely this work of advocacy.

Christians need to urge the political leaders who represent us to specific, policy-based action. Our support for private relief and development activities is wonderful, necessary, and insufficient. We will let Rebecca Blank get the last word:

> Like the human beings that participate in them, both private and public institutions have the potential for good and for evil. Which of these directions they follow depends a great deal on the choices that are made by the people who establish, shape, and participate in these systems.[38]

We are those people. All of us. We are accountable to God for our choices. Judgment begins with the household of faith.

---

37. Stassen and Gushee, *Kingdom Ethics*, 479.
38. Blank, "A Christian Perspective on the Role of Government," 246.

15

Biblical Reflections on a World without Nuclear Weapons

2011

INTRODUCTION

THIS ESSAY OFFERS THEOLOGICAL and ethical framing for the ongoing work of moving toward a world without nuclear weapons. Much of the responsibility for the achievement of this sacred goal rests with the international diplomats, national security experts, and specialists in military doctrine.

My mandate is not to meddle with those issues, but to do something different. I will do some theology.

The way that most Baptists and evangelicals do theology is to turn to Scripture. So that is what I will do—turn to the pages of Scripture for several memorable texts that speak very directly and acutely to the issues raised by nuclear weapons and our quest to remove them from the face of the earth. A transcendently important issue like nuclear weapons needs to be met by transcendently important spiritual, theological, and moral resources. Thus I turn to the Scriptures of the Hebrew Bible and the Christian New Testament.

A THEOLOGY OF DELEGATED RESPONSIBILITY

"The heavens are the LORD's heavens, but the earth he has given to human beings" (Ps 115:16).[1]

---

1. All Scripture citations in this chapter are from the NRSV.

When we try to think about the mass-killing machines humans have invented that we call nuclear weapons, we do well to step back and remember a few things about who we are, and where we are.

According to the Bible, we are the sole species to whom responsibility for the fate of the Earth and its inhabitants has been entrusted. There are between five and one hundred million species on the planet; 1.7 million have been identified and named. There is just one species that is responsible not just for its own well-being but for the well-being of all others. That is *homo sapiens*. Us.

The Bible does not treat the disproportionate role and power of humanity on planet Earth as an accident. Instead that role is described as a divine decision; first to *create* a certain type of creature in the divine image, and then to *entrust* that creature with dominion over the planet as a whole: "Then God said, 'Let us make humankind in our image, according to our likeness, and let them have dominion over the fish of the sea, and over the birds of the air, and over the cattle, and over all the wild animals of the earth, and over every creeping thing that creeps upon the earth'" (Gen 1:26).

There is a theological complexity here that has often tested the capacities of people in the biblical tradition. That has to do with how to make sense *both* of the affirmation that "The earth is the Lord's, and all that is in it" (Ps 24:1) *and* that "The earth he has given to human beings." What ought to be an obvious solution often seems to elude people of faith; that is, that *the second affirmation is dependent on the first*. Human responsibility over the earth and its creatures is delegated responsibility, for which we are answerable to the One who delegated it. It is trusteeship, like when a state elects a senator and entrusts her to represent it, or when a board of trustees elects a university president and entrusts him to manage the affairs of the school. These elected officers hold real responsibility. Their decisions really matter. They are not *seemingly* making important decisions with real consequences. They *are* making important decisions with real consequences. But they hold their power in trust on behalf of others.

That is how it is with us in relation to the Earth and its creatures. This is God's world, over which we humans have been entrusted with enormous responsibility. In that light, the human invention, deployment, use and threat of use of nuclear weapons, and our stubborn slowness in stepping away from these weapons despite their manifest danger to the entire planet, is best viewed as a grotesque violation of our delegated trusteeship over the Earth that God made. But it is not too late to get this right, which is why we gather here this evening.

AN ETHIC OF REFRAINING FROM MASS MURDER

> *"For your own lifeblood I will surely require a reckoning: from every animal I will require it and from human beings, each one for the blood of another, I will require a reckoning for human life"* (Gen 9:5).

It is appropriate when thinking about nuclear disarmament to have all kinds of technical discussions about such matters as the status of the Nuclear Non-Proliferation Treaty, the morality of nuclear deterrence, the feasibility of cooperative missile defenses, and the diplomacy required in relation to countries like Iran and North Korea.

But step back a bit, for one minute, and look at our enterprise perhaps in a new way. Here we are, all of us: men and women in nice clothes at a prestigious university carrying briefcases containing carefully prepared essays reflecting on quite interesting and difficult issues of technology, international relations, and national security policy. A person could feel pretty good about being asked to participate in a meeting like this at the University of Notre Dame.

But I hope that these biblical passages help us to remember that what we are talking about are weapons capable of inflicting the greatest mass slaughter in the history of the world. We are talking about mass murder. We are talking about creatures made in the image of God, using their special, God-given powers of rationality and creativity in order to dream up weapons that can obliterate millions in a single flash in order to create, not a bloodbath, but something worse—more like an evaporation of infinitely precious human beings whom God *loves*. If we were not involved in attempting to *eliminate* these ghastly weapons from the face of the earth I would think we should run screaming from the room at the very thought of what we are talking about.

Because we are talking about murder. The Hebrew Bible regularly treats the murder of one human being by another as the gravest of all sins. A reckoning will be required, says God in Genesis 9, for the lifeblood of every murdered creature (even the animals!). Every life matters enough for there to be both human and divine accountability for its murder. What does that say, then, to a species that since 1945 has carefully developed the means to kill not millions but billions, and has held tightly onto those means since the day they were developed? What kind of accountability could there be for a species like that? We like to compare ourselves favorably to the animals, as when we use such negatively evaluative phrases as "what a beastly act" or "he became such an animal." But only *humans* have the ability to create, deploy, and use weapons like the ones we are talking about here. Do you think maybe the animals, in the secret languages they speak to one another in our imaginations or a good C. S. Lewis novel, ever say of especially creative and murderous fellow animals, "what a human act," or "he became such a human back there"? I think we have done an injustice to the animals with our language of beastliness. For in this way we are much, much worse.

Never let it be forgotten that what we are talking about here is helping our fellow human beings, including the leaders of our own nation, slowly back away from the brink of mass murder. That is what the use of nuclear weapons is, or what it would be, however we dress it up in the morally exculpatory languages we have created. This is a word of warning to all of us, especially those of us operating in the just war tradition. In these traditions killing is not necessarily murder if it is done in self-defense, and the acquisition and threat of weapons is not necessarily evil if these acts deter those who would harm the innocent. This perfectly natural, perfectly logical moral-legal system bumps up against its outer limits here. Mass murder is mass murder, however it is labeled or justified. It will be cold comfort to the dead in a nuclear exchange if we label them as collateral damage in a morally justified act of self-defense. They will still be just as dead.

PEACEMAKING AND CIVILIZATION

"As he came near and saw the city, he wept over it, saying: 'If you, even you, had only recognized on this day the things that make for peace! But now they are hidden from your eyes'" (Luke 19:41–42).

There are two things about this passage that I want to highlight.

The first is that Jesus wept over Jerusalem. It appears that he is anticipating its coming destruction, which occurred a generation after his ministry in a cataclysmic war with Rome. In that war Jerusalem and her temple were destroyed and perhaps a million of her people killed. Many biblical scholars suggest that these New Testament texts are actually retrospective, looking back on the unthinkable destruction of the place, in Jewish tradition, where heaven met earth, the holiest place in the world, in the holiest city. The fact is that rebellions against Rome brought Jerusalem two rounds of mass devastation in the first and second centuries. It took many centuries for the city to be rebuilt, and of course the remnants of that earlier destruction remain visible in the Holy City.

Nuclear weapons target cities. That is somehow horribly appropriate, for nukes, like cities, represent human civilization at its height. It is commonplace to note in Christian theology that the Bible begins in a garden and ends in a city. Cities are the quintessential human product, unique to us, entirely dependent on our sociability, creativity, and technology. Only humans could build cities. And only humans could unbuild cities in a single instant, as with, say, a nuclear attack.

To work for a world without nuclear weapons is at the same time an effort to protect our cities from our own self-destructiveness. Let's not forget what is at stake here. I often remember it when I am in the world's major cities. Maybe it's because I am a child of the latter days of the Cold War, but I never forget when I am in New York or Los Angeles or Washington or London or Paris that these cities could be gone in the blink of an eye.

And yet, Jesus says, "If you had only *recognized* the things that make for peace..."

This may mean, this must mean, that there are things that we can do to *make peace*. And it may mean, indeed it must mean, that we have *the capacity to discover what these are*.

There are people who already have discovered and practiced some of the things that make for peace, the things that save our cities from our own self-destructive fears. I think of Glen Stassen and others who have worked on just peacemaking theory. And so, for example:

- *Nuclear peacemakers know* that so long as possessing nuclear weapons is seen as the best way to secure one's regime or nation from destruction, leaders and nations will seek them. So we need to find ways to ensure regimes and nations without nukes.
- *Nuclear peacemakers know* that relationships between nations can easily default to the law of the jungle, unless a fabric of international covenants and treaties observed by all nations weaves the peoples together under a kind of rule of law. So we need to find ways to strengthen that fabric.
- *Nuclear peacemakers know* that weapons of this level of destructiveness have to be quarantined from other kinds of weapons so that their use is delegitimized. So we need to find ways to continue to quarantine nuclear weapons from other types of weapons.
- *Nuclear peacemakers know* that it is not just weapons themselves that matter but also the quality of the relationship between the nations that develop and deploy them. So we need to find ways to reduce fear, generate trust, and build friendships between nations.
- *Nuclear peacemakers know* that the human heart, even the collective human heart as found in nations, dilates between fear and hope. So we need to find ways to reduce fear and build hope, such as employing

unilateral confidence building measures as independent peacemaking initiatives.

- *Nuclear peacemakers know* that if any nation feels insecure, all will in fact be insecure. So we need to find ways to meet the legitimate security needs of every nation for the sake of all nations. And we need to create constant and open channels of communication between nations, even those that view each other as enemies, rather than ever shutting down communication.

- *Nuclear peacemakers know* that fear and anger tend to produce a hostile rhetoric of blame that tends to produce more fear and anger in a vicious cycle. So we need to train ourselves and require of our leaders a posture of rhetorical restraint, articulated respect for other peoples and nations, and a willingness to confess wrongs that have damaged relations in the past.

CONCLUSION

The Damocles sword of nuclear annihilation has hung over our heads since 1945. By God's grace working through responsible human action and restraint, that sword has not fallen. The work of nuclear peacemaking aims to remove that sword from over all of us at last. I can hardly think of a more worthy aspiration, or one more in keeping with the theology and ethics of biblical faith. May God bless this important work, and all who undertake it.

16

Religion, Science, and the Weakening Quest to Save Creation

2012

E.O. WILSON WRITES A LETTER

> Dear Pastor: We have not met, yet I feel I know you well enough to call you friend. First of all, we grew up in the same faith. As a boy I too answered the altar call; I went under the water. Although I no longer belong to that faith, I am confident that if we met and spoke privately of our deepest beliefs, it would be in a spirit of mutual respect and good will . . . I write to you now for your counsel and help . . . you have the power to help solve a great problem about which I care deeply. I hope you have the same concern. I suggest that we set aside our differences in order the save the Creation.[1]

THIS 2006 "LETTER TO a Southern Baptist Pastor," from one of our nation's leading secular scientists, was intended for people like me. I once answered the altar call; I once went under the water; I am an ordained Baptist pastor and ethics professor. For five years I have been involved in an initiative triggered by E. O. Wilson's open letter. I write to tell you about it. I think you will be surprised by what you learn, as I have been surprised by what I have learned.

---

1. Wilson, *The Creation*, 3.

The place to begin is with E. O. ("Ed") Wilson's book. Wilson called this book, which may be the capstone achievement of his illustrious career as one of the world's most eminent biologists, *The Creation: An Appeal to Save Life on Earth.*

In calling his book *The Creation*, Wilson reached back to the religious language of his Southern Baptist childhood in Alabama. He did not call the book *The Environment* or *The Natural World*. He called it *The Creation*. And it was not the first time he had chosen to use this language—so familiar and comforting to religious folks, so alien and disturbing to many secularists.

The biblical book of Genesis begins with these words: "In the beginning, God created the heavens and the earth."[2]

It is among the most fundamental of biblical teachings—this world is a *creation*. It has been *created*. Its *Creator* is God. I remember the formula we were taught in theology class at Southern Baptist Theological Seminary in 1985: "Creator creates Creation." Each term is significant; each is nonsense without the other.

But Wilson disagrees. He makes clear from the first page of his book that he does not believe in a Creator who creates creation. He does not believe that in the beginning God created the heavens and the earth. He writes: "Life was self-assembled by random mutation and natural selection of the codifying molecules."[3] Oh. Let's just say it's not exactly what we teach in Sunday School.

And yet, for Wilson, what has resulted after four billion years of evolution can be called "the Creation." He believes that this Creation has enormous intrinsic value. And he believes in a human moral obligation to take care of it. Turning again to his imagined pastor, he writes:

> Let us see, then . . . if we can . . . meet on the near side of metaphysics in order to deal with the real world we share . . . The defense of living Nature is a universal value. It doesn't rise from, nor does it promote, any religious or ideological dogma. Rather it serves without discrimination the interests of all humanity.[4]

Can there be a creation without a Creator? It seems a question begging for an answer. But in his 2006 letter Wilson asked us to bracket that question. He seemed to assume that there was not time for that old argument because right now, urgently, "The Creation—living Nature—is in deep trouble."[5] The

---

2. All Scripture citations in this chapter are from the NIV.
3. Wilson, *The Creation*, 166.
4. Ibid., 4.
5. Ibid.

issue was not, for Wilson, whether a Creator created creation. The issue was whether humans would turn back from destroying it.

CREATION'S DISTRESS

In this political silly season, when Republican politicians score cheap points by attacking the Environmental Protection Agency,[6] and leading presidential candidates speak of a global warming "hoax" perpetrated on the suffering American taxpayer by grant-hungry scientists,[7] it is worth spending a few more moments in Ed Wilson's company, hearing his description of the major dimensions of the creation's distress.

Wilson never merely lists "environmental problems" in a big clump. In a retrospective on some of his career's journeys, he takes us around the world to visit some of nature's most extraordinary wonders and, in turn, to see current scenes of the creation's distress.

Wilson loves the creation. That love oozes from every page. We see it in pictures of primary rainforest in Costa Rica, Japanese maple trees, and butterflies of the Dominican Republic. We see it in drawings of algae and protozoans, wolverines and the Pacific yew tree, fire ants and roundworms, the extinct slender bush wren and probably extinct ivory-billed woodpecker. We hear it in descriptions of the Sarawaget Mountains of New Guinea, the Boston Harbor Islands National Park Area, the Florida Keys, and the 1,600 different butterfly species at Jari in Brazil. Wilson is a "naturalist." He wants to teach us all how to become naturalists, and how to raise more of them.

This "naturalism" is not a side point for Wilson, and it is not unrelated to creation's distress. The big story he tells hinges on the human tendency to lose meaningful contact with the creation on which we depend, and a part of which we human beings *simply are.*

Wilson traces this human alienation from creation to the founding days of human civilization:

> We strayed from Nature with the beginning of civilization roughly ten thousand years ago. That quantum leap beguiled us with an illusion of freedom from the world that had given us birth. It nourished the belief that that the human spirit can be molded into something new to fit changes in the environment and culture, and as a result the timetables of history desynchronized. A wiser intelligence might now truthfully say of us at this point: here is a chimera, a new and very odd species

---

6. Broder, "Bashing E.P.A. is New Theme in G.O.P Race."
7. Krugman, "Republicans Against Science."

come shambling into our universe, a mix of Stone Age emotion, medieval self-image, and godlike technology. The combination makes the species unresponsive to the forces that count most for its own long-term survival.[8]

For Wilson, we are creatures of nature, of creation, of Earth. We are in every way dependent upon creation's good gifts—such as the air we breathe, the water we drink, the soil we farm, and the billions of other species who share this planet with us. We are therefore totally vulnerable to any degradation, depletion or destruction of the creation.

But the civilizations we have created through our extraordinary intelligence and technological capacity are, in Wilson's phrase, "pauperizing" the earth, and therefore endangering ourselves. We have become the first of creation's species capable of inflicting grave damage on the creation itself. In fact, says Wilson, human beings are in the process of inflicting the sixth great extinction in the last five hundred million years of planetary history. We have developed the power to destroy vast numbers of species and alter the planet's ecological balances, a destructive power that was last witnessed on Earth at the famous meteorite strike sixty-five million years ago. As a species, we are becoming a collective meteor strike. Nice.

All particular environmental concerns that can be separated out for analysis are sub-problems of this broader human disruption of living nature. Wilson names a variety of specific threats. His central ecological concern is the rapid loss of biodiversity, both in species and in ecosystems; not incidentally, long-term human well-being depends on both. This dramatic loss of biodiversity is caused by habitat loss (including that caused by human-induced climate change), invasive species, pollution, human overpopulation, and over-harvesting.

Other scientific observers of the natural world might offer a somewhat different list. One recent book highlights increasingly acute issues related to the global water supply, for example.[9] Some observers would heighten the emphasis on the centrality of climate change. Details of the extent and seriousness of species loss are debated. But this basic picture—*of local ecosystems, humanity, and an entire creation imperiled by human impacts that today threaten its intrinsic but not inexhaustible resilience*—appears to be shared by just about every serious scientist.

Wilson wrote his book hoping to engage influential Christian leaders and those they lead with this disturbing news and to entice our involvement in addressing creation's distress. Five decades of warnings from the world's

---

8. Wilson, *The Creation*, 10.
9. Fishman, *The Big Thirst*.

scientists, naturalists, and environmentalists had not been enough to stop the runaway train of ecological degradation. But, argued Wilson, "Religion and science are the two most powerful forces in the world today, including especially the United States. If religion and science could be united on the common ground of biological conservation, the problem would soon be solved."[10]

SCIENTISTS AND EVANGELICALS UNITE

And so we met.

In late 2005, through intermediaries a meeting was arranged between Eric Chivian, a Nobel Laureate physician who then directed the Center for Health and the Global Environment at Harvard Medical School,[11] and Rich Cizik, then Vice-President for Governmental Affairs at the National Association of Evangelicals.[12] Eventually a friendship began to develop and they discussed ways to bring leaders of their two communities together to address creation's distress.

The idea was counterintuitive and thus extraordinarily appealing because of the long and dismal history of conflict between mainstream science and conservative American Christianity, going back to evolution and the Scopes Monkey Trial. Just getting elite, mainly secular, scientists together with contemporary leaders of fundamentalism's somewhat more reasonable successor, evangelical Protestantism, would be a historic achievement in itself.

Thirty of us met in late November 2006, at the lovely Melhana Plantation in southern Georgia. I was one of the fifteen evangelicals. Our ranks included, besides Cizik, such notables as Duane Litfin, then president of Wheaton College, evangelicalism's flagship university; Joel Hunter, an influential megachurch pastor in Florida; Ken Wilson, a leading Vineyard Church pastor in Michigan; James Jones, Bishop of Liverpool; Jim Ball, president of the Evangelical Environmental Network; Cal DeWitt of the University of Wisconsin, for decades the leading environmental scientist in US evangelicalism; and Steve Bouma-Prediger, a religion professor at Hope College, in some ways the Cal DeWitt of the next generation.

It was a strong evangelical contingent, but on the other side the roster was simply stunning. Besides Chivian and Wilson (whose book had come out in September and was given to everyone who came to the meeting),

10. Wilson, *The Creation*, 5.
11. http://chge.med.harvard.edu/
12. http://www.nae.net/

their fifteen included Jim McCarthy of Harvard, who had been president of the American Association for the Advancement of Science and shared the 2007 Nobel Prize with other leaders of the Intergovernmental Panel on Climate Change (IPCC); Carl Safina, a marine biologist at the Blue Ocean Institute, one of the nation's most highly honored environmental writers; Gus Speth and Peter Raven, two of our nation's leading conservationists: Howard Frumkin, a physician and epidemiologist and at the time director of the National Center for Environmental Health at the Centers for Disease Control; Judith Curry, one of our nation's leading atmospheric scientists, a professor at Georgia Tech; Jim Hansen, still our nation's leading government scientist on climate, working from the NASA Institute for Space Studies; and Rita Colwell, a specialist on global infectious diseases from the University of Maryland and Johns Hopkins, and a former president of the National Science Foundation. These and others were not only specialists in the relevant fields, tenured and chaired at top universities, but collectively they had also served as leaders of most of the science foundations and academies in the United States. It was a scientific all-star team.

The Melhana summit proved to be quite extraordinary for all concerned. The scheduled time focused primarily on hearing reports about the imperiled state of the natural world and strategizing about joint efforts. For me, and I think for most of the nonscientist evangelicals in the room, the brief scientific presentations painted a far more devastating picture of the distress of the creation than I had yet encountered. It wasn't just the issue of human-induced climate change; it was a broad pattern of human damage to the creation leading to a burgeoning degradation of the natural world. And that degradation was already affecting human health and well-being, now, not in some distant far-off apocalyptic future. The epidemiologists and global health specialists were quite important new voices for many of us evangelicals, helping us to see in a decisive new way that creation's distress was a real and present threat to human beings, especially the poorest and most vulnerable around the world.

Such facts on the ground required a moral response. We agreed that working together we might surprise some people and make some progress that we could not have made on our own. We envisioned teams of mainly secular scientists and evangelical pastors or academics touring college campuses with a new message to be delivered together. We thought about ways to take our message to Capitol Hill, the White House, and the nation. And we dreamed that perhaps our unprecedented effort to heal the breach between American science and religion might tip the balance in the national debate about whether to really do anything about climate change and other problems.

At the very end of the meeting we agreed on a joint "urgent call to action"[13] to "protect creation." I remember that text quite vividly because I had about an hour to draft it from various documents and thoughts that emerged at Melhana. The final statement celebrated our "shared sense of moral purpose" to "save the imperiled living world before our damages to it remake it as another kind of planet." It lamented "the unsustainable and short-sighted lifestyles and public policies of our own nation" and called for a "new moral awakening to a compelling demand, clearly articulated in Scripture and supported by science, that we must steward the natural world." We offered the stark declaration that "business as usual cannot continue yet one more day." We pledged to work together "to lead our nation toward a responsible care for creation."

We went public with a January 2007 press event at the National Press Club. At that event we released our statement, and partnership members made additional public comments. We released letters of support from Republican senators Richard Lugar and Olympia Snowe, as well as a letter from a young Democratic senator from Illinois named Barack Obama. We sent the "Call to Action" to the White House, all congressional leaders, and major figures in religion and science. The press conference received massive coverage.

Over the ensuing four years we have indeed worked together, pretty much as promised, though constrained by limited resources. Teams have visited multiple secular and Christian colleges. A quite thoughtful "Creation Care" booklet[14] was developed by Ken Wilson and Joel Hunter and has been distributed to 20,000 evangelical pastors and churches. An expedition to Alaska[15] was arranged for summer 2007 that brought together new leaders from both sides to see both Alaska's natural wonders and encroaching dangers. *Time* magazine honored the partnership between Cizik and Chivian in 2008 by describing them as among the world's one hundred most influential people.[16] Our team's activism for climate legislation climaxed in November

---

13. Gushee, principal author, "An Urgent Call to Action."
14. http://www.creationcareforpastors.com/
15. http://www.pbs.org/now/shows/343/index.html
16. Anderson, "Eric Chivian & Richard Cizik."

2009 with a Senate briefing and a visit to the White House. Along the way friendships have developed that are cherished by all concerned.

There can be little question that, as Steve Bouma-Prediger told me in a conversation recently, in the ensuing five years creation care has gotten a much firmer foothold in the evangelical world, especially among students and young graduates of evangelical colleges. Our initiative surely had something to do with that. Pastors Joel Hunter and Ken Wilson emerged as national creation care leaders, and they told me recently that their congregations have cooperated with them in going green without serious objection. Hunter, in fact, told me that his church "has had a tremendous transformation in the way we do business here," from energy audits to efficiency retrofitting to an ongoing green task force in the church. Young pastoral leaders like Jonathan Merritt[17] and emerging leaders like Ben Lowe[18] have written important books on creation care, and there is little doubt that leaders like them will help many evangelicals take better care of creation.

Even the most corrosive conservative evangelical skeptics, including the pesky Cal Beisner of Knox Theological Seminary, feel it necessary to frame their delay-deny-derail efforts as in fact creation care or ecological stewardship, just with a more theologically conservative and market-friendly approach. Beisner cleverly calls his organization the Cornwall Alliance for the Stewardship of Creation.[19] And, despite their removal of Rich Cizik from his role in 2008—Cizik is now my colleague at the New Evangelical Partnership for the Common Good[20]—the National Association of Evangelicals under its president Leith Anderson retains a commitment to creation care, though the removal of Cizik seems to have taken much of the energy out of that NAE effort.

DEEPER LEVELS OF RESISTANCE

Five years have passed. Despite glimpses of progress, it is hard to overstate the contrast between the optimism our partnership felt in November 2006 and where we find ourselves as a nation today. If we made real progress in bridging the historic gap between mainly secular scientists and Bible-centered evangelicals, and if we worked together in advocacy, why have we not been able to get any kind of climate bill passed? Does anybody even remember the Climate Stewardship Act? What universe was that? Why have

17. Merritt, *Green Like God*.
18. Lowe, *Green Revolution*.
19. http://www.cornwallalliance.org/
20. http://www.newevangelicalpartnership.org/

the climate "hoaxers" gained momentum? Why, in short, are we now moving backward rather than forward?

I want to propose three hypotheses.

#1: *Ed Wilson was wrong in one very important assumption. Religion and science are not in fact "the two most powerful forces in the world today."*

I asked several of the participants in our initiative how Wilson's claim looks five years later. Most thought that he was right, but that the potential of a religion-science partnership had not yet been fully realized. But in the cold light of 2011, it seems more accurate to suggest that corporate power, allied with the political power that it buys, combined with popular economic fears, together with a loss of confidence in scientific research, are collectively far more powerful than religion and science, even were they to achieve a miraculous reconciliation.

Follow the money—it's one of the oldest truisms in politics. It is also a pretty significant theological claim as well, when we take the form of human sin known as greed into account—or, for that matter, the enduring power of simple economic self-interest.

Three years after the near-collapse of our economy, brought on mainly by corrupt business practices on Wall Street, practices whose ruinous implications were so profound that the American taxpayer got the tab so the global economy would (supposedly) not collapse, it is hard not to see that our political system is more a plutocracy than a democracy. The interlocking personal, professional, and political ties between Wall Street and Washington dominate our national life. Distressed scientist Carl Safina put it this way to me: "Big business . . . has enshrined an ethic of greed that brought us everything from the BP blowout to the bank bailouts to a frighteningly shaky national and world economy."[21]

This massive corporate power means, among other things, that the federal government, for now at least, will move more sluggishly than it should to take any steps that might reduce somebody's shareholder value or curtail profit margins at influential corporations. It means regulations will be weaker than they should be and will be under attack as entirely too strict. It means that corporations will have the right to use the runoff of their massive fossil fuel profits to set up "think tanks" and to fund "research" that raises questions about the seriousness of ecological problems like, say, climate change. This money will dwarf the resources available on the other side.

---

21. Safina, Interview by author.

The "merchants of doubt" (as Naomi Oreskes[22] describes the professional eco-skeptics) will go looking for any possible reason to cast doubt on the reality or seriousness of any environmental problem. In these intervening years they found a convenient target when questions began arising about sloppiness in the Intergovernmental Panel on Climate Change and perhaps massaging of the data to fit the story of a climate change crisis. I asked atmospheric scientist Judith Curry about this. Curry is simply the embodiment of an honest scientist, and she carries enormous credibility.

Curry strongly affirms that "climate change being a hoax and people doing it for grant money is ludicrous." But, she does acknowledge that "An inconceivably complex scientific issue became oversimplified. I have been uneasy about this for awhile . . . I don't think it will be any evidence of scientific misconduct by anybody," but "the policy got out ahead of where the science was,"[23] and consequently scientists faced pressure to speak at levels of certainty that were somewhat higher than they should have been. This was a mistake, and Curry has not hesitated to say so.

Of course, one reason climate scientists felt the need to do this was because well-funded doubts about the entirety of climate science (or environmental science generally) were slowing public awareness and policy response to what the evolving science was discovering, a problem that has grown dramatically worse in the last few years. Curry is calling scientists back to their own core vocation of "continually challenging our assumptions and questioning everything we do"—leaving it to policymakers and moral leaders to do *their* job of providing prudent national leadership based on what we *do* know. Instead, says Safina, we are currently being led by those who simply "do not like what the science is telling us" about what our use of fossil fuels is doing "to lands, water, forests, the climate, the acidity of the ocean, and the options of people yet to be born."[24]

The seemingly chronic weakness of the American economy also seems to have trumped the power of religion and science. When our rapacious laissez-faire capitalist system goes bonkers, throwing people out of work and out of their homes and out of their retirements, as ours has recently done, a fearful and exhausted and impoverished populace will be all the more unresponsive to governmental actions to protect the creation—if they cost the taxpayer anything, or can be accused of costing us anything, especially jobs.

---

22. Oreskes and Conway, *Merchants of Doubt*.
23. Curry, interview by author.
24. Safina, interview by author.

#2: *Christianity, still the dominant religion in the United States, is not easily turned to care of the creation.*

Here I can speak with the expertise born of nearly thirty years in Christian ministry and twenty years in seminary and college teaching. I can say categorically that despite the shelves full of fine Christian books about creation care, despite numerous excellent conferences and symposia, despite valuable activist organizations doing their very best work, despite progress among the younger generation, most everyday Christians simply have not moved "the creation" to the center of their religious consciousness.

Few pastors regularly teach or preach on ecological issues or creation care. Few Bible study classes ever engage creation care issues. Few small groups meet to do creation care work. Few Christians wake up each day asking "what can I do to address the creation's distress today?"

There are many reasons for this, and I will be honest about them. For those Christian communities in which the Bible remains the central source of authority and the sacred text studied and preached each week, the inherent limits of the Bible's creation-care resources are significant. Yes, I and others have done what we can to extract and lift up for attention those biblical teachings and texts that are most instructive and helpful for learning to care for creation, but—though this point is disputed by Christian environmentalists like Bouma-Prediger—it is hard to claim that creation care is *the* or even *a* central narrative strand of the Bible. Most days, most people who read most parts of the Bible will not be drawn toward care of God's creation.

The Bible primarily tells a story about God's relationship with humanity. Two-thirds of the canonical Christian Bible concerns God's covenant relationship with Israel; one-third tells the story of Jesus and the spread of the early church. Creation frames the story at the front end, and a "new/renewed heaven and earth" frames the story at the back end. Good scholarly work is being done right now to move these creation/new creation themes closer to the center of Christian understanding. But the beating heart of the story—at least, as it has been understood in centuries of Christian tradition—is a particular telling of God's redemptive love for human beings.

And that is still what people come to church to hear. Most who step into a church on a Sunday do so in order to hear the good news that God loves them. They seek resources for thriving or at least surviving their daily lives. They come broken and beaten down, weary and stressed, hoping for enough "spiritual food" to get through the week. They don't want to hear about biodiversity. They want to hear that they are okay, that God is on their side, that all will be well. They want some ideas for how to cope with their lives. They want community, people praying for them and caring about them.

So far, creation care is a boutique issue in American Christianity. However much the leaders of any sector of Christianity try to change this, it does not seem to be changing fast enough. We have to acknowledge the deep unlikelihood that, absent severe and overwhelmingly obvious ecological crisis, the concerns of most churches and Christians will recenter toward creation care any time soon.

#3: Human beings are deeply alienated from the Creation. We do not love it.

Ed Wilson tells us that alienation from creation is a civilizational problem. It goes with the "betrayal of nature" that has always been required to create human civilizations, beginning with the very first agricultural settlements and certainly the first cities. This human alienation from creation is therefore a 10,000-year-old problem. Wilson also reminds us that the West's major religions were born in this nexus and with its biases. I once read that you can develop a habit in forty days. A 10,000-year-old habit is, let's say, a pretty well-established one.

But it is perhaps better understood as an acutely modern problem. Fewer human beings live in any significant organic contact with the creation than at any time in human history. The family farm is a distant memory for most. We live in near total disconnection from nature. We are creatures entirely of civilization and its barely comprehensible technical and bureaucratic processes and structures.

Let me practice my religion and do some painful Christian confession here. I now see how much I have been a full-on nature-alienated suburbanite. I grew up in the cozy northern Virginia suburbs (ironically enough, as the son of an environmental policy analyst for the Congressional Research Service). My father was so connected to his own New England agricultural heritage that he planted extensive vegetable gardens and we ate homegrown beans and such. He spent as much time outside as he could. Yet I had no interest in any of that. Ed Wilson says, "every child is a beginning explorer naturalist."[25] But my closest connection to nature was the Little League baseball field.

I went fishing once. I caught a boot. I only recently started learning the names of the flowers my wife grows. Even though I live on a lake I couldn't tell you one bird call from another. The author Richard Louv[26] has worried that this generation of children has "nature-deficit disorder." I am nearly

---

25. Wilson, *The Creation*, 139.
26. Louv, *Last Child in the Woods*.

fifty, and I am now mortified to have to acknowledge that I have had such a condition since childhood. I discovered this through meeting "secular" scientists who are decidedly not afflicted by said condition.

As a Christian, I love God. Theologically, I love the creation. But I haven't loved it deeply, not from the heart. Ed Wilson is a self-proclaimed secular humanist. But he loves the creation, in its details, in its majesty. His posture toward creation is one of engaged reverence. He loves God's actual physical creation, as a secular humanist, better than I have loved it, as a Christian. I say this with deep sorrow.

Ed Wilson reached out to Christian leaders like me in 2006 and proposed that together we could save the creation. He assumed that his kind of scientific expertise coupled with our kind of Christian values would be enough to make the breakthrough we need before it is too late.

I hope he was right. But I wonder. Most of us do not make sacrifices for people or causes that we do not really love. I will sacrifice all kinds of things to pay for *my* child's college tuition, but not *your* child's tuition, because though I love your child in theory, I love my child in reality. It may be that the ultimate reason why good science and humane religion may not succeed in saving the Creation is because there are not enough human beings who actually *love* this good yet distressed world.

It may be that from a long-term ecological perspective the most important line that divides human beings is not that between religious believers and unbelievers, but between those who love the Creation and those who do not. This line cuts across religious traditions and goes right to the human heart. And many Christians are among those who need to be converted. This is what I have learned from Ed Wilson and his scientific friends—so reticent to speak of God, so devoted in their love of God's creation.

17

America's Unfinished Racial Reconciliation

2012

INTRODUCTION

THIS ESSAY CONTRIBUTES TO research on how peoples tell the truth about their own collective wrongdoing in the past, repent and if possible "make right" those wrongs, and move toward contemporary intergroup reconciliation. Truth-telling, repentance/making right, and reconciliation—in a world filled with collective wrongdoing that continues to bear grave contemporary consequences, this is critically important work. And it is work that occurs at the intersection of religion and politics; or, at least, it is political work to which theology has the capacity to contribute, if it makes use of its own rich resources.

I will focus here on the ongoing challenge of racial truth-telling, confession, and reconciliation in the United States. My thesis is that the United States of America, as a national community, has very slowly been coming to terms with a national history that included more that 250 years of race-based slavery (1609–1865), and 100 years of de facto and de jure segregation and terror against black Americans (1865–1968), leaving a legacy of second-class citizenship for blacks, and the assassination in 1968 of America's leading African American fighter for racial justice and reconciliation, Dr. Martin Luther King, Jr. Truthful speech about the collective wrongdoing of especially southern, white slaveholding, and segregationist America remains difficult. Repentance and making right of that wrongdoing remains incomplete. Forgiveness for that wrongdoing therefore remains unfinished. And yet, evidence from a variety of sources reveals progress in recent years. America's work of racial memory, repentance, and reconciliation remains incomplete, but it does continue to inch forward little by little.

There are many tantalizing avenues I could pursue in this paper to support aspects of my thesis. I could speak about the way the election of President Barack Obama marked progress in race relations but also has "troubled the waters" on race in the United States and revealed how much work still remains to be done. I could speak about the subterranean role of race in everyday American politics at both the local and the national level. I could point to numerous policy arenas, such as public education, affirmative action, and criminal justice, in which race is implicated in policy disputes, as well as numerous symbolic arenas, such as how our Civil War and its leaders are memorialized. I could speak of how our bipolar political system has in many ways become racialized, with the Democrats now the party of a surging multi-racial America and the Republicans at risk of becoming the party of anxious white resentment.

For this paper, though, I have decided to focus on an examination of ways in which governmental bodies in the United States have officially addressed our history of slavery and segregation. I will briefly explore governmental deliberations about this history, including struggles over whether to offer an apology, whether to extend some form of reparations to the descendants of the enslaved, and whether to enact a holiday to honor Dr. Martin Luther King after his 1968 murder. I will also take a brief glimpse at religious, corporate, and state efforts to apologize and make amends as well. The evidence offered will support my thesis that we are making gradual progress toward coming to terms with our racial history, but that there is still much more to do.

APOLOGIZING FOR SLAVERY AND JIM CROW

One would think that it would not be difficult for the citizens of the United States to acknowledge wrongdoing when it comes to our history of slavery. Approximately 650,000 Africans were brought to (what became) the United States. By 1860 the slave population was four million.[1] These millions of human beings were owned by other human beings, who used their labor without recompense and who exercised near absolute control over their

---

1. Behrendt, "Transatlantic Slave Trade."

lives, bodies, and families. This is not even to mention the countless victims who never survived the passage between Africa and North America.

After Emancipation, deeply entrenched racism in attitudes and social structures, especially but not only in the South, gave birth to a legal and cultural regime of disenfranchisement and discrimination. Black Americans were treated as second-class citizens, especially but not only in the South. Perhaps the greatest symbol of black powerlessness was lynching, a form of mob vigilantism that terrorized blacks for decades.

Remembering and apologizing for slavery is made more difficult because of how slavery ended. The South fought a Civil War in part to preserve the institution of slavery, and therefore memory of slavery in the South is tied up intimately with the humiliating memory of a lost war. It has been hard for southerners to apologize for slavery without apologizing for the very existence of the Confederacy as a political entity—and therefore apologizing for the broader white Southern way of life; parts of which some, at least, remember quite fondly. Thus, for some white Southerners, to apologize for slavery seems tantamount to apologizing for their own heritage and even their collective identity.

For the winning side of the United States Civil War, an apology is a different matter. Descendants of those who fought on the Union side often feel that they have nothing to apologize for—they had abolished slavery in their territory, and their victorious war helped end it across the continent. An apology would be somebody else's responsibility.

African-Americans themselves have not always been eager to take up the issue of a slavery apology. Many would prefer to leave the past in the past and not to aggravate relations with their neighbors, especially in the South.

These are several plausible factors, at least, that might help to explain why it took until July 2008 (143 years after the thirteenth Amendment abolished slavery) for the United States House of Representatives to issue an apology for slavery (and Jim Crow segregation). The Senate did the same nearly a year later.[2]

The House resolution read as follows:

H. RES. 194

Whereas millions of Africans and their descendants were enslaved in the United States and the 13 American colonies from 1619 through 1865;

---

2. Thompson, "Senate Backs Apology for Slavery"; Welna, "Senate Apologizes for Slavery."

Whereas slavery in America resembled no other form of involuntary servitude known in history, as Africans were captured and sold at auction like inanimate objects or animals;

Whereas Africans forced into slavery were brutalized, humiliated, dehumanized, and subjected to the indignity of being stripped of their names and heritage;

Whereas enslaved families were torn apart after having been sold separately from one another;

Whereas the system of slavery and the visceral racism against persons of African descent upon which it depended became entrenched in the Nation's social fabric;

Whereas slavery was not officially abolished until the passage of the 13th Amendment to the United States Constitution in 1865 after the end of the Civil War;

Whereas after emancipation from 246 years of slavery, African-Americans soon saw the fleeting political, social, and economic gains they made during Reconstruction eviscerated by virulent racism, lynchings, disenfranchisement, Black Codes, and racial segregation laws that imposed a rigid system of officially sanctioned racial segregation in virtually all areas of life;

Whereas the system of de jure racial segregation known as "Jim Crow," which arose in certain parts of the Nation following the Civil War to create separate and unequal societies for whites and African-Americans, was a direct result of the racism against persons of African descent engendered by slavery;

Whereas a century after the official end of slavery in America, Federal action was required during the 1960s to eliminate the dejure and defacto system of Jim Crow throughout parts of the Nation, though its vestiges still linger to this day;

Whereas African-Americans continue to suffer from the complex interplay between slavery and Jim Crow—long after both systems were formally abolished—through enormous damage and loss, both tangible and intangible, including the loss of human dignity, the frustration of careers and professional lives, and the long-term loss of income and opportunity;

Whereas the story of the enslavement and de jure segregation of African-Americans and the dehumanizing atrocities committed against them should not be purged from or minimized in the telling of American history;

Whereas on July 8, 2003, during a trip to Goree Island, Senegal, a former slave port, President George W. Bush acknowledged slavery's continuing legacy in American life and the need to confront that legacy when he stated that slavery "was . . . one of the greatest crimes of history . . . The racial bigotry fed by slavery did not end with slavery or with segregation. And many of the issues that still trouble America have roots in the bitter experience of other times. But however long the journey, our destiny is set: liberty and justice for all.";

Whereas President Bill Clinton also acknowledged the deep-seated problems caused by the continuing legacy of racism against African-Americans that began with slavery when he initiated a national dialogue about race;

Whereas a genuine apology is an important and necessary first step in the process of racial reconciliation;

Whereas an apology for centuries of brutal dehumanization and injustices cannot erase the past, but confession of the wrongs committed can speed racial healing and reconciliation and help Americans confront the ghosts of their past;

Whereas the legislature of the Commonwealth of Virginia has recently taken the lead in adopting a resolution officially expressing appropriate remorse for slavery and other State legislatures have adopted or are considering similar resolutions; and

Whereas it is important for this country, which legally recognized slavery through its Constitution and its laws, to make a formal apology for slavery and for its successor, Jim Crow, so that it can move forward and seek reconciliation, justice, and harmony for all of its citizens: Now, therefore, be it Resolved, That the House of Representatives—

> (1) acknowledges that slavery is incompatible with the basic founding principles recognized in the Declaration of Independence that all men are created equal;
>
> (2) acknowledges the fundamental injustice, cruelty, brutality, and inhumanity of slavery and Jim Crow;
>
> (3) apologizes to African Americans on behalf of the people of the United States, for the wrongs committed against them

and their ancestors who suffered under slavery and Jim Crow; and

(4) expresses its commitment to rectify the lingering consequences of the misdeeds committed against African Americans under slavery and Jim Crow and to stop the occurrence of human rights violations in the future.[3]

This appears to be quite a historic declaration. It is indeed significant. But I would be remiss if I failed to note a few important details that somewhat diminish its impact. First, of the 435 members of the United States House, there were only 121 co-sponsors, a relatively small number; and only two of them were Republicans. Roughly half of the US Congress was not fully reconciled to this resolution, reflecting the racial polarization of our two main parties. Further, it was offered, and passed, during a time when Democrats controlled the House of Representatives, thus giving Democrats procedural control. Scouring the Congressional Record this became clear. We see Representative Steve King, Republican of Iowa, speaking against the resolution, and protesting that a quorum was lacking when it was approved by voice vote upon the ruling of the chair.[4]

A similar Senate resolution passed a year later.[5] The Democrats also controlled the Senate at the time. The Congressional Record recorded a unanimous "voice vote," but the Senate was, according to news reports, nearly empty at the time. Picture it this way—not every senator at his desk and a full gallery of witnesses like in the movies, but instead an empty Senate and a few men talking to cameras before hastening on to the rest of the day's duties. The same basic picture had prevailed in the Senate four years earlier (June 13, 2005) when it issued an apology for repeatedly failing to pass anti-lynching legislation despite the lobbying efforts of seven US presidents and the passage of such legislation three times in the House. In 2005, as in 2009, few senators were present and there was no roll call vote.[6]

The significance of an apology is real. But it cannot be measured merely by the words on the page or the fact of passage. Those who know the US political system can tell the difference between a small step forward such as this—a Democratic-driven apology for slavery and Jim Crow passed in largely empty congressional halls and receiving relatively little attention—and the kind of high profile national coming-to-terms with slavery that has,

3. Congressional Record: House 7224–7227.
4. Congressional Record: House 7227.
5. Congressional Record: Senate 6761–6768.
6. Thomas-Lester, "A Senate Apology for History on Lynching."

in fact, not yet occurred. One could be forgiven for the surmise that our federal politicians concluded as of 2008–2009 that black Americans needed to see passage of an apology, but white Americans were sufficiently queasy about it that our legislators did not want to make too much of a fuss about it.

THE PROBLEM OF REPARATIONS

I want to call attention to a small feature of the 2009 Senate slavery apology that might help explain the reticence to do more:

(2) DISCLAIMER.—Nothing in this resolution—

(A) authorizes or supports any claim against the United States; or

(B) serves as a settlement of any claim against the United States.[7]

Under international human rights law, the right to reparation for gross wrongs is well-established. Such reparations can take the form of "restitution, compensation, rehabilitation, and satisfaction and guarantees of non-repetition."[8] The question of reparations is one of the most explosive issues at stake whenever a collectivity such as a nation owns up to wrongdoing against its own people or against another people. Fear of the costs of reparation is one reason why collectivities are so reticent to admit human rights violations.

Reparations are in fact one logical entailment of acknowledging wrongdoing. But besides African-Americans, there is almost no constituency for reparations for slavery, lynching, Jim Crow, and segregation. Every politician who faces white voters knows that to speak up for reparations is to say goodbye to one's political career. This may be one very good reason why President Barack Obama is on the record in opposition to reparations.[9]

The closest the United States has come to the matter is the introduction in each Congress since 1989 of a bill to establish a commission to study reparation proposals. This has been spearheaded by the stalwart African-American legislator John Conyers (D-MI) and has never passed.[10] Notice that this is not legislation to pay reparations but simply to study various reparation proposals. It has gone nowhere.

Reparations for slavery and segregation would be problematic at a practical level, even in identifying to whom such reparations should be paid.

7. Congressional Record: Senate 6762.
8. http://nuweb9.neu.edu/civilrights/reparations/.
9. Wills, "Obama Opposes Slavery Reparations."
10. Berkowitz, "Conyers Fights to Pass Slave Reparation Bill."

But it is interesting to compare this utter lack of progress on reparations for the descendants of slaves with how the United States government related to World War II Japanese-American internment victims. The 1988 Civil Liberties Act apologized to Japanese Americans who were unjustly interned and authorized $20,000 per person in reparations (and delivered over 1.5 billion dollars), to the affected Japanese Americans and their descendants.[11] African Americans were not the only ones to wonder why temporary internment of Japanese Americans during World War II merited reparations, while reparations for generations of permanent enslavement and discrimination against African Americans could not be seriously discussed.

THE MARTIN LUTHER KING HOLIDAY

The United States civic calendar contains a number of federal holidays that bless most workers with a day off from work while noting events or persons of especially profound significance in our national life. Our calendar honors our Presidents George Washington and Abraham Lincoln; our workers, veterans, and war dead; Columbus Day and Independence Day; and even our unique Thanksgiving Day.

No holiday honored a black American until after the assassination of civil rights leader Martin Luther King on April 4, 1968. Four days after that terrible murder, John Conyers (then a very young congressman from Michigan) introduced legislation to establish a federal holiday in honor of King.

The legislation went nowhere for about a decade, despite intensive organizing on behalf of a King Holiday from King's widow Coretta as well as King's surviving civil rights organization, the Southern Christian Leadership Conference. In 1971 they presented a petition to Congress with three million signatures asking for a holiday. Then-President Jimmy Carter offered his support for the legislation, but in 1979 the bill was defeated in the House by five votes. The push was renewed in 1980 with another massive petition drive, and this time it passed the House overwhelmingly, 338–90.

However, as often happens in our politics, the bill was blocked in the Senate for another few years. Leading the opposition was North Carolina Republican Jesse Helms, a classic old-school Southern white conservative who was notorious for his race-baiting. On October 8, 1983, Helms presented his opposition to the King Holiday on the Senate floor by reading a paper called "Martin Luther King, Jr.: Political Activities and Associations," which recycled old charges that King was tied to Communism. The paper also mentioned King's "alleged sexual dalliances." This attack on the martyred

---

11. Brophy, *Reparations: Pro and Con.*

hero of the civil rights movement created outrage. Ten days later, the bill passed 78–22, with Republicans voting in favor 37–18 and Democrats 41–4. The bill was signed into law by President Ronald Reagan in November 1983, and the King birthday became a federal holiday beginning in 1986.

At the state level, debates were sometimes equally acrimonious. It took until 2000 for all of our fifty states to grant a King Holiday at the state level. South Carolina was the last US state to do so.[12]

As with everything else associated with race in America, the debate over a King Holiday was laden with symbolism on all sides. For black Americans, a King Holiday symbolized their hard fight for full inclusion as Americans. Many women and men had fought hard for dignity and equality for black Americans, but King had become the leading symbol of the movement and was its most visible victim, dying on a Memphis hotel balcony from a white assassin's bullet. He was only thirty-nine years old at the time. It is sad to note that progress on the social and economic justice issues that King was working on ground to a near halt after his death, and the civil rights movement never really recovered. They were united on this one thing, though—the quest for a holiday in honor of King—and this they achieved.

For white Americans, King was a much more divisive and ambiguous figure. There were and still are white Americans, especially in the South, who believed that King had actually created racial problems in their communities when all had been fine before. False charges that he was affiliated with Communists were predictable given the rabid Cold War anti-Communism of the era. Pretty much every agitator for social change was accused of being a Communist. Notorious FBI director J. Edgar Hoover authorized spying and wiretaps on King, from which the sexual dalliance accusations were derived. Every effort was made to discredit King in his lifetime, and to resist honoring him after his death. But finally the King Holiday passed, despite the grumblings of resentful whites.

PRIVATE EFFORTS

Efforts at truth-telling, apologizing, and reconciling our troubled racial history have not been confined to the federal government.

Religious bodies have sought to come to terms with their complicity with slavery and segregation. The Southern Baptist Convention and the Presbyterian Church USA have issued resolutions expressing their regrets

---

12. Wolfensberger, "The Martin Luther King, Jr. Holiday"; Romero, "A Brief History of Martin Luther King Jr. Day."

for past actions. I was a part of the drafting committee for the SBC resolution in 1995.[13]

A number of universities have studied their own ties to slavery, with some offering apologies. These include some of our most prestigious national universities, such as Yale, Vanderbilt, Emory[14] and, most thoroughly, Brown University.[15] The state universities of Alabama, Mississippi, North Carolina, South Carolina, and Virginia have undertaken investigations and/or offered apologies. The University of Alabama, for example, explicitly apologized for the university's ownership of slaves and abuse of slaves by faculty members.[16]

The Hartford Courant newspaper apologized for placing ads related to runaway slaves.[17] Banks such as JP Morgan Chase and Wachovia have apologized for their involvement with slavery. Chase set up a five million dollar restitutionary scholarship fund.[18] Insurance companies such as Aetna have disclosed and apologized for their insurance policies on slaves' lives. California requires insurance companies to disclose their former policies on slaves, and now has a statewide database for this purpose.[19] Chicago, Detroit, and Los Angeles have ordinances requiring companies that do business in their cities to disclose their past ties to slavery.[20]

At the state level, Alabama,[21] Connecticut,[22] Florida,[23] New Jersey,[24] North Carolina,[25] Maryland,[26] and Virginia,[27] have offered apologies for slavery and segregation, while others have offered subtly weaker expressions of *regret*. Similar legislation is under consideration in other states, including Tennessee, Missouri, and Georgia.[28]

13. http://www.sbc.net/resolutions/amResolution.asp?ID=899
14. "Emory Issues 'Regret' for Slavery Role."
15. Goldschmidt, "Colleges Come to Terms with Slave Owning Past."
16. "University of Alabama Apologizes for Slave Past."
17. Brophy, *Reparations*, Table 2.1.
18. http://nuweb9.neu.edu/civilrights/reparations/.
19. http://www.insurance.ca.gov/0100-consumers/0300-public-programs/0200-slavery-era-insur/.
20. Brophy, *Reparations*, Table 2.1.
21. Rawls, "Alabama Governor Signs Slavery Apology."
22. http://www.cga.ct.gov/2009/TOB/H/2009HJ-00001-R01-HB.htm.
23. Colavecchio-Van Sickler, "Florida Apologizes for Role in Slavery."
24. http://www.njleg.state.nj.us/2006/Bills/ACR/270_I1.PDF.
25. "North Carolina Senate Apologizes for Slavery."
26. "Maryland Issues Apology for its Role in Slavery."
27. O'Dell, "Virginia Apologizes for Role in Slavery."
28. http://nuweb9.neu.edu/civilrights/remediation/.

Going even further, the state legislature in Florida in 1994 voted 2.1 million dollars in compensation funds for survivors of the notorious 1923 Rosewood race massacre.[29] In 2001 the state legislature of Oklahoma studied an infamous 1921 race riot in Tulsa and voted monies for a memorial, scholarship fund, and redevelopment authority in the area of the riots.[30] These are especially notable moves because of their specificity and the commitment of money.

CONCLUSIONS

I would like to venture a thesis as this study concludes: to echo Reinhold Niebuhr, I suggest that even as it is difficult for individuals to acknowledge the truth, confess, and seek reconciliation related to their own sins, it is all the harder for collectivities to do so. As Niebuhr said, groups have even less moral capacity than individuals do.[31] Therefore groups especially struggle to do the hard moral work of truth-telling, repentance, and reconciliation.

White Americans, especially white southerners, have struggled mightily to come to terms with racism, which has been called America's original sin. During slave days, most southern whites told themselves there was nothing morally wrong with slavery. After slavery, most southern whites told themselves that while maybe slavery wasn't so great, there was nothing morally wrong with white supremacy and segregation. During the civil rights movement, most southern whites told themselves that while maybe segregation wasn't so great, Martin Luther King and his movement weren't really necessary. After King's assassination, whites told themselves that while maybe it was a shame that King got killed, blacks really needed to stop complaining that racism was still such a big problem in their lives. And so on. Even today, white support for either an apology for slavery or reparations is dramatically lower than black support (for apology—30 percent white support/79 percent black support; for reparations—4 percent/67 percent).[32]

Dr. King himself liked to say that while the arc of the universe is long, it bends toward justice. Very slowly, very gradually, at least the leadership class of white Americans, including in the South, has begun to do the work of truth-telling, repentance/making right, and reconciliation. It really is significant when legislatures in states like Virginia and Alabama—and

29. Fallstrom, "Senate Oks $2.1 million for Rosewood Reparations."
30. Ford, "Race Riot Memorial Funding Bill Signed"; Ford, "House Passes Race Riot Act."
31. Niebuhr, *Moral Man and Immoral Society*.
32. Hodder, "The Price of Slavery," 12–13.

Washington—tell the truth about the past and express real regret. It is encouraging that this culture of remembrance has begun to spread to the private sector. It is important that specifically egregious details are coming into view for collective acknowledgment and repentance, such as the Rosewood Massacre or the placing of ads for runaway slaves in a Hartford newspaper. Vague acknowledgment that maybe things weren't so great is giving way to focused acknowledgment of specific sins. That is real progress.

Each truth/confession/reconciliation proposal evokes controversy. Each elicits hateful or outrageous comments from newspaper readers, legislators, and everyday citizens that make the rest of the citizenry groan in embarrassment. But each occasion seems to lance the boil of unconfessed social sin a little bit more. People have their say, and we move forward.

Certainly America's work of racial reconciliation is unfinished. The travails of President Barack Obama have provided a case in point. The very fact of a black man serving as president of the United States is shockingly offensive to many millions of white Americans. But most know that it is no longer acceptable to say this directly. And it appears likely that he will be serving for another four years, re-elected by a predominantly white nation. The unthinkable has become normal. As a racial matter, that is progress, even while a long journey of racial reconciliation remains before us.

18

Christian Public Theology and Israel-Palestine

2013

INTRODUCTION

A RECENT ARTICLE IN the *Christian Century* began with this very true statement: "It's not possible to say anything about Israel and Palestine without offending someone." So, of course, we will be speaking about Israel-Palestine and about a Christian public theology in relation to the Israeli-Palestinian situation, and therefore will be offending many people, undoubtedly. But this is what we do in public theology, in the search for some advance in understanding and in doing God's will.

I will try to do three basic things:

1. Offer enough context and history related to the establishment of the modern state of Israel to raise questions about the wisdom of too quickly moving to a definitive theological interpretation of the significance of this or any new nation-state. In other words, I want to help evangelicals re-engage real history in its bloody complexity and to some extent demythologize the state of Israel.

2. Offer an interpretation of the current state of affairs in Israel and the occupied Palestinian territories that can help ground a claim as to what moral responsibilities are incumbent upon persons of good will who might advocate or intervene in the region.

3. Offer some claims related to the ways in which US evangelicals could involve themselves constructively in the Israel-Palestine question.

In all of this, my reflections are offered with humility and without any undue sense of certainty or pride.

A QUICK AND DIRTY HISTORICAL ACCOUNT OF WHAT WE ARE CALLING ISRAEL-PALESTINE

I consider the Israel-Palestine situation the knottiest geopolitical and diplomatic problem in the world. I do not consider myself any kind of expert on it. Two trips to the region and a bunch of reading do not make anyone an expert on this area and its problems. But I am trying, and here is what I see.

Israel is one of scores of new countries born in the world since 1945. At the birth of the United Nations there were fifty-one member states; today there are 193. Some of the countries that existed in 1945 don't exist now; most that exist now did not exist then. Each new nation has its own story. Most of the new nations founded since 1945, though by no means all, resulted from decolonization, as the Western colonial powers gradually loosed their grip on—or had their grip forced loose from—their former colonies in the Global South. Certainly from the perspective of many Arabs, the birth of Israel marks a last gasp of European colonization. But of course such a claim is also easily contested, as is every claim one could make about Israel-Palestine.

The history of the land that today we call Israel is an ancient one with many layers. A large part of the relevant history is certainly colonial. The region that today encompasses Israel was controlled by the Turkish Ottoman Empire for 400 years, from 1517 to 1917. It came under British control in 1920. If the region had followed more common global trends, the eventual receding of the British Empire and the collapse of colonialism's legitimacy after World War II would have left the land between the Jordan and the Mediterranean to its local inhabitants.

In a sense, that *is* what happened. The issue in this case was that the local inhabitants were not one people. While a relatively small number of Jews had for centuries lived in what eventually became the modern state of Israel, and while Israel had been the Jews' ancient homeland, Jewish numbers increased dramatically due to waves of immigration inspired by the Zionist movement beginning in the late nineteenth century. Zionism was born in part out of the ancient Jewish attachment to *Eretz Israel*, in part as an expression of nineteenth-century European nationalism, and in part as a response to the evident and terrible anti-Semitism of European Christian civilization (so-called). The British put their stamp of approval on the Zionist project with the Balfour Declaration of 1917.

Yet this declaration was by no means welcomed by the area's Arab populations, and for most of the time of the British "Mandate of Palestine" the Brits actually did little to advance a new Jewish state. Eventually they favored a single binational Arab and Jewish state, an idea that surfaces sometimes today either as a dream or a nightmare. Eventually, the growing Jewish nationalist movement ended up in open military conflict with the British, while also having to cope with violence from the local Arab population, which also resented the British, and which gradually evolved both a local Palestinian nationalism and a broader pan-Arab, anti-Zionist, and anti-British nationalism. It was Jews and Arabs struggling with each other and both struggling with the Brits. That is the situation already in the late 1930s.

Then of course came World War II and the horrible evil of the genocidal Nazi and collaborator assault on the Jews that we know as the Holocaust, which claimed six million Jewish lives as partial fulfillment of an exterminationist plan. Meanwhile, the Middle East seethed. After World War II, an exhausted Britain was ready to get out. The Brits handed the Israel-Palestine problem to the new United Nations. On November 29, 1947 the UN General Assembly passed Resolution 181, which offered a partition plan involving an Arab state, a Jewish state, and an internationally controlled Jerusalem. This plan was accepted by the Zionists but not by the Arabs. Palestinian fighters attacked Jewish communities the very next day, though it is not as if this was the first such attack or the first intercommunal violence. The Zionists counterattacked beginning in April 1948. With British power ebbing, and the infant UN attempting to find some kind of resolution, the forces on the ground were already in an Arab-Jewish civil war. On May 14, 1948, the day the British Mandate ended, Jews declared an independent state of Israel, commencing what Palestinians still call the *naqba*, or catastrophe.

After the declaration of independence the next round of the fighting commenced. Local and regional Arab enemies attempted but were not able to strangle the newborn state in its cradle. Many on both sides died in the fighting, which lasted until early 1949. Massive population movements occurred as Jews flooded into the new Jewish state and Arabs left and were forced out. Still, when the dust settled in 1949 the Jews had fought their way successfully to an internationally recognized state (though with unsettled borders, and not recognized by Palestinians or surrounding Arab states). Wartime victories meant Israel controlled territory that was 30 percent bigger than in the 1947 UN partition plan. Palestinians had no state of their own, as the new "Hashemite kingdom of Jordan" annexed the region west of the Jordan, while Egypt retained occupation of what became known as the Gaza Strip. Israel's near neighbors signed armistice deals rather than peace agreements. They had not come to terms with the existence of the new Jewish state.

The rest of the story is somewhat more familiar. In 1967 Israel's enemies were preparing to attack once again. This time, in a war lasting only six days, Israel prevailed decisively, conquering the Golan Heights in the north, the Sinai Peninsula near Egypt, the Gaza Strip, and most significantly the Jordanian-controlled area west of the Jordan, including East Jerusalem. This profoundly changed the balance of power in the region, and has done so to this day. As is customary in international law, occupied territories remained under military rule pending a negotiated settlement. UN Security Council Resolution 242 in November 1967 called for the establishment of a lasting peace based on Israeli withdrawal from all territories occupied in the June war in return for an end to the state of belligerence, respect for the sovereignty of all states in the region, and the right of all to live in peace within secure, recognized boundaries. This resolution has been the basis for all subsequent peace negotiations.

Treaties in 1979 with Egypt and in 1994 with Jordan gave hope that the Arab states could one day come to terms with the permanence of Israel in the region or even make a real peace. The Oslo Accords (negotiated in 1993, finalized in Washington in 1995), seemed to signal that Israel and the Palestinian national movement could come to terms. The 1995 Israeli-Palestinian Interim Agreement, which is as close as the parties and the world have come to an internationally recognized negotiated settlement of the conflict, allowed the PLO leadership to relocate to the occupied territories, granted autonomy to the Palestinians but not yet a state (though providing the framework for negotiating final issues related to a state), and committed the Palestinians to abstain from terror and change their charter, which had called for the elimination of the state of Israel. A final deal was to be negotiated by May 1999.

That deal has never been consummated, and courageous Israeli Prime Minister Yitzhak Rabin paid with his life when he was killed by an Israeli religious extremist who opposed the Oslo Accords. Meanwhile, according to recent reporting, the very same Yasser Arafat who signed the Oslo deal planned the second intifada of 2000–2002, further deepening the immense difficulty Israelis have in believing that the Palestinians will ever accept their existence. Today we still live in the seemingly endless time between the times—between the establishment of an interim Palestinian Authority and Israeli-Palestinian Agreement, and the formation of a State of Palestine and a final peace agreement.

So what does this history mean? I would say that the modern state of Israel was born and survived due to a combination of a rising Jewish nationalism after centuries as a persecuted minority in Christian Europe, refugee desperation that intensified as European anti-Semitism worsened, superior Zionist and then Israeli military performance both before and after the declaration of the State of Israel, and just enough international legitimation for Israel to get up on its feet—provided first by the British and then by the United States and the new United Nations. Coming so soon after the devastation of European Jewry during the Holocaust, it was hard for onlookers not to view the birth of the Jewish state as a kind of miracle of resurrection, though an unambiguous religious narrative of that type has never prevailed in Israel.

Of course, a miracle of resurrection was not exactly how either local or regional Arab populations viewed the birth of modern Israel. The Arabs lost territory, ever more with each successive military conflict and subsequent effort to craft a peace treaty; they lost face; many lost their homes; and of course in war many lost their lives, as was also true on the Jewish side. With defeat after defeat, with the gradual economic and military strengthening of Israel over against the chronic weakness of the Palestinians and the relative weakness of the Arab world, some also lost contact with reality. Revanchists dreamed and sometimes still dream of pushing the Jews out of Palestine altogether, no matter how absurd is and was that hope; and Palestinian "leaders" became the romanticized terrorists who were only good at the routine use of attacks on civilians to express anger and inflict misery on Israelis. Every round of attacks struck directly at the Jewish state's post-Holocaust trauma and insecurity.

Any review of the spate of nation-birthing and nation-dying since 1945 inspires a healthy respect for the contingent nature of nation-states. They come and go, usually in a flow of blood. Each story is unique but each is all too human.

This may suggest that attaching any ultimate significance, including theological significance, or ascribing any existential purity or innocence, to any particular nation-state with any particular territory and any particular political regime, is unwise. This is true whether we speak of the US, the USSR (remember them?), or Israel. These are very human creations with very bloody births and deaths. These are stories of blood and iron.

I challenge evangelicals to try to learn how to examine the history and politics and conflicts of Israel-Palestine and the region without always jumping to overlay some kind of theological interpretation on it. Ethnic groups fight each other. Nations are born in bloody, conflicted ways. Territorial disputes abound. A just peace that honors the sacred worth of each person and allows everyone to go about their daily lives in security amidst such constant bloody conflicts should always be our goal as Christians.

I am asking us to examine the conflicts and challenges of Israel-Palestine the way we would examine the conflicts and challenges of any other region of the world, and to apply the same moral standards and peacemaking practices there as we would anywhere else. Here I believe our particularized public theology of Holy Land, or holy Israel, or even primal Palestinian Christian community, needs to give way to a more universal Christian public ethic of justice, peace, and just peacemaking.

In saying this I am not altogether repudiating what we attempted to do in the infamous (Glen) Stassen/Gushee "Open Letter on Christian Zionism."[1] I do still believe that a certain kind of Christian Zionism hurts the situation in this particular region because its theology hinders the capacity of large numbers of American Christians to apply standard Christian public ethics to the Israeli-Palestinian conflict. In other words, I am suggesting that mythologizing the modern state of Israel by overlaying a certain reading of the Old Testament land texts, or of biblical apocalyptic texts, has made it more difficult for millions of evangelical Christians to understand our ethical obligations right here, right now, in the real world of real bloody history.

What we attempted to do about that in our "Open Letter" was to get into the weeds of the same Old Testament texts and suggest a different, more inclusive interpretation of those texts, such as that the descendants of Abraham and the heirs of the land promised to him include Arabs and not just Jews. And we turned to prophetic writings, together with the lament of Jesus over Jerusalem, to rather literally suggest that Israel might face divine judgment for its unjust mistreatment of the Palestinians. We went beyond what today I am calling standard Christian public ethics. And I don't know what Glen Stassen is planning to do, but I think that I won't do this again.

Instead, I will try to stop treating Middle East conflicts as if they were existentially or theologically any different from conflicts over other contested land, such as the Kashmir region or Kosovo. I will take seriously the way in which people's theological beliefs affect how they act in conflict zones.

---

1. Gushee and Stassen, "An Open Letter to America's Christian Zionists."

But I will not do any form of Land Theology in relation to Israel-Palestine again. I will do just peacemaking ethics, and that only.

I have been told by a committed Israel-Palestine peacemaker that while this is an interesting suggestion it may not be a wise one for the evangelical community. Evangelicals need to be told that we should care about a just peace in Israel-Palestine especially because it is the Holy Land, the land that Jesus walked, because we are told in Scripture to pray for the peace of Jerusalem, and so on. I am coming to believe that while this might and should affect our moral drive in some special ways, the Israel-Palestine problem is historical, geopolitical, diplomatic, and ethical, and the overall principles of cooperative conflict resolution and other tenets of just peacemaking are where we ought to focus our attention.

THE PROBLEM OF MILITARY OCCUPATION, SETTLEMENTS, AND EXTREMIST (RELIGIOUS) ZIONISM

If we summarize the history of the land we are discussing as consisting of the burgeoning and then new Israel outmaneuvering and outfighting Palestinians and regional Arab groups and states, over time changing the facts on the ground in her favor, gradually acquiring more and more power relative to the Palestinians in the normal way of the world, gradually claiming irreversible and internationally recognized control over more and more of the territory between the Jordan and the Mediterranean—has anything really changed in recent years? Does the Israel-Palestine problem have a new dimension worthy of our attention?

I am persuaded by a number of books by American and Israeli Jews—such as those by Peter Beinart and Gershom Gorenberg[2]—that Israel as a whole has grown accustomed to a permanent military occupation of another people, and is at risk of abandoning her founding commitment to partitioning the land with the Palestinians. The Oslo Accords promise such a partition and the negotiations to accomplish it. Deals to make such a partition happen have come very close to being accomplished more than once since 1995, most recently in 2008. But leaders openly calling for an abandonment of any kind of two-state peace deal, such as Israeli official Naftali Bennett, have moved from the margins to the mainstream in Israeli politics in the past decade.

---

2. Beinart, *The Crisis of Zionism*; Gorenberg, *The Unmaking of Israel*.

The expansion of Jewish communities in the area of an envisioned Palestinian state has created facts on the ground that risk making a viable Palestinian state impossible. Primary responsibility for permitting and in fact subsidizing these settlements, which in some cases are in fact mid-size cities and include more than 300,000 inhabitants (over 500,000 if one counts East Jerusalem), belongs to the government of Israel, both through omission and commission. Gorenberg shows that Israel stumbled rather than rushed headlong into the policies she has undertaken, but by now these policies have developed a deeply loyal constituency and a momentum of their own that is very difficult to break. (Many settlers would almost certainly fight their own Israeli Army if a peace deal required them to move. Many soldiers would not follow orders to evacuate settlers, polls show.)

Meanwhile, these settlements need to be protected. Because Palestinian territory is under military occupation, which consists for Palestinians of a life of permits, checkpoints, walls, prisons, property and natural resource seizures, settler abuses, and often fierce IDF repression of even nonviolent protests, the face of Israel for much of the world is an unsavory combination of occupation troops and militant settlers. Both Beinart and Gorenberg, together with a new book by Yuval Elizur and Lawrence Malkin,[3] decry the emergence of a militant ultra-orthodox Judaism that is especially strong among the settlers and sometimes the military in the Occupied Territories, but is also becoming a major factor in Israel proper. Gorenberg suggests that in keeping and then settling occupied territories, Israel has invited the religious and political radicalization of a significant portion of her population, and that this cannot be contained to that part to be found on the Palestinian side of the wall. This part of the population is not especially interested in protecting the principles of Israeli democracy, and its understanding of religion is not in keeping with the humane justice orientation of the best Jewish religious traditions.

When a religion under the name Judaism becomes a force for denying the human worth, needs, and rights of those outside the group, it is not true Judaism, or at least not the truest Judaism. Christians are under no obligation to defer to that kind of religious sensibility, but instead must protest it. And to the extent that there is a version of Christianity that also becomes a force for denying the human worth, needs, and rights of, say, Palestinians in the occupied territories, it is not the truest Christianity and we must protest it. (Just as we must protest any mutant strain of Christianity anywhere else. Or a similarly problematic Islam.) This kind of religion becomes a justifying

---

3. Elizur and Malkin, *The War Within*.

ideology for the rule of force rather than the rule of law or the standards of justice and peace, and it must be resisted in Christ's name.

Certainly Arab and then Palestinian leaders bear a significant share of responsibility for not seizing peace deals when they had the opportunity (beginning at least in 1947). Their own inability to accept sharing the land in the times before the situation mutated to what it is today is most unfortunate. But the situation that now exists on the ground is that Israel is in essence creating a two-headed Jewish state, one a quite sophisticated first-world state in internationally recognized territory with an Israeli Arab population that has considerable legal protections if not totally equal treatment, and one a rather brutal occupying power in territory with a Palestinian population that is under military rule. The trend lines appear to me to be exacerbating extremist Palestinian nationalism of the Hamas type and weakening the legitimacy of the more reasonable Palestinian Authority leaders now aging and soon to leave the scene. I am not saying that endless military occupation *creates* Palestinian voices that do not recognize the legitimacy of Israel; I am saying that such an occupation raises the profile and popularity of such voices over against the more moderate voices, such as PA president Mahmoud Abbas, prepared to make peace with Israel.

It is still UN and US policy to press for a negotiated two-state solution, with an autonomous and viable Palestinian state next to a secure, recognized Israel. But as I learned in a detailed presentation from a former Israeli negotiator in 2012 in Israel, the level of complexity involved in trying to arrange land swaps in order to accommodate apparently immovable Israeli settlements, while still giving a future Palestine enough land, and enough contiguity, to be a viable state, makes the 1947 partition look like child's play by comparison. A number of articles in US publications on the eve of President Obama's 2013 visit to Israel discussed the apparently closing window of opportunity for a negotiated two-state solution.

The basic Christian ethics of just peacemaking emphasizes respect for international institutions and the rule of law. It calls for negotiated win-win conflict resolution. It emphasizes shared responsibility for serious conflicts and for resolving them. Its brand of religiosity is interested in transforming initiatives that turn enemies into friends and spirals of conflict into cycles of peacemaking.

It is hard for me to see how Christians could not support adherence to the essential structure of UN resolutions encouraging a two-state solution, together with the Oslo Accords, together with the stated preference of the US for a negotiated two-state solution, together with respectful discussion of and with responsible participants on all sides. To the extent that there are Christians who look at the situation with a theological framework that repudiates any Palestinian claim on any land between the Jordan and the Mediterranean, or who do not respect the authority of the legal and treaty structures that have emerged to help bring some order to this situation, or who mythologize the Jewish side and demonize the Palestinian side (or vice-versa), they are not contributing constructively to Christian public ethics with relation to Israel-Palestine.

WHAT'S US EVANGELICAL CHRISTIANITY GOT TO DO WITH IT

US evangelicals bring some distinctive characteristics into the global discussion and potential resolution of the Israel-Palestine problem. Some of these characteristics are constructive; some are a double-edged sword; and some are destructive:

US evangelicals are among the last population in the world whose moral imaginations are so suffused with the stories of Scripture that the land we are talking about still remains "Holy Land" to them.

US evangelicals have also been remarkably better than most European Christians were in developing a positive theology of and relationship to the Jewish people. Historic Christian anti-Semitism is more often among us a contemporary Christian philosemitism. This is indeed a welcome development, except for where it precludes a philo-Palestinianism; e.g., where it trains some Christians in a one-sided love.

US evangelicals, like many other Americans, take the Holocaust seriously. It looms large in their understanding of World War II and of the twentieth century, and it helps shape a desire to assure that the Jewish people never stand alone in the world again when confronted by an enemy. I hope that everyone knows that I share deeply in that concern, as a Holocaust scholar and one who serves the US Holocaust Memorial Museum in an official capacity.

A significant minority of US evangelicals (and fundamentalists) has embraced a theological framework in which the birth of the modern state of Israel is an important part of the timetable of events preceding the imminent return of Jesus Christ. And the "Israel" they have in mind is not the negotiated Israel of UN resolutions and treaties but the Davidic/Solomonic Israel in the maps in the back of their Bibles.

Many US evangelicals undertake Holy Land tours that are structured in such a way as to appeal to their religious sensibilities while carefully steering clear of the problems associated with the occupied territories.

Meanwhile, US evangelicals are such an important part of the US population that our very strong instinctual and theological support for the modern state of Israel has a profound impact on US foreign policy.

More recently, of course, more and more US evangelicals have come into relationship with Palestinians, including Palestinian Christians. These have come to understand the claims of Palestinians on (parts of) the land. They have come to care about the suffering of Palestinians under occupation. They have taken dual narrative Holy Land tours that have taken them through the separation barrier and checkpoints and into the Occupied Territories. They are likely to take seriously the significance of modern history and the legal-ethical-treaty framework promising/demanding a two-state solution. And they are sometimes so changed by their visits to the region that this type of evangelical polarizes toward an anti-Israel/pro-Palestinian posture.

I believe that the proper posture for evangelicals is to be pro-Israel, pro-Palestine, and pro-(just) peace. We do best not when we take sides but when we function as a third side, a just-peace side. We are best postured when we are friends who come up alongside squabbling brothers and help them make peace, not when we come up on squabbling brothers and take sides.

Evangelicals who care about Israel and Palestine need to engage individuals, groups, and cultures on both sides, which is not easy, because the entire conflict somehow seems structured to keep you on one side or the other. We need to partner with constructive just peacemakers wherever we find them, and lift their voices up for special attention and emulation. We need to speak up constantly for win/win solutions. We need to help our government take a balanced and constructive role that tracks very closely with the steps I just mentioned for us as evangelicals.

What is good Christian public theology in relation to Israel-Palestine? Good historical realism. Good modern respect for the rule of law. Good love of the God who makes each life sacred. Good love of each sacred individual life and each sacred people. Good, skillful just peacemaking—so that soon there will be a just peace in the land between the Jordan and the Mediterranean.

19

Closing Reflections
David Gushee's Compassion and Realism, with Concreteness

GLEN H. STASSEN

IN THE FRAY IS wonderfully concrete. David Gushee gives us insightful and specific guidance on many of the most salient issues of our time. Reading *In the Fray*, I am wishing I had written more concretely, as David does.

Indeed, people are largely formed by their perceptions of concrete, specific contentious issues. How they perceive these contentious issues forms their ethics as a whole. This book will be formative for many readers.

My goal in this brief interpretive essay is not to describe where David Gushee comes out on each of the salient issues. You can see what they are in the Table of Contents. You will want to read them for yourself to find out where he comes out and how it can make your own ethics and your own spiritual formation more faithful. I do not want to spoil your your reading with a far less interesting summary of his conclusions.

I want to dig a little deeper. I want to ask what it is that leads David Gushee to be so very helpful, so very insightful, so very faithful, and so very interesting to read.

In the Fray begins with an essay on the Holocaust and the rescuers in which the first paragraph is basically a call to repentance: "preyed upon by the most powerful nation in Europe, murdered by some of their neighbors, abandoned by almost all of the rest of them, and largely unaided by the world, the Jews of Europe were slaughtered." This is a call for all of us to repent for bystanderism.

And the second paragraph is an expression of compassion:

> The spirit of an examination of the Holocaust, it seems to me, ought to be something like the spirit of an investigation of a fatal airplane crash (though, of course, even this metaphor is not nearly grave enough). As tears sting the eyes and the stench of death overwhelms the senses, the investigators nonetheless pick through the rubble, in search of the answer to two critical questions: Why did this catastrophe happen? How can another disaster like this be prevented in the future?

And these two themes—compassion and a call to repentance—continue not only through the essay, but in fact through the whole book. I think here we see major clues to the strength of David Gushee, essayist and ethicist.

> The piety of religiously motivated Christian rescuers . . . began with a faith characterized by compassion and an orientation to others' needs. All aspects of piety reinforced this basic orientation. The search for God's will and the commitment to obeying it deepened the compassion and empowered Christians to act on it, as did the desire to please God and the fear of God's displeasure . . . Those of us who live and work among Christian people know that there are among us certain people consistently involved in acts of love, compassion, and justice on behalf of others. One finds that not only do such people believe an authentically compassionate version of Christianity but they also practice a piety that empowers them to do what they believe.

Notice that David's book, *Getting Marriage Right*, was inspired by his own compassionate getting to know thirty of his students who were children of the tragedy of divorce. They came to him initially, I believe, because they learned that he had compassion and insightfulness.

Notice the connection between his strong commitment to the sacredness of human life, and to human rights for everyone, and Christian compassion. You see it in his recent book, *The Sacredness of Human Life*. The vision for that book began in his outstanding essay (chapter 10 here) that founded Evangelicals for Human Rights:

> We ground our commitment to human rights in the core Christian theological conviction that each and every human life is sacred. This theme wends its way throughout the Scriptures: in Creation, Law, the Incarnation, Jesus' teaching and ministry, the Cross, and his Resurrection. Concern for the sanctity of life

> leads us to vigilant sensitivity to how human beings are treated and whether their God-given rights are being respected.

He writes that Jesus' compassion "was especially apparent in the way he treated the marginalized: women, the sick, the dead, the poor, people of bad reputation, children, and enemies of Israel such as tax collectors, Roman soldiers, and Gentiles in general."

Christ's command that we love our neighbors, especially the most despised and rejected, includes our homosexual neighbors.

> We must treat them as we would want to be treated. We must remember that as we do to them, we do to Jesus (Matt 25:31ff). We must oppose their harassment and bullying in schools, churches and clubs—everywhere . . . We must teach Christian parents of gay children to communicate unconditional love and under no circumstances evict them from either their hearts or their homes, no matter what they believe about the moral significance of homosexual inclination.

David's heartfelt compassion for the powerless leads him to search for "a biblical theology for the United States government serving the economic and survival needs of the poorest outside our national borders."

Throughout, David writes with passion. He is aware of his own passions, and aware of others' passions. He is no abstract, impersonal, rationalistic writer.

I think it helps that David is left-handed, and therefore more in touch with the right side of his brain than many of us. It also helps that he is deeply Christian, a follower of Jesus, who takes seriously Jesus' own compassion and Jesus' call for us to love God with all our hearts, minds, and strengths, and to love our neighbors as ourselves.

It also helps that his dissertation and first book were a deeply compassionate study of the Holocaust, and of the rescuers, while beginning with repentance that there were so few rescuers.

David writes: "Christian rescuers were convinced that their faith demanded compassion and love on behalf of the oppressed, and this is a conviction we rightly celebrate." Here I think is the key to his ethics. I do not know whether David's writing his dissertation on the suffering of the Holocaust and the rescuers got him started writing ethics based on compassion for people who are being deprived of their basic human rights, or whether his own native compassion caused him to choose to write his dissertation on the suffering of the Holocaust and the rescuers. Probably both are true, and probably the compassion came first.

The theme of repentance comes on behalf of the churches he cares so compassionately about:

> The argument of several essays is directed against what I consider to be the sometimes aberrant or unconstructive public ethics of my co-religionists in this vast sector of the American religious community. I do not write as a disdainful outsider but instead as an insider who contests one primary version of evangelical public ethics—that represented by our most reactionary and narrow elements. I hope that my love for the church of Jesus Christ, and my desire for greater fidelity to Christ's lordship on the part of the church, is apparent in and through my criticisms.

In this, he takes Dietrich Bonhoeffer as a model. He writes that Bonhoeffer

> lifted up the centrality of the church as the primary community/polity for Christian people . . . and reminded the church of its allegiance to Christ alone . . . It is partly my loyalty to Bonhoeffer's model that has inspired me as an evangelical to take what I would call small steps of resistance in our own context.

Indeed, throughout *In the Fray*, David identifies as himself a centrist evangelical. He says he found with Ronald Sider and ESA "the kernel of a social-political vision that has never left me—pro-life, pro-justice, pro-peace, pro-poor, pro-creation care." He has written for *Christianity Today*, he founded Evangelicals for Human Rights (against torture), he grew up Christian as a Southern Baptist, and wrote books mostly calling on evangelicals for a more Christian, a more faithful, a more responsible Christian ethic: *A New Evangelical Manifesto*, *The Future of Faith in American Politics*, *The Scholarly Vocation and the Baptist Academy*. His *The Sacredness of Human Life*, *Righteous Gentiles of the Holocaust*, *Getting Marriage Right*, and *Only Human* are aimed not only at evangelicals but at a wider Christian audience. And of course, our jointly authored *Kingdom Ethics: Following Jesus in Contemporary Context* is published by an evangelical press (Intervarsity), but we intend it for a Christian ethics generally, that wants to participate in the new Reformation we are calling for, recovering the way of Jesus for Christian ethics.

David also knows that evangelicals deeply need a responsible political ethic. He observes much that is going wrong when evangelicals are co-opted by a political ideology that feigns Christian loyalties but acts to disempower the poor and to shift money to the wealthy political donors. You see that in his book, *The Future of Faith in American Politics*, and in several essays in *In the Fray*.

Many essays in *In the Fray* contribute mightily to the recovery of a responsible political ethic. David says so much that is helpful and indeed incisive that I cannot try to summarize it here. This is the biggest missing element in my interpretive essay. What I am saying is that as you read this, I urge you to keep David's basic loyalties front and center: compassion, awareness of our need for continuous repentance, loyalty to churches as faithful to Jesus Christ as Lord, Christ-centeredness, and loyalty to Bonhoeffer's Christ-centered witness. David observes that the rescuers were more likely to embrace a democratic and pluralistic patriotism than were nonrescuers. "There is a kind of patriotism that complements rather than contradicts authentic Christian beliefs. This is a patriotism that is inclusive, democratic, compassionate, and just in its orientation."

And one more thing: the dangerous temptation of churches to seek power by receiving favors from the politically powerful. David's ethics has realism about the power-temptations that lead churches astray. In his essay on "The Quest to Save Creation," he writes:

> Three years after the near-collapse of our economy, brought on mainly by corrupt business practices on Wall Street, practices whose ruinous implications were so profound that the American taxpayer got the tab so the global economy would (supposedly) not collapse, it is hard not to see that our political system is more a plutocracy than a democracy.

I want to emphasize David's Christ-centeredness, not merely as a slogan, but as paying attention to Jesus' concrete teachings and deeds.

> The church's primary obligation is to follow Jesus (Matt 10:38–39). As a community of Christ-followers, the church exists to worship God-in-Christ, to preach the Word, to make disciples, to serve the least of these, to love God with all we have and likewise love our neighbors as ourselves. We dare not drift from our core mission.

This is one reason he and I share such strong loyalty to Dietrich Bonhoeffer as mentor for our ethics:

> Dietrich Bonhoeffer taught and modeled unrelenting loyalty to Jesus Christ . . . His was a Christ-centered theology and ethic. This clarity about his loyalties left Bonhoeffer far better prepared to resist the siren song of loyalty to race, Volk, nation, party, state, and Führer than were most German Christians.

He writes that the most important resource in the evangelical debate over torture was

> a passionate commitment to the person and work of Jesus Christ. Some evangelicals, at least, operated from the recognition that the gracious Savior whose forgiveness we claim is also the sovereign Lord who demands our entire lives, who taught justice and mercy, who requires our setting aside of all ideologies, loyalties, and fears that hinder our faithfulness to his will, and demands our embodied love for the enemy, the alien, and the abandoned of the earth.

One other important dimension of David Gushee's essays on whichever concrete issue he takes up is his deep commitment to fair-mindedness. (See what he writes about his own father, whose influence is seen clearly here. Think also of his education at William and Mary, an outstanding liberal arts college.) He works carefully not to distort any perspective that he is criticizing. He treats what I consider the embarrassing distortions of Calvin Beisner both on what science is clearly saying and what Scripture is clearly saying concerning care of the creation and justice in distribution with remarkable gentleness. He shows respect that I share for southerners who are working more deeply than many northerners to grow in loyalty to racial justice and healing. He treats his fellow evangelicals always with respect, even where he is calling for repentance for getting entangled in the ideologies of those who have political and economic power.

In his concluding essay, there is one intriguing indication of a shift in his thinking. As he notes in his last essay, he had joined with me in an "Open Letter to Christian Zionists," which I had drafted. We pointed out that in Genesis 17, God says to Abraham:

> This is my covenant with you: You shall be the ancestor of a multitude of nations . . . I have made you the ancestor of a multitude of nations. I will make you exceedingly fruitful, and I will make nations of you . . . And I will give to you, and to your offspring after you, the land where you are now an alien, all the land of Canaan, for a perpetual holding.

We offered no complicated interpretation. We said "a multitude of nations" means many nations. "The land of Canaan" means the land of Canaan. God's covenant says as clearly as possible, as literally as possible, that the land of Canaan belongs to many nations, not one single nation. We wrote this to call Christian Zionists to desist from claiming that God's covenant gives all the land only to Israel, and that Palestinians have no human rights in the land of Canaan.

In drafting it, I knew that Christian Zionists were basing their arguments not on international law, but on their claim that the Bible says all the land belongs to Israel. I wanted to dialogue with Christian Zionists on the basis of the very kind of claim that they have been making, and to call them to desist from supporting the denial of Palestinians their basic human rights. The argument was thoroughly biblical, very concrete, completely literal: a multitude of nations means a multitude of nations. Not one nation.

David has not rejected the argument. But he says he will not write that way anymore. Instead, he now proposes that we

> examine the conflicts and challenges of Israel-Palestine the way we would examine the conflicts and challenges of any other region of the world, and to apply the same moral standards and peacemaking practices there as we would anywhere else . . . Our particularized public theology of Holy Land, or holy Israel . . . needs to give way to a more universal Christian public ethic of justice, peace, and just peacemaking.

I wonder why he made this shift? The biblical teaching is so absolutely clear. And none of the many responses that I saw refuted the biblical teaching, or even dealt with it.

My hypothesis is that David senses that entangling biblical interpretations in partisan power struggles complicates emotions so much that it makes resolution harder to find. Furthermore, David's deep compassion for Jewish loyalties, shown in his first book, *Righteous Gentiles of the Holocaust*, and throughout his life, caused him to back off from an argument that could be offensive to some Jews, as seen in some of the responses to our open letter. (I want to make as clear as I can that I share those loyalties very, very deeply. In 1955, my father was awarded the B'nai B'rith annual award for support for Israel. He had to be away negotiating arms control with the Soviet Union, so, as a young student, I received the award on my father's behalf, and was deeply impressed. This is the kind of family I was raised in. My sister's husband was a wonderfully ethical Jew whom we all loved, Martin Berger. Sadly, he has now died of cancer. I am a Bonhoeffer scholar, deeply committed to what David writes in *Righteous Gentiles of the Holocaust*. I share deep loyalty to the security and survival of Israel; and also to human rights and justice for Palestinians.)

David's deep commitment to fair-mindedness causes him not to want to write what could be offensive to some Jews. So he backs off and instead supports "an ethic of justice, peace, and just peacemaking." The ethic of justice, peace, and just peacemaking is of course my ethic. I support this advocacy completely. I think David's shift on how to make this argument gives us an intriguing window into his deep loyalties of compassion, justice, peacemaking, fair-mindedness, and defense of Jews who have been so horribly attacked throughout Christian history, culminating in the Holocaust.

I encourage you to admire David Gushee's loyalties, passions, and ethics all the more deeply, and to go and do likewise. Read this book and let yourself be formed more like David Gushee.

Works Cited

"Active Duty Military Personnel Strengths by Regional Area and by Country." U.S. Department of Defense, December 21, 2007, 1–4. *Globalpolicy.org*. Online: http://www.globalpolicy.org/images/pdfs/1232militarypersonnel.pdf.

Allen, Joseph L. "Covenant." In *The Westminster Dictionary of Christian Ethics*, edited by James F. Childress and John Macquarrie, 136–37. Philadelphia: Westminster, 1986.

Anderson, Leith. "Eric Chivian & Richard Cizik." The 2008 *Time* 100, *Time*, May 12, 2008. Online: http://content.time.com/time/specials/2007/article/0,28804,1733748_1733754_1736213,00.html.

Anderson, Sarah, and John Cavanagh. "Top 200: The Rise of Corporate Global Power." *Institute for Policy Studies*, December 4, 2000. Online: http://www.ips-dc.org/reports/top_200_the_rise_of_corporate_global_power.

Aristotle. *Nicomachean Ethics*. Translated by W. D. Ross. In *Great Books of the Western World* 9, edited by Robert Maynard Hutchins, 339–436. Chicago: Encyclopedia Brittanica, Inc., 1952.

Baranowski, Shelley. "The Confessing Church and Antisemitism: Protestant Identity, German Nationhood, and the Exclusion of Jews." In *Betrayal: German Churches and the Holocaust*, edited by Robert P. Ericksen and Susannah Heschel, 90–109. Minneapolis: Fortress, 1999.

Baron, Lawrence. "The Holocaust and Human Decency." *Humboldt Journal of Social Relations* 12, nos. 1–2 (1985/1986) 237–51.

Behrendt, Stephen. "Transatlantic Slave Trade." In *Africana: The Encyclopedia of the African and African American Experience*, edited by Kwame Anthony Appiah and Henry Louis Gates, Jr., 1865–77. New York: Basic Civitas, 1999.

Beinart, Peter. *The Crisis of Zionism*. New York: Picador, 2013.

Berkowitz, Jeremy. "Conyers Fights to Pass Slave Reparation Bill." *The Michigan Daily*, February 4, 2002. Online: https://www.michigandaily.com/content/conyers-fights-pass-slave-reparation-bill.

Blank, Rebecca M. "A Christian Perspective on the Role of Government in a Market Economy." In *Global Neighbors: Christian Faith and Moral Obligation in Today's Economy*, edited by Douglas A. Hicks and Mark Valeri, 224–47. The Eerdmans Religion, Ethics, and Public Life Series. Grand Rapids: Eerdmans, 2008.

Blankenhorn, David. *Fatherless America: Confronting Our Most Urgent Social Problem*. New York: Basic Books, 1995.

Bravin, Jess. "The Conscience of the Colonel." *Wall Street Journal*, March 31, 2007, A1.

Broder, John M. "Bashing E.P.A. is New Theme in G.O.P. Race." *New York Times*, August 17, 2011. Online: http://www.nytimes.com/2011/08/18/us/politics/18epa.html?_r=2&.

Brophy, Alfred L. *Reparations: Pro and Con*. New York: Oxford University Press, 2006.

"Bumper Subsidy Crop for US Cotton Producers: African Farmers Suffer." Oxfam International, November 2005. Online: http://www.oxfam.org/en/news/pressreleases2005/pr051019_wto.

"Burkina Faso: Cotton Story." Oxfam International. Online: http://www.oxfam.org/en/campaigns/trade/real_lives/burkina_faso.

Bush, George W. "Commencement Address." United States Military Academy at West Point. *New York Times*, June 1, 2002. Online: www.nytimes.com/2002/06/01/international/02PTEX-WEB.html.

———. "Signing of the *Military Commissions Act of 2006*." Washington, D.C., October 17, 2006.

Carter, Phillip. "A Few Bad Apples?" Intel Dump: Phillip Carter on National Security and the Military, May 24, 2008. Online: voices.washingtonpost.com/inteldump/.

Cavanagh, John, and Jerry Mander, eds. *Alternatives to Economic Globalization*, 2d ed. San Francisco: Berrett-Koehler, 2004.

Chilton, David. *Productive Christians in an Age of Guilt-Manipulators: A Biblical Response to Ronald J. Sider*. Tyler, TX: Institute for Christian Economics, 1985.

Clements, Ronald E. "Psalm 72 and Isaiah 40–66: A Study in Tradition." *Perspectives in Biblical Studies* 28, no. 4 (Winter 2001) 333–41.

Colavecchio-Van Sickler, Shannon. "Florida Apologizes for Role in Slavery." *Tampa Bay Times*, March 26, 2008. Online: http://www.tampabay.com/news/politics/state/florida-apologizes-for-role-in-slavery/432823.

Cornwell, John. *Hitler's Pope: The Secret History of Pius XII*. New York: Viking, 1999.

"DoD Releases Fiscal 2010 Budget Proposal." U.S. Department of Defense, May 2009. Online: http://www.defense.gov/releases/release.aspx?releaseid=12652.

Elizur, Yuval, and Lawrence Malkin. *The War Within: Israel's Ultra-Orthodox Threat to Democracy and the Nation*. New York: Overlook Duckworth, 2013.

"Emory Issues 'Regret' for Slavery Role." Associated Press, January 21, 2011. *The Augusta Chronicle*. Online: http://chronicle.augusta.com/latest-news/2011-01-21/emory-apologizes-slavery-role.

Ericksen, Robert P. and Susannah Heschel, eds. *Betrayal: German Churches and the Holocaust*. Minneapolis: Fortress, 1999.

Evans, Robert A., and Alice Frazer Evans. *Human Rights: A Dialogue Between the First and Third Worlds*. Maryknoll, NY: Orbis, 1988.

Fallstrom, Jerry. "Senate Oks $2.1 million for Rosewood Reparations." *Sun Sentinel*, April 9, 1994. Online: http://articles.sun-sentinel.com/1994-04-09/news/9404080701_1_rosewood-descendants-rosewood-bill-reparations.

Farley, Margaret A. *Personal Commitments: Beginning, Keeping, Changing*. New York: HarperCollins, 1990.

Fishman, Charles. *The Big Thirst: The Secret Life and Turbulent Future of Water*. New York: Free Press, 2012.

Fleischner, Eva. "Can the Few Become the Many?" In *Remembering for the Future*, vol. I, edited by A. Roy Eckardt and Alice Eckardt, 233–47. London: Pergamon, 1989.

Fogelman, Eva. "The Rescuers: A Sociopsychological Study of Altruistic Behavior During the Nazi Era." PhD diss., City University of New York, 1987.

"For the Health of the Nation: An Evangelical Call to Civic Responsibility." In *Toward an Evangelical Public Policy*, edited by Ronald J. Sider and Diane Knippers, 363–75. Grand Rapids: Baker, 2005.

Ford, Brian. "House Passes Race Riot Act." *Tulsa World*, May 23, 2001. Online: http://www.tulsaworld.com/site/printerfriendlystory.aspx?articleid=010523_ne_a11house.

———. "Race Riot Memorial Funding Bill Signed." *Tulsa World*, June 2, 2001. Online: http://www.tulsaworld.com/article.aspx/Race_riot_memorial_funding_bill_signed/010602_ne_11a1race2.

Friedman, Philip. *Their Brothers' Keepers*. New York: Holocaust Library, 1957.

Gerlach, Wolfgang. *And the Witnesses Were Silent: The Confessing Church and the Persecution of the Jews*. Translated and edited by Victoria J. Barnett. Lincoln: University of Nebraska Press, 2000.

Geneva Convention (III): Relative to the Treatment of Prisoners of War. Geneva: August 12, 1949.

Glendon, Mary Ann. *Rights Talk*. New York: Free Press, 2004.

Gold, Mitchell, and Mindy Drucker, eds. *Crisis: 40 Stories Revealing the Personal, Social, and Religious Pain and Trauma of Growing Up Gay in America*. Austin, TX: Greenleaf Book Group, 2008.

Goldschmidt, Debra. "Colleges Come to Terms with Slave Owning Past." *CNN*, May 23, 2011. Online: http://www.cnn.com/2011/US/05/23/university.slavery/index.html.

Gorenberg, Gershom. *The Unmaking of Israel*. New York: Harper Perennial, 2012.

Gushee, David P. "Against Torture: An Evangelical Perspective." *Theology Today* 63, no. 3 (October 2006) 349–64.

———. "All Things Jewish." *Books and Culture* 6, no. 6 (November/December 2000) 6–11.

———. "An Urgent Call to Action: Scientists and Evangelicals Unite to Protect Creation." National Press Club, 2007. Washington D.C.

———. "Five Reasons Torture Is Always Wrong." *Christianity Today* 50, no. 2 (February 2006) 32–37.

———. *The Future of Faith in American Politics: The Public Witness of the Evangelical Center*. Waco, TX: Baylor University Press, 2008.

———. "Many Paths to Righteousness: An Assessment of Research on Why Righteous Gentiles Helped Jews." *Holocaust and Genocide Studies* 7, no. 3 (Fall 1993) 372–401.

———. *The Righteous Gentiles of the Holocaust: A Christian Interpretation*. Minneapolis: Augsburg Fortress, 1994.

———. *The Sacredness of Human Life: Why an Ancient Biblical Vision Is Key to the World's Future*. Grand Rapids: Eerdmans, 2013.

Gushee, David P., and Cliff Kirkpatrick. "Rights of Detainees Must Not Be Violated." *Memphis Commercial Appeal*, September 27, 2006.

Gushee, David P. and Glen H. Stassen. "An Open Letter to America's Christian Zionists." The New Evangelical Partnership for the Common Good. Online: http://newevangelicalpartnership.org/?q=node/139.

Gushee, David P., Jillian Hickman Zimmer and J. Drew Zimmer, eds. *Religious Faith, Torture and Our National Soul*. Macon, GA: Mercer University Press, 2010.

Hallie, Philip. *Lest Innocent Blood Be Shed*. New York: Harper and Row, 1979.

Hauerwas, Stanley. *With the Grain of the Universe: The Church's Witness and Natural Theology.* Grand Rapids: Brazos, 2001.

Haugen, Gary A. "Silence on Suffering." *Christianity Today*, October 17, 2005. Online: http://www.christianitytoday.com/ct/2005/octoberweb-only/12.0b.html.

Heschel, Susannah. "When Jesus Was an Aryan: The Protestant Church and Antisemitic Propaganda." In *Betrayal: German Churches and the Holocaust*, edited by Robert P. Ericksen and Susannah Heschel, 68–89. Minneapolis: Fortress, 1999.

Hicks, Douglas A. "Global Poverty and Bono's Celebrity Activism: An Analysis of Moral Imagination and Motivation." In *Global Neighbors: Christian Faith and Moral Obligation in Today's Economy*, edited by Douglas A. Hicks and Mark Valeri, 43–64. The Eerdmans Religion, Ethics, and Public Life Series. Grand Rapids: Eerdmans, 2008.

Hicks, Douglas A., and Mark Valeri, eds. *Global Neighbors: Christian Faith and Moral Obligation in Today's Economy.* The Eerdmans Religion, Ethics, and Public Life Series. Grand Rapids: Eerdmans, 2008.

Hodder, Harbour Fraser. "The Price of Slavery." *Harvard Magazine*, May–June 2003. Online: http://harvardmagazine.com/2003/05/the-price-of-slavery.html.

Hollinger, Dennis P., and David P. Gushee. "Evangelical Ethics: Profile of a Movement Coming of Age." *Annual of the Society of Christian Ethics* 20 (2000) 181–203.

Horton, Scott. "Justice After Bush: Prosecuting an Outlaw Administration." *Harper's Magazine*, December 2008, 49–60.

Hugenberger, Gordon P. *Marriage as a Covenant: Biblical Law and Ethics as Developed from Malachi.* Grand Rapids: Baker, 1998.

"Human Development Indicators." In *United Nations Human Development Report 2007/2008*, 229–354. Online: hdr.undp.org/en/reports/global/hdr2007-2008/chapters/.

"Human Intelligence Collector Operations." *U.S. Army Field Manual* 2-22.3. September 6, 2006.

Huneke, Douglas. "Glimpses of Light in a Vast Darkness: A Study of the Moral and Spiritual Development of Nazi-Era Rescuers." In *Remembering for the Future*, vol. I., edited by A. Roy Eckardt and Alice Eckardt, 486–93. London: Pergamon, 1989.

Ignatieff, Michael. "Evil Under Interrogation." *Financial Times*, May 15, 2004.

International Covenant on Civil and Political Rights. United Nations General Assembly Resolution 2200A. September 15, 2006.

Kertzer, David I. *The Popes Against the Jews: The Vatican's Role in the Rise of Modern Anti-Semitism.* New York: Alfred Knopf, 2001.

Krugman, Paul. "Republicans Against Science." *New York Times*, August 28, 2011. Online: http://www.nytimes.com/2011/08/29/opinion/republicans-against-science.html?scp=3&sq=global%20warming%20&st=cse.

Lewy, Guenter. "Pius XII, the Jews, and the German Catholic Church." In *Betrayal: German Churches and the Holocaust*, edited by Robert P. Ericksen and Susannah Heschel, 129–48. Minneapolis: Fortress, 1999.

Limburg, James. *Psalms.* Westminster Bible Companion, edited by Patrick D. Miller and David L. Bartlett. Louisville: Westminster John Knox, 2000.

Long, Edward LeRoy, Jr. *Academic Bonding and Social Concern: The Society of Christian Ethics.* Notre Dame: Religious Ethics, Inc., 1984.

Louv, Richard. *Last Child in the Woods: Saving Our Children From Nature-Deficit Disorder.* Chapel Hill, NC: Algonquin, 2008.

Lowe, Ben. *Green Revolution: Coming Together to Care for Creation*. Downers Grove, IL: InterVarsity, 2009.

Marshall, Christopher D. *Crowned with Glory and Honor: Human Rights in the Biblical Tradition*. Studies in Peace and Scripture, vol. 6. Telford, PA: Pandora Press U.S., 2001.

Marshall, Paul. "Human Rights." In *Toward an Evangelical Public Policy*, edited by Ronald J. Sider and Diane Knippers, 307–22. Grand Rapids: Baker, 2005.

"Maryland Issues Apology for its Role in Slavery." Associated Press, March 27, 2007. *NBCnews.com*. Online: http://www.nbcnews.com/id/17813609/ns/us_news-life/t/maryland-issues-apology-its-role-slavery/#.UkM9cH_hfVU.

Mason, Mike. *The Mystery of Marriage*. Sisters, OR: Multnomah, 1985.

Mayer, Jane. *The Dark Side*. New York: Doubleday, 2008.

Merritt, Jonathan. *Green Like God: Unlocking the Divine Plan for Our Planet*. Nashville: FaithWords, 2010.

Mertus, Julie A. *Bait and Switch: Human Rights and U.S. Foreign Policy*. New York: Routledge, 2004.

Meusel, Marga. "The Meusel Memorandum." In Wolfgang Gerlach, *And the Witnesses Were Silent: The Confessing Church and the Persecution of the Jews*, 81–86. Translated and edited by Victoria J. Barnett. Lincoln, NE: University of Nebraska Press, 2000.

Military Commissions Act of 2006. 120 Statutes at Large 2600. Public Law 109-366. October 17, 2006.

Miller, J. Maxwell, and John H. Hayes. *A History of Ancient Israel and Judah*, 2d ed. Louisville: Westminster John Knox, 2006.

Miller, Patrick D. "The Prophetic Critique of the Kings." *Ex Auditu* 2 (1986) 82–95.

Mohler R. Albert, Jr. "Torture and the War on Terror: We Must Not Add Dirty Rules to Dirty Hands." December 2005. Online: http://www.albertmohler.com/2005/12/20/torture-and-the-war-on-terror-we-must-not-add-dirty-rules-to-dirty-hands/.

Monera, Arnold T. "The Christian's Relationship to the State according to the New Testament: Conformity or Non-conformity?" *Asia Journal of Theology* 19, no.1 (April 2005) 106–42.

Munoz, Eric. "More than Aid: Partnership for Development." *Bread for the World Briefing Paper*, no. 5, August 2008.

National Conference of Catholic Bishops. *The Challenge of Peace: God's Promise and Our Response*. Washington D.C.: United States Catholic Conference, 1983.

"New Day, New Way: U.S. Foreign Assistance for the 21st Century." Modernizing Foreign Assistance Network. *Center for Global Development*, June 10, 2008. Online: http://www.cgdev.org/publication/new-day-new-way-us-foreign-assistance-21st-century.

Nicholson, Ernest W. *God and His People: Covenant Theology in the Old Testament*. Oxford: Clarendon Press, 1986.

Niebuhr, Reinhold. *Moral Man and Immoral Society: A Study in Ethics and Politics*. New York: Scribner's, 1934.

Noll, Mark. *The Scandal of the Evangelical Mind*. Grand Rapids: Eerdmans, 1994.

"North Carolina Senate Apologizes for Slavery." Associated Press, April 5, 2007. *USA Today*. Online: http://usatoday30.usatoday.com/news/nation/2007-04-05-nc-senate-slavery_N.htm.

O'Dell, Larry. "Virginia Apologizes for Role in Slavery." Associated Press, February 25, 2007. *Washington Post*. Online: http://www.washingtonpost.com/wp-dyn/content/article/2007/02/25/AR2007022500470.html.

Oline, Pamela. "Rescuing the Hidden Story." *Books & Religion* 18, no. 2 (Summer 1991) 4–7, 11.

Oliner, Samuel P., and Pearl M. *The Altruistic Personality*. New York: Free Press, 1988.

Oreskes, Naomi, and Erik M. Conway. *Merchants of Doubt: How a Handful of Scientists Obscured the Truth on Issues from Tobacco Smoke to Global Warming*. New York: Bloomsbury, 2011.

Paldiel, Mordecai. "Hesed and the Holocaust." *Journal of Ecumenical Studies* 23, no. 1 (Winter 1986) 90–106.

Pavlischek, Keith. "Human Rights and Justice in an Age of Terror: An Evangelical Critique of An Evangelical Declaration Against Torture." *Books and Culture*, September 2007, 1–10. Online: http://www.booksandculture.com/articles/webexclusives/2007/september/ept24a.html.

———. "Just War Theory and Terrorism: Applying the Ancient Doctrine to the Current Conundrum." Family Research Council. Online: http://www.frc.org/get.cfm?i=WT01K2.

Peters, Rebecca Todd. "Economic Justice Requires More than the Kindness of Strangers." In *Global Neighbors: Christian Faith and Moral Obligation in Today's Economy*, edited by Douglas A. Hicks and Mark Valeri, 89–108. The Eerdmans Religion, Ethics, and Public Life Series. Grand Rapids: Eerdmans, 2008.

Phayer, Michael. *The Catholic Church and the Holocaust, 1930–1965*. Bloomington, IN: Indiana University Press, 2000.

Pope John Paul II. *The Gospel of Life*. New York: Random House, 1995.

Pulliam, Sarah. "Richard Cizik Resigns from the National Association of Evangelicals." *Christianity Today*, December 2008. Online: http://www.christianitytoday.com/ct/2008/decemberweb-only/150-42.0.html

Rawls, Phillip. "Alabama Governor Signs Slavery Apology." Associated Press, May 31, 2007. *Huffingtonpost.com*. Online: http://www.huffingtonpost.com/huff-wires/20070531/slavery-apology/.

"Religion and Genocide." *Commonweal* (July 13, 2001) 5–6.

"Report on Detainee Treatment." Task Force on Detainee Treatment. Washington, D.C.: The Constitution Project, 2013.

Roach, Erin. "Ethicist: NAE Torture Declaration 'Irrational.'" *Baptist Press*, March 2007. Online: http://www.bpnews.net/bpnews.asp?id=25190.

Romero, Frances. "A Brief History of Martin Luther King Jr. Day." *Time*, January 18, 2010. Online: http://content.time.com/time/nation/article/0,8599,1872501,00.html.

Sauvage, Pierre. Interview with Bill Moyers. Arlington, VA: PBS, 1989.

———. *Weapons of the Spirit*. VHS. Directed by Pierre Sauvage. Los Angeles: Chambon Foundation, 1989.

Second Committee General Assembly. "UN General Assembly Resolution 2626." Twenty-fifth Session, October 1970.

Sharkey, Joe. "Word for Word/The Case Against the Nazis; How Hitler's Forces Planned to Destroy German Christianity." *New York Times*, January 13, 2002. Online: http://www.nytimes.com/2002/01/13/weekinreview/word-for-word-case-against-nazis-hitler-s-forces-planned-destroy-german.html?pagewanted=all&src=pm.

Shrader, Katherine. "U.S. has Detained 83,000 in War on Terror." Associated Press, November 16, 2005.
Sider, Ronald J. "For the Common Good." *Sojourners* 36, April 2007, 24–29.
———. *Rich Christians in an Age of Hunger: A Biblical Study*. Downers Grove, IL: InverVarsity, 1977.
Stackhouse, Max L. *Covenant and Commitments: Faith, Family, and Economic Life*. Louisville: Westminster John Knox, 1997.
Stassen, Glen H. "Foreword." In Christopher D. Marshall, *Crowned with Glory and Honor: Human Rights in the Biblical Tradition*, 11–14. Studies in Peace and Scripture, vol. 6. Telford, PA: Pandora Press U.S., 2001.
———. *Just Peacemaking: Transforming Initiatives for Justice and Peace*. Louisville: Westminster John Knox, 1992.
Stassen, Glen H., and David P. Gushee. *Kingdom Ethics: Following Jesus in Contemporary Context*. Downers Grove, IL: InterVarsity, 2003.
Sundman, Per. "Human Rights, Justification, and Christian Ethics." Ph. D. diss., Uppsala University, 1996.
Stiglitz, Joseph E. *Globalization and Its Discontents*. New York: Norton, 2003.
Tec, Nechama. *When Light Pierced the Darkness*. New York: Oxford University Press, 1986.
Thatcher, Adrian. *Marriage After Modernity: Christian Marriage in Postmodern Times*. New York: New York University Press, 1999.
"The Report of the Constitution Project's Task Force on Detainee Treatment." *The Constitution Project*. Online: detaineetaskforce.org/report/.
Thomas-Lester, Avis. "A Senate Apology for History on Lynching." *Washington Post*, June 14, 2005. Online: http://www.washingtonpost.com/wp-dyn/content/article/2005/06/13/AR2005061301720.html.
Thompson, Krissah. "Senate Backs Apology for Slavery." *Washington Post*, June 19, 2009. Online: http://articles.washingtonpost.com/2009-06-19/politics/36855638_1_congressional-apology-resolution-slavery.
Tooley, Mark D. "The Evangelical Left's Nazi Obsession." *Frontpagemag.com*, October 2008. Online: www.frontpagemag.com/Articles/Read.aspx?GUID=13825700-A2AF-4EEA-91AC-662512B7276D.
"Top Commodity and Conservation Programs in United States, program years 2003–2005." Environmental Working Group: Farm Bill 2007 Policy Analysis Database. Online: http://farm.ewg.org/sites/farmbill2007/index.php.
Tucker, Gene M. "The Book of Isaiah 1–39: Introduction, Commentary, and Reflections." In *The New Interpreter's Bible: A Commentary in Twelve Volumes*, vol. VI, edited by Leander E. Keck, 25–306. Nashville, Abingdon, 2001.
UN General Assembly. Twenty-fifth Session, Second Committee. "Resolution 2626: International Development Strategy for the Second United Nations Development Decade," 39. October 24, 1970. In *Resolutions Adopted on the Reports of the Second Committee*. Official Record. New York, 1970.
United Nations High Commission on Human Rights. *Civil and Political Rights Including the Questions of Torture and Detention*. Geneva: United Nations Department of Public Record, December 23, 2005.
"University of Alabama Apologizes for Slave Past." Associated Press, April 20, 2004. *NBCnews.com*. Online: http://www.nbcnews.com/id/4759657/ns/us_news-life/t/university-alabama-apologizes-slave-past/#.UkM2xH_hfVU.

US Senate. One-hundred-eleventh Congress, second session. *Foreign Assistance Revitalization and Accountability Act of 2009.* S. 1524. Senate Report 111-12. 2 February 2010.

Vatican Council II. "Gaudium et Spes [Pastoral Constitution on the Church in the Modern World]." In *The Conciliar and Postconciliar Documents*, edited by Austin Flannery, 903–1001. December 7, 1965.

Vere, D. W. "Sanctity of Human Life." In *New Dictionary of Christian Ethics & Pastoral Theology*, edited by David J. Atkinson, et al., 757–58. Downers Grove, IL: InterVarsity, 1995.

Wallerstein, Judith S., and Sandra Blakeslee. *Second Chances: Men, Women, and Children a Decade After Divorce.* New York: Ticknor & Fields, 1989.

Webb, Stephen. Review of *Go and Do Likewise: Jesus and Ethics*, by William C. Spohn. *Books and Culture* 7, no. 5 (2001) 21–22.

Weiser, Artur. *The Psalms.* The Old Testament Library. Translated by Herbert Hartwell. Philadelphia: Westminster John Knox, 1961.

Weitzman, Lenore J. *The Divorce Revolution: The Unexpected Social and Economic Consequences for Women and Children in America.* New York: Free Press, 1985.

Welna, David. "Senate Apologizes for Slavery." All Things Considered. *NPR*, June 18, 2009. Online: http://www.npr.org/templates/story/story.php?storyId=105620620.

White, Michael Westmoreland. "Setting the Record Straight: Christian Faith, Human Rights, and the Enlightenment." *Annual of the Society of Christian Ethics* (1995) 75–96.

Whitehead, Barbara Dafoe. *The Divorce Culture.* New York: Knopf, 1996.

Wiesel, Elie. "Acceptance Speech for 1986 Nobel Peace Prize." Oslo, Norway, December 10, 1986.

Wills, Christopher. "Obama Opposes Slavery Reparations." Associated Press, August 2, 2008. *Huffingtonpost.com.* Online: http://www.huffingtonpost.com/2008/08/02/obama-opposes-slavery-rep_n_116506.html.

Wilson, E. O. *The Creation: An Appeal to Save Life on Earth.* New York: Norton, 2007.

Wolfensberger, Don. "The Martin Luther King, Jr. Holiday: The Long Struggle in Congress." Woodrow Wilson International Center for Scholars, January 14, 2008, 1–10. Online: http://www.wilsoncenter.org/sites/default/files/King%20Holiday-essay-drw.pdf.

Wright, N. T. "The Letter to the Romans: Introduction, Commentary, and Reflections." In *The New Interpreter's Bible: A Commentary in Twelve Volumes*, vol. X, edited by Leander E. Keck, 393–770. Nashville: Abingdon, 2002.

Zuccotti, Susan. *Under His Very Windows: The Vatican and the Holocaust in Italy.* New Haven, CT: Yale University Press, 2000.

www.ingramcontent.com/pod-product-compliance
Lightning Source LLC
Chambersburg PA
CBHW031807220426
43662CB00007B/562